MD

Washington, D.C.

WV

VA

Surry

Louisville

KY

Owensboro

TN

APPALACHIA

Asheville

NC

Chattanooga

SC

Memphis

Decatur

Atlanta

GA

Greenwood

WHITE BBQ SAUCE

AL

Charleston

LOWCOUNTRY

Tuskegee

Vidalia

MS

St. Augustine

New Orleans

Apalachicola

FL

Tampa

OF MEXICO

EVERGLADES

Miami

THE
SOUTHERNER'S
COOKBOOK

ALSO BY DAVID DiBENEDETTO
AND THE EDITORS OF *GARDEN & GUN*

The Southerner's Handbook
Good Dog

THE SOUTHERNER'S COOKBOOK

RECIPES, WISDOM,
AND STORIES

*David DiBenedetto with Phillip Rhodes
and the Editors of*

GARDEN&GUN

HARPER WAVE

An Imprint of HarperCollinsPublishers

HarperCollins books may be purchased for educational, business,
or sales promotional use. For information, please e-mail the Special Markets
Department at SPsales@harpercollins.com.

FIRST EDITION

Designed by Laura Palese

Photographs copyright © Peter Frank Edwards

Library of Congress Cataloging-in-Publication Data

The Southerner's cookbook : recipes, wisdom, and stories / David DiBenedetto and
the editors of Garden & Gun.—First edition.

pages cm

ISBN 978-0-06-224241-9

1. Cooking, American—Southern style. 2. Food habits—Southern States. I.
DiBenedetto, David. II. *Garden & Gun.*

TX715.2.S68S688 2015

641.5975—dc23

2015025009

ISBN 978-0-06-224241-9

15 16 17 18 19 OV/RRD 10 9 8 7 6 5 4 3 2 1

"As anyone who grew up on the food can attest, life without a little South in your mouth at least once in a while is a bland and dreary prospect."

JOHN EGERTON

CONTENTS

INTRODUCTION

THE SOUTHERN BOUNTY

David DiBenedetto

WHEN NOT AT SCHOOL OR PRACTICING SPORTS during my teenage years, I could often be found on a small boat in the coastal waters near my Savannah, Georgia, home. I loved being on the water, but I really loved to fish. My season would usually start in April as the water temperature pushed toward the 70s and fish of all stripes showed up. Whiting, a small bottom-feeding fish, arrived first, and while they didn't necessarily offer much sport, they tasted good. I often pan-fried them for lunch, coated in House Autry seafood breader, and, once on the plate, drenched in vinegar. Refined cooking this was not. But providing a meal and then delivering it to the table brought me a level of satisfaction that I had not yet known. And it was fresh. These were not the fish I would see at the supermarket, their eyes cloudy and skin drained of color, with flesh that would hold the indentation of your finger if you applied pressure. Those fish, I thought, were hardly suitable for bait much less lunch.

And so it is. We Southerners are picky about our ingredients. Almost snooty. We'll drive out of the way to get to a farm stand where we know the peaches are ripe and the tomatoes are still warm from the field. I've witnessed heated debates on the best oyster for a roast: the prevailing opinion in the Lowcountry of South Carolina, where I live now, being Beaufort Clusters. (And how dare you steam them too long!) When the local farmers' market gets green peanuts—the best for making boiled goobers, aka boiled peanuts—our cell phones buzz with text messages. "They're here."

We're also attuned to the land around us. When June rolls around you'll find me poking around the woods of my hunt club in search of the first chanterelles of the season. I love to sauté the fleshy, apricot-scented mushrooms with Vidalia onions in butter and white wine and pair them with homemade pasta. Since they don't freeze well, the surplus gets divvied up in brown paper lunch bags for friends, the foraging equivalent of dropping off a sack of tomatoes from the garden on your neighbor's doorstep. In the fall during certain moon tides, the jumbo white shrimp leave the Charleston Harbor en masse before the onset of cold weather. Those willing to brave the cold and backbreaking work cast weighted nets in deep water to intercept them. The payoff is the freshest shrimp you've ever tasted.

But you don't need to live in the South to cook like a Southerner. As the editor in chief of *Garden & Gun* magazine I'm lucky to spend time with chefs who supplied the fuel for the recent rocket-like ascendancy of Southern food to national prominence. And I've learned that while good ingredients are important, tips and techniques help, too. The farm-to-table movement has taught us much about the pleasures of eating seasonally, but what's left out of the phrase is the cook. Chef Chris Hastings of Birmingham's Hot and Hot Fish Club showed me that a dry brine of kosher salt tames the gaminess of a wild turkey breast before

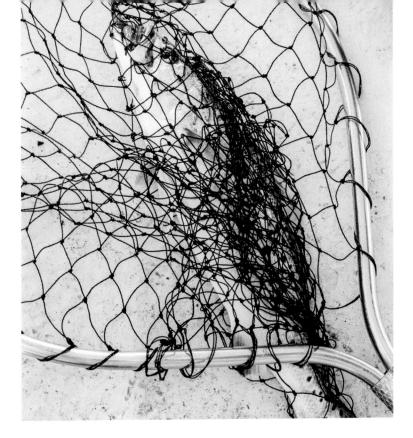

you toss it on the grill. And my go-to Thanksgiving dish, a sweet potato casserole, comes courtesy of Chef Tandy Wilson of City House in Nashville, Tennessee. Wilson brilliantly swaps the standard marshmallow topping for a crumbly and very Southern combination of chopped peanuts and sorghum. These are the same chefs we rely on in the pages of the magazine and who helped inform this cookbook. And while every one of them will tell you that they're riding on the backs of the chefs and home cooks who came before them, they're also expanding the boundaries of Southern food. It has never been more vibrant.

Hopefully you'll find this book is as much a celebration of the South's foodways as it is a guide to our region's bounty and how to prepare it. The more than one hundred recipes cover a range of Southern traditions, from barbecue to entertaining to our love affair with vegetables and our appreciation of wild game. And, yes, there are a few potent drink recipes, too. (Throwing a bash? Try the Charleston Brown Water Society Punch.) You'll find plenty of classics (fried chicken, country ham with red-eye gravy, biscuits) but also new takes on traditional Southern dishes and

ingredients (kil't greens with bacon jam, collard pesto, duck poppers with goat cheese). If you grew up in the South and are familiar with Southern food, I hope it will help expand your repertoire and provide some new favorites. If you're new to Southern cooking, it's a great primer to the scope of the region's traditions and why eating here is such a joy. No matter where you live, time at the table—whether at home, a hunt club, a dinner party, or a church hall—has the power to bring us all together in a sacred and intimate moment.

For the record, I still love to fry fish. But these days I take a cue from Chef Justin Devillier of La Petite Grocery in New Orleans. I no longer rely on House Autry but instead dip fillets of freshly caught sea trout in a mix of three eggs, one cup of milk, and several dashes of hot sauce, dredge them in seasoned cornmeal, pan fry them, then add an over-easy egg atop the fillets. A few more healthy shakes of Crystal hot sauce and a squeeze of lemon replace the vinegar shower of old. It's a simple recipe that lets the fish shine, and it has become my favorite weekend breakfast to share with family and friends. I hope this book inspires lots of new ideas to share with yours.

THE SOUTHERN LARDER

Critical as they are to some of the best-loved dishes in
the Southern canon, bacon and butter are as
much at home in Michigan as Mississippi. But when you
see White Lily Flour or any of the following
ingredients in the pantry or fridge, you know
you're in a Southerner's kitchen.

1 BUTTERMILK

The grocery store down the street probably sells buttermilk. Take a look at the fine print, though. It's usually just cultured milk, and that bears little resemblance to the tart liquid that runs off a batch of fresh butter—and makes the best possible biscuits and cornbread. Look for the real thing from a local dairy.

2 CANE SYRUP AND/OR SORGHUM SYRUP

Hard to find nowadays but well worth seeking out. The most reliable cane syrup producer in the country is Steen's, in Abbeville, Louisiana, which was once smack dab in the heart of cane-growing country. Cane syrup's darker, more complex cousin is the pressed juice of sorghum cane, reduced into a sweet syrup. Poured over buttered biscuits and otherwise enlisted as a substitute for cane syrup or honey, it's an ingredient with more than a century of Southern history.

3 DUKE'S MAYONNAISE

If you think all mayonnaise tastes more or less the same, you haven't tried Duke's. Cooks elsewhere may waver between Hellmann's and Miracle Whip, but below the Mason-Dixon line, Duke's, which was invented in Greenville, South Carolina, is the clear favorite. That's not only because it has been around for about a century, but also because it's the only big-name mayonnaise with no added sugar, which means its vinegar tang sings loud and clear when slathered on a tomato sandwich.

4 FAMILY-SIZE TEA BAGS

When Southerners brew tea, it's more often than not bound for a gallon-size pitcher in the back of the refrigerator. A family-size tea bag—of basic black tea, not green—is the equivalent of three or four regular bags, depending on the manufacturer. When you brew as much tea as we do, you might as well consolidate.

5 HOT SAUCES

What grows together goes together, they say, and the same basic principle applies to hot sauce pairings. Splash Louisiana-made Crystal on fried seafood po' boys and Bayou-country Tabasco in a Bloody Mary. Texas Pete, which is actually from Winston-Salem, is a fine dressing for North Carolina barbecue—eastern or western. For more adventurous cooks, small-batch options abound, made with unusual regional chiles like Chesapeake fish peppers or datil peppers from St. Augustine, Florida.

6 JARRED PIMENTO PEPPERS

One 4-ounce jar of diced pimentos is all you need to make a crowd-pleasing batch of pimento cheese, tubs of which are another common item found in Southern refrigerators.

7 PEANUT OIL

Think cooking oil doesn't matter? Try a chicken breast fried in canola oil and another fried in peanut oil. The latter fat has a higher smoke point and is nearly flavorless, which is a good thing when you're aiming for bird that tastes not of oil but of crisp skin and perfectly seasoned meat.

8 QUALITY GRITS AND CORNMEAL

The first lesson of Southern cooking: instant grits don't cut it. Neither does dried-out old cornmeal. For dishes that would make your great-grandmother proud, invest in grits and cornmeal milled from good crop, like those from South Carolina's Anson Mills or Alabama's McEwen & Sons. And for goodness' sake, store both in the freezer to keep them nearly as fresh as the day they were ground.

9 SOUTHERN SODAS

You probably know Nehi. But what about Blenheim Ginger Ale, Cheerwine, or Grapico? The region that birthed Coca-Cola and Mountain Dew has no shortage of local soft drinks, enjoyed on ice but also as ingredients in sauces, baked goods, and—of course— cocktails.

10 WINTER WHEAT FLOUR

Southern expats lugging home heaving bags of flour must raise eyebrows in airports these days. They'll tell you it's worth the trouble. When it comes to biscuitry, few other brands can compete with the likes of White Lily and Martha White, made from low-protein, low-gluten soft winter wheat flour, which gives Southern buttermilk biscuits that perfectly light-on-the-inside, crisp-on-the-outside texture.

1

PARTY BITES

&

APPETIZERS

GRACIOUS PLENTY

———◆———

Two simple words perfectly sum up the Southern approach to entertaining

MATT LEE AND TED LEE

FOR MOST OF THE 1980S AND '90S, OUR GRANDMOTHER, Elizabeth Maxwell, rented a tiny brick house hidden behind a grander home on Meeting Street in Charleston, South Carolina. Her stocky dwelling had served in the eighteenth and nineteenth centuries as the separate kitchen house for the large stucco mansion directly in front of it—detached, so that the occasional hearth or chimney fire (a result of the open-flame cooking method of the period) wouldn't engulf the entire property. The place was perfectly suited to our Gran, partly because of its size—she'd been widowed since 1971—but more so because she was a passionate cook and an ardent recipe collector and she loved to entertain.

In 1997, Gran's landlady and friend, Elizabeth Young, who lived in the big house, became a widow too, and for several years the two of them were very much in demand on the South-of-Broad reception, wedding, and cocktail circuit, attending a party—if not two, and often three—most nights. Heels clacking, pocketbooks swinging, they'd set out around 6 p.m. in Mrs. Young's black Taurus, always parked in front of the wrought-iron gate, for a leisurely evening of open bars, cheese bites, finger sandwiches, and shrimp every which way.

People would casually remark—We don't know where they get the energy! At their age!

We knew exactly where. Gran was in her late eighties by then, and Mrs. Young her late seventies. Both were spending less and less time in their own kitchens, so these parties functioned as dinner. But beyond the sustenance (and the frugality), these nights out were the energy that kept them going. Think about it: what true Southerner wouldn't compose an entire evening of cocktail parties if she could?

There's something about the first drink and bites of the evening that focus the crackling effervescence of great hospitality. It's why we tend to find twentieth-century regional cookbooks, from Natchez to New Orleans to North Augusta, to be front-heavy, with generous chapters covering drinks and hors d'oeuvres. And it makes a certain sense: smart hosts and hostesses want those first impressions to be the most lasting ones (and not simply because the power of memory tends to fade with the fourth gin and tonic . . .). And while some might argue that cocktail hour is the most memorable stretch of an evening simply because that's when our memories are least compromised, we believe it goes beyond that, to the very nature of cocktail party food.

The iconic Southern finger foods are never dull, always memorable, intensely flavored, designed to pack into one (maybe two) bites a surfeit of sensations. Think of rich, spicy Southern hero hors d'oeuvres like Deviled Eggs and Pimento Cheese, the smoky-buttery-salty wallop of Bacon Crackers, or the vinegary, sweet crabbiness of Mobile's favorite, West Indies Salad. Salty, pickly flavors unite in Salt-Baked Shrimp dunked in piquant Mississippi Comeback Sauce, and the Benedictine that's Kentucky's other genius cocktail-hour concoction (besides the mint julep, that is) alternates the fire of raw onion and peppery cress with cool cucumber. You'll find all these recipes—and many more—in this chapter, which truly bears out the wisdom of putting the fireworks first.

We're not sure that Gran and Mrs. Young (may they rest in peace) would recognize the entire array of finger sandwich recipes included here—mini muffulettas, hot browns, and cubanos—but we're quite certain that if they got word they were being served, they'd be polishing their shoes, packing their compacts (and some zip-top bags) into their purses, and firing up the Taurus for another night on the town.

BACON CRACKERS:
CLASSIC, HERBED, & BROWN SUGAR

MAKES 48 CRACKERS;
serves 12

THESE DANGEROUSLY ADDICTIVE LITTLE BITES FUELED COUNTLESS 1950s AND
'60s bridge parties from Greenwood, Mississippi, to Greenville, South Carolina, before being rescued
from recipe-box oblivion by modern Southern cooks like Martha Hall Foose. And thank goodness.
Magic happens when a cracker slowly sops up the fat from smoky, crisping bacon; it transforms into
something more akin to piecrust. Unadorned, bacon crackers are pure pork perfection. The addition of
a tiny bundle of rosemary needles makes for a fancified version, while topping the "belt" of bacon with a
bit of brown sugar adds a hint of sweet to the smoke.

INGREDIENTS

- 12 bacon slices (not thick-cut)
- 48 saltines or buttery crackers, such as Club brand
- 48 fresh rosemary tips (for Herbed Bacon Crackers)
- 6 teaspoons dark brown sugar (for Brown Sugar Bacon Crackers)

PREPARATION

Preheat the oven to 250°F. Line the bottom of a broiler pan with foil for
easy cleanup.

Cut the bacon slices in half lengthwise and then crosswise to create 4
long strips.

Arrange the crackers on a work surface and wrap a bacon strip around
each cracker, overlapping the ends on top.

If making Herbed Bacon Crackers, tuck a base of rosemary tips under
overlapping ends of bacon. If making Brown Sugar Bacon Crackers,
carefully sprinkle ⅛ teaspoon brown sugar on the bacon on the top side
of each cracker, pressing to help it adhere (avoid getting sugar on the
cracker or it will burn).

Set a perforated rack on top of the foil-lined broiler pan and arrange the
crackers seam-side down ½ inch apart in a single layer and bake for 1 to
1½ hours, until the bacon is at your desired level of crispness. Transfer
the crackers to a cooling rack and cool completely before serving.

"CLASSIC" PIMENTO CHEESE

MAKES 1 PINT

HERE'S A BIT OF HERESY: PIMENTO CHEESE, ONE OF THE SOUTH'S MOST BELOVED food icons, may be an import. Food historians have traced the origins of the "pâté of the South" to late-1800s New York City, where it was made with Spanish peppers and creamy Neufchâtel-like cheese. The dish most likely only began its association with the South in the 1930s and '40s, when Georgia became a top domestic producer of pimentos and Depression-era Southerners were pressing the whey out of cottage cheese and molding the solids into "hoop" cheese. Still, we made pimento cheese what it is today by using mayonnaise to bind the cheese into something spreadable and, yes, adulterating the trio of cheese, mayo, and peppers with other ingredients. Every Southerner's treasured family recipe has a secret twist—perhaps a teaspoon of sharp yellow mustard, a pinch of garlic powder, or a splash of sherry.

But first, the immutable elements: extra-sharp cheddar (it has slightly less moisture than regular cheddar, which is key to achieving the right texture) and Duke's mayonnaise, a Southern standard bearer. Our secret twists? First: a little grated Vidalia onion, which distributes evenly throughout the mayo mixture, nearly disappearing but leaving a trace of sweet-sharp flavor. Second: Worcestershire sauce; its combination of malt vinegar, anchovy, and soy sauce—among many other ingredients—adds savory depth.

INGREDIENTS

- ½ cup mayonnaise, preferably Duke's
- 1 (4-ounce) jar diced pimentos, drained
- 1 tablespoon grated Vidalia onion with juice
- 1 teaspoon Worcestershire sauce
- ½ teaspoon kosher salt
- ½ teaspoon freshly ground black pepper
- ⅛ teaspoon cayenne pepper
- 1½ cups lightly packed coarsely shredded extra-sharp yellow cheddar cheese
- 1½ cups lightly packed coarsely shredded extra-sharp white cheddar cheese

PREPARATION

In a medium bowl, whisk the mayonnaise, pimentos, onion, Worcestershire sauce, salt, pepper, and cayenne together. Fold in the cheeses with a rubber spatula to thoroughly combine. Transfer to a container, cover, and refrigerate for a few hours before serving to allow the flavors to meld. Use within 1 week.

TIP: **An 8-ounce block of cheddar will yield 3 to 4 cups of shredded cheese depending on how firmly you pack it.**

3 VARIATIONS ON "CLASSIC" PIMENTO CHEESE

SPICY PICKLE PIMENTO CHEESE

Diced pickles—spicy dill chips, not sweet bread-and-butters—along with a teaspoon of juice brings some brininess to the party.

INGREDIENTS

- 1 teaspoon pickle juice
- 1 batch "Classic" Pimento Cheese (page 13)
- ⅓ cup drained diced spicy pickle chips

PREPARATION

Whisk the pickle juice into the pimento cheese base when you add the mayo. Fold in the pickle chips as you add the cheddar cheese.

COUNTRY HAM PIMENTO CHEESE

Ham always goes with cheese. Here, extra-salty, smoky country ham goes *in* the cheese. Save the neat slices of ham for breakfast and use scraps or end pieces here. If you're using a single plastic-wrapped slice from the grocery store, it will likely be more moist than traditional country ham. Let it air-dry in the refrigerator unwrapped overnight. It will be easier to chop, and the drier texture will hold up better in the creamy pimento cheese.

INGREDIENTS

- ½ cup finely diced country ham (about half of a trimmed steak)
- 1 batch "Classic" Pimento Cheese (page 13)

PREPARATION

Fold the ham into the pimento cheese base as you add the cheddar cheese.

CHARRED ONION & PECAN PIMENTO CHEESE

Think of this as kin to a nut-rolled holiday cheese ball; char brings out the sweetness of the onions, and toasting deepens the crunch of the pecans.

INGREDIENTS

- 1 (1-inch-thick) Vidalia onion slice, skin removed
- ⅓ cup pecan halves
- 1 batch "Classic" Pimento Cheese (page 13)

PREPARATION

Place a cast-iron skillet over high heat until smoking. Add the onion slice and cook for 5 minutes, until charred on the underside, then flip and cook for 5 minutes more, until charred on the other side and tender all over. Transfer to a plate to cool, then finely chop and transfer to a bowl.

Reduce the heat to medium, add the pecans, and toast them for 5 to 7 minutes, until fragrant, stirring or shaking the pan occasionally. Transfer to a plate to cool, then finely chop the pecans and add them to the bowl with the chopped onions. Fold the mixture into the pimento cheese base as you add the cheddar cheese.

CRAB HUSH PUPPIES

SERVES 20

CHARLESTON CATERER CALLIE WHITE KNOWS THE BEST WAY TO FEED A CROWD: one bite at a time. Along with her daughter, Carrie Morey, White built a baked-goods empire, Callie's Charleston Biscuits, on the bite-size ham and cinnamon-sugar biscuits she's baked for parties all over the Lowcountry. She's found that downsizing works with other classic party foods too. In this recipe White shrinks hush puppies down to a pop-in-your-mouth size and sweetens them with lump crabmeat.

INGREDIENTS

Peanut oil for frying

3 cups buttermilk cornmeal mix, preferably White Lily

1 cup self-rising flour, preferably White Lily

1 teaspoon baking soda

2 teaspoons kosher salt

4 teaspoons freshly ground black pepper

1 cup chopped scallions

2½ cups full-fat buttermilk

1 pound lump crab-meat, picked over

1 large egg, lightly beaten

Tartar sauce (page 240) for dipping

PREPARATION

Fill a Dutch oven or a large, deep-sided cast-iron skillet with 1 inch of oil. Clip a frying thermometer to the side of the pot, place over medium-high heat, and bring the oil to 375°F. (The temperature will drop when the hush puppy batter is added; you'll want to regulate the heat to maintain a temperature of between 350 and 375°F while you are frying.)

In a large bowl, whisk all the ingredients together. Working in batches, drop by scant tablespoons into the oil and fry until golden and crisp, 3 to 4 minutes, turning occasionally for even browning. Remove with a spider or slotted spoon and drain on paper towels. Serve with a bowl of tartar sauce for dipping.

TIP: **These will go fast, so you might as well make a double batch. After frying, arrange your second (or third) pass on a cooling rack set onto a baking sheet in a 200°F oven. The rack will keep air circulating all around the hush puppies so they don't become soggy.**

SALT-BAKED SHRIMP

SERVES 8 TO 10

ATLANTA CHEF ADAM EVANS HAS A DEEP AND ABIDING RELATIONSHIP WITH Gulf shrimp—not uncommon for people like him who grew up in Alabama, where drives to the shore punctuate nearly every childhood. Now he serves up signature seafood dishes at the Optimist. His salt-baked shrimp is like classic beach-bar peel-and-eat shrimp, except instead of steaming flavor away, it's concentrated in a dish that's as simple to prepare as it is spectacular to serve to guests. Bake three pounds of rock salt tricked out with coriander, star anise, garlic, and a few other intense flavors, then bury the shrimp in it. Pop the whole thing back in the oven for ten more minutes or so, and it's done. "It's a great technique and makes so much sense," Evans says. "You have seafood in whatever form—a whole fish or whole shrimp—coming out of salt."

INGREDIENTS

- 3 pounds rock salt
- 1 tablespoon coriander seeds
- 2 tablespoons black peppercorns
- 4 bay leaves
- 3 star anise
- 10 sprigs fresh thyme
- 1 head garlic, cloves smashed and skin removed
- 1 jalapeño, sliced, with seeds
- 2 lemon wedges
- 2 pounds head-on shrimp (20 to 25 count)
-   Comeback Sauce (page 237) for dipping

PREPARATION

Preheat the oven to 475°F.

Combine the rock salt, coriander, peppercorns, bay leaves, star anise, thyme, garlic, jalapeño, and lemon wedges in a large bowl and mix well.

Pour half of the salt-spice mixture into a large, oven-safe baking dish (or two smaller dishes) and place it in the oven to preheat for 10 to 12 minutes, until the salt becomes hot. Remove from the oven, lay the shrimp in the salt, and add the remaining salt to cover the shrimp. Return the pan to the oven and bake for an additional 8 to 12 minutes, until the shrimp are just cooked through. Using tongs, remove the shrimp from the salt and transfer to a plate. Serve with a bowl of Comeback Sauce for dipping.

SIMPLE SLICE-AND-BAKE CHEESE WAFERS

MAKES 36 WAFERS;

serves 12

CHEESE STRAWS ARE THE ELEGANTLY SLENDER COUTURE MODELS OF SOUTHERN party appetizers. And like couture models, they can't just be put together at a moment's notice. Typically the dough is carefully rolled and cut or extruded from a pastry bag or vintage hand-cranked cookie press. Tasty but not easy. Enter the cheese wafer, the cheese straw's good-time, slice-and-bake cousin. Like a proper straw, this recipe binds the least amount of flour possible into the most possible amount of butter and cheese and accomplishes the feat without a lot of fuss. Keep a log of cheese wafer dough in the fridge and in twenty minutes you can have a hot, salty, savory appetizer to serve guests, expected or otherwise.

INGREDIENTS

- ½ cup (1 stick) unsalted butter, sliced
- 2 cups coarsely grated extra-sharp cheddar cheese
- ½ cup finely grated Parmesan cheese
- ½ teaspoon kosher salt, plus more for sprinkling on top
- ¼ teaspoon cayenne pepper
- 1 cup all-purpose flour

  Optional garnishes: pecan halves, sliced Manzanilla olives, thyme leaves

PREPARATION

Combine the butter, cheeses, salt, cayenne, and flour in a food processor and pulse several times until crumbly, then process for 30 seconds, until a mass of dough forms. Transfer the dough to a sheet of parchment paper and roll into a log about 2 inches in diameter, wrap in Tootsie-Roll fashion, and refrigerate for at least 1 hour or overnight.

Preheat the oven to 350°F.

Cut the chilled dough into ¼-inch slices and arrange them on a parchment-lined baking sheet. Top with any of the garnishes if you like. Bake for 12 minutes, or until golden and crisp. Immediately sprinkle with salt, then transfer to a wire rack to cool. The wafers can be stored in an airtight container for up to 1 week.

TOMATO ASPIC & SHRIMP SALAD

FOR MANY SOUTHERNERS OF A CERTAIN AGE, NO GATHERING WAS COMPLETE without a wobbly tomato aspic or some other sort of gelatin coagulation. And though the popularity of jellied salads has faded since the 1950s, they're a fun throwback ripe for revival. This recipe comes from Gilchrist, a classic Southern lunch counter in Mountain Brook, Alabama, that's been serving aspic since 1928. Current owner Leon Rosato says the kitchen turns out more than a hundred individual aspic molds per week, and his brother Jody makes most of them. Here, Gilchrist's time-tested recipe—made ever so slightly sweet and fragrant with brown sugar and cloves—is paired with a simple shrimp salad. Together they make a refreshing party centerpiece on a hot summer day.

INGREDIENTS

FOR THE ASPIC

Crisco for greasing the mold

1 (46-ounce) bottle tomato juice (Clamato juice also works nicely)

10 whole cloves

½ cup brown sugar

1 small white onion, cut into chunks

1 celery stalk, cut into chunks

3½ tablespoons powdered gelatin (3½ envelopes)

½ cup cold water

1 cup boiling water

Juice of ½ lemon

FOR THE SALAD

2 pounds cooked bay shrimp or larger shrimp, cut into pieces

8 celery stalks, thinly sliced

12 scallions, white and light green parts only, thinly sliced

⅔ cup mayonnaise

½ cup sweet pickle relish

2 tablespoons grainy Dijon mustard

Kosher salt and freshly ground black pepper

Freshly squeezed lemon juice

Bibb lettuce leaves and fresh parsley or celery leaves for garnish

PREPARATION

FOR THE ASPIC Lightly grease a 6½-cup ring mold or gelatin mold with Crisco.

Combine the tomato juice, cloves, brown sugar, onion, and celery in a large saucepan. Place over high heat and bring to a boil; reduce the heat to low, simmer for 15 minutes, stirring to dissolve the sugar, then strain.

Sprinkle the gelatin over the surface of the cold water and let sit for 1 minute. Slowly whisk in the boiling water to dissolve the gelatin, add lemon juice, then continue whisking for 1 minute. Pour the gelatin into the hot tomato juice mixture and stir well to combine. Pour the mixture into the prepared mold and transfer to the refrigerator to chill until set, 4 to 6 hours or overnight.

Carefully loosen the gelatin from the sides of the mold with the tip of a moistened knife. Unmold by carefully dipping the mold into warm but not hot water to just beneath the surface of the gelatin for 5 to 10 seconds. Tap the mold a few times to release the suction, then invert it onto a serving dish, gently shaking to help release the aspic from the mold without breaking it.

FOR THE SALAD In a large bowl, mix the shrimp, celery, and scallions. Add the mayonnaise, pickle relish, and mustard, season with salt, pepper, and lemon juice, and stir well to combine. Place in the refrigerator and chill until ready to serve. Line the center of the molded aspic with lettuce leaves and spoon in the shrimp salad to serve. Garnish with fresh celery or parsley leaves.

DELTA-STYLE HOT TAMALES

MAKES 36 TO 48,

depending on the size of the cornhusks

DEPOSITED BY MEXICAN MIGRANT WORKERS IN WHAT'S OFTEN CALLED "the most Southern place on Earth" in the early 1900s and embraced by the local African-American population, Mississippi Delta–style "hots" diverge from their south-of-the-border brethren in several ways: they are simmered more often than steamed; the filling is more likely to be made with ground cornmeal than *masa harina;* and they're smaller and often open-ended, which makes eating a bundle easy—squeeze the filling toward the top, just like a push-up pop.

Beyond those similarities, however, no two Delta tamale recipes are the same, in the same city or, sometimes, even at the same purveyor. "I always tell folks, hot tamale[s] is like making corn whiskey," Shine Thornton, the late proprietor of Maria's Famous Hot Tamales in Greenville, told the Oxford-based Southern Foodways Alliance back in 2005. "You never get the same thing out twice." And then there are the secret ingredients that season the meal, the meat, and the simmering broth. Everybody has one, and nobody's telling.

Making a batch isn't a quick affair. "With tamales, the first thing you need to keep in mind is [that] it is a long process, a lot of work, and if you don't have the time, don't try doing it," says two-time Delta Hot Tamale Festival winner Hattie Brown Johnson of Jodie's Hot Tamales in Greenville. But they're also a great excuse for throwing a party. Prep the meat and dough several days ahead and refrigerate them. Then, whenever you're ready, call the crowd to start rolling and steaming.

This recipe is an amalgamation of recipes we've studied, what we've learned from cooks we've interviewed, and hots we've sampled. The three "secret" ingredients here actually are quite basic. First, a bit more minced meat in the tamale than some—about a two parts cornmeal to one part meat ratio—for more textural contrast inside the husk. Second, your favorite spicy Bloody Mary mix, which infuses the meat cooked in it with the acidity of tomatoes to balance the luxuriousness of the lard- and butter-filled meal mixture, along with an extra dose of heat from horseradish. Third, courtesy of Hattie, a spoonful of lard in the simmering liquid, a final hedge against the saddest of all fates that could befall a tamale: a dry filling. RECIPE FOLLOWS ▶

2 (8-ounce) bags cornhusks (about 4 dozen)

FOR THE MEAT AND BROTH

⅓ cup vegetable oil

2 pounds boneless pork shoulder, cut into cubes

Kosher salt and freshly ground black pepper

4 onions

1 cinnamon stick, broken in half

6 garlic cloves, smashed and peeled

1 tablespoon chili powder

2 teaspoons onion powder

1 teaspoon ground cumin

1 teaspoon cayenne pepper

1 teaspoon dried oregano

3 cups proper Southern Bloody Mary mix, such as Tabasco or Oxford Falls Bootlegger

Reserved stock from cooking the pork

FOR THE DOUGH

1 cup lard, plus 1 tablespoon for the simmering liquid

4 tablespoons (½ stick) softened unsalted butter

4 cups fine-ground white or yellow cornmeal

2 teaspoons baking powder

2 teaspoons kosher salt

½ teaspoon cayenne pepper

Hot sauce (optional)

FOR THE MEAT AND BROTH Place a Dutch oven over medium-high heat and add 2 tablespoons of the oil. Season the pork generously with salt and pepper and brown the meat on all sides, 5 to 6 minutes, working in batches if necessary and removing the meat to a plate as it's ready. Pour a splash of water into the pan and scrape up the browned bits from the bottom, then return the meat and any collected juices to the pan and add water to just below the surface of the meat. Peel and cut 2 onions in half, stud with the cinnamon stick halves, and nestle them in the pot. Add the garlic and bring to a boil, then reduce the heat to low, cover, and gently simmer for 1 hour, until tender. Strain the liquid through a fine-mesh sieve (you should have at least 2 cups liquid), cool the liquid, and refrigerate. Discard the onion halves and cinnamon sticks. When the meat is cool enough to handle, finely chop it and set aside.

To make the sauce for the meat, dice the remaining 2 onions. Put the remaining oil in the Dutch oven over medium-high heat. Add the diced onions and sauté 5 minutes, until softened. Stir in the chili powder, onion powder, cumin, cayenne, oregano, and ½ teaspoon salt and cook, stirring, for 2 minutes. Add 2 cups of the Bloody Mary mix and the browned pork, bring to a simmer, then reduce the heat to low and simmer for 20 minutes. Remove from the heat and set aside.

FOR THE DOUGH In a large bowl, beat the 1 cup lard and the butter with an electric mixer until light and fluffy. In a separate large bowl, whisk together the cornmeal, baking powder, salt, and cayenne. Gradually beat the dry ingredients and 2 cups of the reserved cooled pork stock into the whipped fat, alternating dry ingredients and stock, to create a dough similar in texture to mashed potatoes.

TO ASSEMBLE AND COOK THE TAMALES Soak the cornhusks in hot water to cover for at least 30 minutes. Drain the cornhusks and sort them, selecting whole, clean husks (tear irregular husks into strips for tying the tamales), and arrange them on a work surface. Spoon 2 tablespoons tamale dough vertically down center of the top two-thirds of each open husk. Top with a heaping tablespoon of the pork mixture, more or less depending on the size of the husks. Add a dash of hot sauce if you like. Fold the bottom third of the short end of the husk up over the filling, then fold one long side toward the center of the package, then roll the tamale like a cigar, lightly squeezing it to evenly distribute the filling. Tie with strips of soaked husk to secure. Repeat with remaining husks, dough, and filling.

In a large stockpot, arrange the tamales vertically, closed side down. Carefully add the remaining 1 tablespoon lard, remaining 1 cup Bloody Mary mix, and any remaining stock and sauce, then add water until the tamales are three-quarters submerged. Bring to a boil over high heat, then cover, reduce the heat to low, and simmer for 1½ hours. To test for doneness, sample a tamale—the filling should be smooth, with no traces of graininess. Any remaining tamales may be cooled and frozen in zip-top bags for up to 3 months.

PICKAPEPPA PECANS

MAKES ABOUT 4 CUPS;

serves 16

WHILE PICKAPEPPA HOT SAUCE ACTUALLY HAILS FROM JAMAICA, ITS FLAVOR profile—spicy-salty-sweet with the oaky undertones that come from barrel aging—meshes perfectly with Southern standbys from barbecue to Bloody Marys. When it collides with pecans, it's a match made in Southern cocktail-hour heaven.

INGREDIENTS

- 1 pound (about 4 cups) pecan halves
- 1 (5-ounce) bottle Pickapeppa sauce
- ¼ cup water
- ¼ cup brown sugar
- 1 teaspoon kosher salt
- 1 teaspoon smoked paprika

PREPARATION

Place the pecans in a large bowl. In a glass measuring cup, whisk together the Pickapeppa sauce, water, brown sugar, salt, and smoked paprika. Pour over the pecans and let sit for 1 hour, tossing occasionally to mix. Drain.

Preheat the oven to 350°F. Arrange the drained nuts in a single layer on a parchment-lined baking sheet and bake for 20 minutes, tossing once, until fragrant. Let cool on the baking sheet. The nuts will keep stored in an airtight container for up to 1 week.

TIP: **For a sweeter spin, sprinkle the nuts with an additional ¼ cup brown sugar just before you put them in the oven.**

DEVILISH EGGS

MAKES 24;

serves 12

WHEN CHEF TREVOR HIGGINS WAS GROWING UP IN CLEVELAND, TENNESSEE, deviled eggs were a tradition at family get-togethers, as they still are at gatherings across the South and beyond. "My grandmother had those neat old platters, and she would bring out tons of deviled eggs for us to snack on before the meal," says Higgins, who serves his own ramped-up version of the dish at his restaurant, Roost, in Greenville, South Carolina. "I go classic with mustard and mayonnaise, but I add bacon fat and a drop of Sriracha." We'll take a dozen, please.

INGREDIENTS

- 12 large grade-A eggs
- 2 tablespoons white wine vinegar
- ½ cup mayonnaise
- 1½ teaspoons grainy mustard
- 1 tablespoon Sriracha
- 1½ teaspoons bacon grease

  Kosher salt and freshly ground black pepper
- 2 ounces smoked salmon, cut into small slices (optional)

  Snipped fresh chives for garnish (optional)

PREPARATION

Place the eggs in a stockpot and add water to cover by 1 inch. Add the vinegar. Place over high heat, bring to a boil, then reduce the heat to medium and simmer for 10 minutes more (you're looking for a firm yolk). Remove the pot from the heat, put it in the sink, and run cold water over it for 1 to 2 minutes to cool the eggs a bit, then transfer the eggs to an ice-water bath and chill (about 20 minutes), until cooled completely. Remove the eggs from the water, peel them, then cut them in half lengthwise and scoop out the yolks.

Combine the egg yolks, mayonnaise, mustard, Sriracha, and bacon grease in a medium bowl and season to taste with salt and pepper. Whisk the ingredients until smooth. Fill a piping bag with the mixture and pipe it into the egg yolk halves. Top each with a small slice of salmon and snipped chives, if using. Serve immediately.

TIP: There are all kinds of tales about how best to avoid divots or craters when peeling eggs, but these are the methods we've found work best: First, save just-laid eggs for another recipe; older eggs peel more easily. Second, let the eggs chill completely. (They contract slightly, making peeling easier.) Third, gently roll the egg around on your countertop with enough pressure to thoroughly crack the shell without breaking the egg. Start peeling at the air pocket, using the membrane to help lift bits of broken shell.

OLD-FLORIDA SMOKED FISH DIP
WITH SMOKED MULLET & MINORCAN MAYONNAISE

SERVES 4 TO 6

GREG BAKER IS MORE THAN A CHEF—HE'S A CULINARY ANTHROPOLOGIST. HIS Tampa restaurant, Fodder & Shine, is a shrine to the staples of old Florida: smoked mullet, frog legs, rabbit and dumplings, and mayonnaise. Yes, mayonnaise. According to Baker, there's a strong chance one of the South's favorite condiments might have been introduced to the Americas by the Minorcans who made their way from the Mediterranean to St. Augustine, Florida. The theory might help explain the prevalence of mayonnaise-based fish dips in the Sunshine State. One of the most cherished fish is smoked mullet, a working-class staple along Florida's Gulf Coast for generations.

INGREDIENTS

- 1 pound Smoked Mullet (recipe follows) or prepared smoked fish of your choice
- ¼ cup minced onion
- ¼ cup minced celery
- ¼ cup thinly sliced scallions
- Juice of ½ large lemon
- 2 datil peppers, minced (or substitute 1 seeded habañero)
- ½ cup Minorcan Mayonnaise (recipe follows)
- 1 teaspoon kosher salt or sea salt
- ½ teaspoon freshly ground black pepper

PREPARATION

Shred the smoked fish into chunks, discarding the skin and removing the bones (if you're using mullet, there will be *many* bones). Combine the fish, onion, celery, scallions, lemon juice, peppers, mayonnaise, salt, and pepper in large bowl and stir until well combined. Taste and adjust the seasoning if needed.

SMOKED MULLET

Although frequently described with words like "lowly" and "humble," mullet makes fine eating. It smokes especially well because of its high oil content.

INGREDIENTS

- 1 mullet (about 2 pounds) or other fish, head removed and butterflied
- ¼ cup sea salt or kosher salt
- 2 tablespoons freshly ground black pepper
  Soaked wood chips

PREPARATION

Place the fish skin-side down on a wire rack set on a baking sheet. Combine the salt and pepper and liberally coat the flesh of the fish. Place the baking sheet in the refrigerator and allow the fish to sit in the salt for 30 to 45 minutes to drain. Rinse the fish to remove the salt mixture. Drain any accumulated water from the baking sheet, place the mullet back on the rack, and refrigerate for 1 hour.

Prepare a smoker with soaked wood chips (Chef Baker recommends citrus, mangrove, or oak) according to the manufacturer's instructions. When the temperature reaches 130 to 150°F, place the fish skin-side down in the center of the rack above the drip pan and smoke for 1 to 2 hours, until the flesh starts to pull away from edges of the skin, replenishing the wood chips if necessary. Remove the fish from the smoker.

MINORCAN MAYONNAISE

Makes 1 generous cup

Chef Baker's mayonnaise is slightly more lemony than most standard homemade recipes, likely a vestige of its Mediterranean origin. When used to bind the dip, the extra acidity contrasts nicely with the fattiness of the smoked fish.

INGREDIENTS

- 2 egg yolks
  Juice of ½ lemon
- 1 garlic clove, minced
- ½ cup good olive oil
- ½ cup vegetable oil
  Kosher salt or sea salt and freshly ground black pepper

PREPARATION

Combine the egg yolks, lemon juice, and garlic in a medium bowl. Using a whisk, beat until the yolks are fluffy and start to stiffen, about 1 minute.

Combine the olive and vegetable oils and add to the bowl—a few drops at a time at first to homogenize the yolk mixture, whisking constantly, then in a slow steady stream, again whisking constantly, until the oils are completely homogenized into the yolk mixture (about 8 minutes). If the mixture starts becoming too thick, it may be thinned with a drop or two of water. Season with salt and pepper to taste. Store in an airtight container, refrigerated, for up to 3 days.

BENEDICTINE

MAKES 1 CUP

BENEDICTINE, A KENTUCKY COCKTAIL-SANDWICH SPREAD INVENTED IN THE late 1800s by famous Louisville hostess "Miss Jennie" Carter Benedict, isn't like raita, tzatziki, or any other kind of fresh cucumber condiment we're familiar with today. It's delightfully strange—the spread tastes like onion-spiked cucumber, but no onions or cukes are visibly discernible in the mint green–colored mix, which gets its hue from a shot of food coloring. You can certainly prepare the recipe without it—the peels from the cucumber will add a faint greenish tinge—but it won't look nearly as appealing when slathered in between dainty triangles of white sandwich bread (crusts removed, of course). Benedictine goes in the same file as another colorful Southern classic—red velvet cake. Sure, you could try to make the cake with beet juice or something, but why?

INGREDIENTS

1 slicing or English cucumber
½ small Vidalia onion
1 (8-ounce) package cream cheese, softened
1 teaspoon kosher salt
Pinch of cayenne pepper
2 drops green food coloring

PREPARATION

Wash and dry the cucumber, then grate it, peel and all, using a fine grater set over or into a bowl. Drain the grated cucumber in a fine-mesh sieve set over a bowl, pressing on the cucumber pulp to extract at least 3 tablespoons of juice. Discard the solids. In a separate bowl, repeat the grating and juicing process with the onion to yield at least 1 tablespoon of juice.

Combine the cream cheese, 3 tablespoons cucumber juice, 1 tablespoon onion juice, salt, cayenne, and food coloring in a medium bowl and mix with a rubber spatula, pressing the mixture against the sides of the bowl to incorporate all the components and coloring. Scrape down the sides of the bowl, transfer to a serving bowl, and serve. If not using right away, transfer the mixture to an airtight container and place in the refrigerator, where it will keep for up to 1 week.

SAUSAGE BALLS

MAKES 36;

serves 12

LET'S BE HONEST: MANY OF THE SAUSAGE BALLS SET OUT ON PARTY PLATTERS could take down a horse if shot from a musket. Most often made from just three ingredients—sausage, cheese, and boxed baking mix—they're low effort and, too often, low reward. But it doesn't have to be that way. With just a dollop of ingenuity and not much more work, you can build a better ball. Pack them with Southern ingredients like cornmeal, tangy buttermilk, brown sugar, and real-deal hot country sausage. Then build on that solid foundation with grated sweet onion, a good sharp cheddar, and a blend of fresh herbs and spices that amp up the flavors of the sausage.

INGREDIENTS

- 1 cup fine-ground cornmeal
- 1½ teaspoons baking powder
- 1 tablespoon brown sugar
- ½ teaspoon kosher salt
- ½ teaspoon freshly ground black pepper
- ½ teaspoon red pepper flakes
- 2 teaspoons minced fresh sage
- 2 tablespoons sliced fresh chives
- 1 (10-ounce) block extra-sharp cheddar cheese, grated
- 1 pound bulk spicy breakfast sausage
- 2 tablespoons grated onion
- 2 tablespoons buttermilk

PREPARATION

Preheat the oven to 350°F.

Whisk together the cornmeal, baking powder, brown sugar, salt, pepper, red pepper flakes, sage, and chives in a large bowl. Add the cheese and toss with the cornmeal mixture to evenly coat and distribute. In a separate bowl, combine the sausage, onion, and buttermilk. Pour the cornbread and cheese mixture into the sausage mixture and mix with your hands to thoroughly combine.

Roll packed tablespoons of dough into 1-inch balls and arrange them on a parchment-lined baking sheet. Bake for 22 to 25 minutes, until bubbly, cooked through, and golden brown.

TIP: **The flat side created as the sausage balls bake will help keep them from rolling around on a serving tray, but if you want a rounder ball, turn them halfway through baking.**

WEST INDIES SALAD

SERVES 24 AS A DIP,
or 10 to 12 as a starter salad

ODDLY ENOUGH, WEST INDIES SALAD IS ACTUALLY NATIVE TO ALABAMA.
Bayley's Seafood Restaurant, specifically, on Mobile Bay, where Bill Bayley put the onion-studded crab ceviche on the menu in 1947. Nowadays, you'll find variations at restaurants all along the Gulf Coast. At Fisher's in Orange Beach, Alabama, Bill Briand, a protégé of Emeril Lagasse and Donald Link, serves a version that doesn't stray too far from the original. "This is a very simple and traditional recipe, with one exception," he says. "I use red onions instead of white onions because I think they taste better, and they're prettier." That tiny tweak, along with a sprinkling of lemon zest and a garnish of mint, brings new life to an often-overlooked regional classic.

INGREDIENTS

- 1 small red onion, finely diced
- 1 pound fresh lump crabmeat
- 3 ounces vegetable oil (scant ½ cup)
- 3 ounces apple cider vinegar (scant ½ cup)
- 6 tablespoons ice water
- ½ teaspoon kosher salt
- ½ teaspoon freshly ground black pepper
- 1 tablespoon thinly sliced mint
- Zest of ½ lemon

ACCOMPANIMENTS AND GARNISHES

- Saltines
- Satsuma segments when in season, clementines, or any small, seedless tangerine
- Mizuna or arugula

PREPARATION

Spread half of the onion over the bottom of a large bowl. Cover with the crab, then add the remaining onion. Add the oil, vinegar, and ice water in that order. Do not mix. Add the salt and pepper, then cover and refrigerate for 2 hours. Toss lightly, then taste and adjust the seasonings if needed. Top with the mint and lemon zest. Spoon into a serving bowl and serve as a dip with saltines, or serve over a bed of mizuna or arugula with satsuma segments as a starter salad.

THREE SOUTHERN SANDWICHES, PARTY-STYLE

No matter how you slice it (although we have some specific recommendations for that),
any one of these classics will feed—and please—a crowd.

KENTUCKY HOT BROWNS

MAKES 16 FINGER SANDWICHES

AFTER A NIGHT OF DANCING INTO THE WEE HOURS DURING THE ROARING
Twenties, revelers in Louisville would stop by the Brown Hotel's restaurant, where Chef Fred Schmidt
concocted an open-faced turkey sandwich smothered in classic Mornay sauce that helped keep the
good times going—or fortify the start of a workday. His rich and refined dish has endured as the hotel's
signature menu item. Our recipe makes only one alteration to the basic formula: thick Texas toast
provides a more solid foundation for the gravy-topped goodness.

INGREDIENTS

- 2 tablespoons unsalted butter
- 2 tablespoons all-purpose flour
- 2 cups heavy cream
- ½ cup grated Pecorino Romano cheese
- Pinch of freshly grated nutmeg
- 1 teaspoon kosher salt
- ½ teaspoon finely ground black pepper
- 4 thick-cut slices Texas Toast, crusts removed, toasted
- 16 slices roasted turkey
- 4 Roma tomatoes, cored and chopped
- 8 cooked thick-cut bacon slices, chopped
- Chopped fresh parsley
- Paprika

PREPARATION

Preheat the broiler.

Melt the butter in a small saucepan over medium-high heat. Add the
flour and whisk until combined. Cook, whisking, until a light golden
roux comes together, about 1 minute. Slowly whisk in the cream and
cook, stirring often, for 2 to 3 minutes, just until the mixture comes to
a simmer, then remove from the heat. Whisk in ¼ cup of the cheese, the
nutmeg, salt, and pepper.

Toast the bread under the broiler for 30 seconds to 1 minute, until
browned to your liking. Place each toasted bread slice in the bottom
of an individual ovenproof dish. Top each piece of toast with 4 slices
of turkey. Spoon a scant ½ cup sauce over each and evenly sprinkle the
remaining cheese on top. Place under the broiler and broil until lightly
browned and bubbly, 2 to 3 minutes. Remove from the oven and top
with the tomatoes and bacon.

Place a toothpick or skewer in each of 4 quadrants of each sandwich,
then cut in between them to create 4 squares. Sprinkle with parsley, a
light dusting of paprika, and a little extra salt and pepper and serve.

CUBANOS WITH MARINATED PORK

MAKES 32 FINGER SANDWICHES

CLASSIC KEY WEST, MIAMI, AND YBOR CITY *PLANCHA*-**PRESSED CUBANOS ARE** a celebration of pork two ways: thinly sliced ham and pork roast marinated in traditional flavors of garlic, citrus, and oregano. This sandwich is often re-created using crusty French bread, which can shred the roof of your mouth, or Hawaiian bread, which is much too sweet and moist. Spongy Cuban bread works best, and you can find it at most grocery stores.

INGREDIENTS

FOR THE MARINATED PORK

- 1 (2.5-pound) pork sirloin roast
- 2 teaspoons kosher salt
- 1½ teaspoons freshly ground black pepper
- 1½ teaspoons dried Mexican oregano
- 2 teaspoons ground cumin
- 1 shallot, thinly sliced
- 10 garlic cloves, minced
- ¾ cup freshly squeezed lime juice
- ¼ cup freshly squeezed lemon or Seville orange juice

FOR THE CUBAN PORK SANDWICH

- 1 loaf Cuban bread
- 4 tablespoons (½ stick) unsalted butter, softened
- ½ teaspoon garlic powder
- 1 tablespoon yellow mustard
  Dill pickle slices
- 8 ounces thinly sliced deli ham
- 8 ounces sliced Swiss cheese
  Olive oil for toasting

PREPARATION

FOR THE PORK Pierce the pork roast all over with tines of a fork. Place the pork in a quart-size zip-top bag with the remaining ingredients. Seal and massage the meat well. Refrigerate for at least 4 hours or preferably overnight, turning the meat over once or twice to evenly distribute the marinade.

Preheat the oven to 325°F.

Place the pork on a wire rack set over a baking sheet and roast for 45 minutes to 1 hour, until a meat thermometer registers 140°F. Remove from the oven and let the meat rest for 15 minutes before slicing.

FOR THE SANDWICHES Slice the loaf in half horizontally. Brush both cut sides of bread with butter and sprinkle each half with ¼ teaspoon garlic powder. Spread the mustard on one half and arrange dill pickle slices in an even layer on top. Slice the pork roast about ¼ inch thick and arrange the slices on top of the pickles. Top the pork with the ham slices, followed by the cheese. Place the remaining half of the bread on top and cut the sandwich in half crosswise.

Place a large cast-iron skillet or griddle over medium heat and add the oil. Add 1 sandwich half and top with a smaller, heavy skillet or cast-iron sandwich press. Press the sandwich while it cooks for 5 to 7 minutes per side. Repeat with the remaining sandwich half, adding more olive oil if needed. Transfer to a cutting board and let rest for 3 to 5 minutes.

Slice the sandwich halves lengthwise in half again. Evenly place 8 toothpicks or skewers through each sandwich quarter, then cut in between them to create bite-size squares and serve.

MUFFULETTAS WITH OLIVE-ARTICHOKE RELISH

A MASSIVE MOUND OF MEAT, CHEESE, AND TANGY PICKLED VEGETABLE RELISH on a round sesame roll, the muffuletta has been a cornerstone of New Orleans cuisine for more than a century. It's generally made with muffuletta bread—a sesame-topped round that's dense and sturdy enough to soak up the deliciously oily, fatty, cheesy fillings. That's all well and good if you can get your hands on some. If not, substitute ciabatta or a sesame semolina loaf and follow the slicing instructions for the Cubanos on page 37.

INGREDIENTS

- 1 (10-inch) round muffuletta loaf, ciabatta, or sesame semolina loaf
- 8 slices provolone cheese
- 3 ounces ham
- 3 ounces capocollo
- 3 ounces mortadella
- 3 ounces Genoa salami
- 3 ounces prosciutto
- 1 cup Olive-Artichoke Relish (recipe follows)

PREPARATION

Preheat the oven to 350°F.

Slice the bread in half horizontally. Create a cavity in both bread halves by removing all but about ½ inch of soft interior from each.

Arrange a layer of 4 slices of cheese on one half of the bread. Top with a layer of ham, followed by capocollo, mortadella, salami, and prosciutto. Spoon the Olive-Artichoke Relish on top and top with the remaining cheese. Place the remaining bread half on top. Wrap the sandwich in foil, place in the oven, and bake for 15 to 20 minutes, until the sandwich is heated through and the cheese has melted. Transfer to a cutting board and let rest for 3 to 5 minutes.

Evenly place 16 toothpicks or skewers in a circle through the sandwich, then cut in between them to create individual wedges and serve.

OLIVE-ARTICHOKE RELISH

Makes about 2 cups

Cutting the traditional olive spread with lemony artichokes doesn't make this muffuletta any less salty and good, but it does make enjoying a second helping a slightly less blood-pressure-raising proposition.

INGREDIENTS

- ½ cup drained sliced pimento-stuffed Manzanilla olives
- ½ cup drained sliced kalamata olives
- ½ cup drained giardiniera (pickled vegetables)
- 3 canned artichoke hearts, drained
- 1 tablespoon drained capers
- 1 garlic clove, chopped
- 1 tablespoon olive oil
- 1 tablespoon red wine vinegar, or to taste
- ¼ teaspoon dried oregano, crushed
- ¼ teaspoon red pepper flakes, or to taste
- 1 celery stalk, finely chopped

PREPARATION

Combine all the ingredients except the celery in the bowl of a food processor and pulse several times to coarsely chop or, alternatively, chop them by hand. Transfer to a bowl and fold in the celery. Taste and adjust the seasoning and acidity by adding more red pepper flakes or a bit more vinegar if needed. Transfer to an airtight container and refrigerate for at least 24 hours before using to allow the flavors to meld. Leftover relish will keep refrigerated for up to 1 week.

BOURBON BALLS

MAKES 48;

serves 24

BOURBON BALLS FUNCTION AS THE ULTIMATE EASY DESSERT FOR SOUTHERN cocktail parties, and they put a sweet, slightly boozy finish on any get-together. Think of them as an edible digestif. Crushed vanilla wafers hold all the chocolatey goodness together. Buy an 11-ounce box and remove two dozen wafers to save for another use, like the Banana Pudding on page 202.

INGREDIENTS

- 2 cups crushed vanilla wafers (about 8 ounces)
- 1 cup finely chopped toasted pecans
- 8 ounces bittersweet chocolate, such as Nashville-made Olive & Sinclair 67% cacao chocolate, chopped
- ½ cup heavy cream
- ¼ cup light corn syrup
- 1 teaspoon ground cinnamon
- ⅓ cup bourbon

OPTIONAL COATINGS

Finely ground vanilla wafers

Finely chopped pecans or other nuts

Dusting of cocoa powder, cinnamon-sugar, or confectioners' sugar

PREPARATION

Combine the crushed wafers and pecans in a large bowl. Place the chopped chocolate in a separate bowl.

In a small saucepan, combine the cream, corn syrup, and cinnamon, place over medium heat, and bring just to a boil, stirring constantly. Immediately pour the mixture over the chopped chocolate and whisk to blend in the cream as the chocolate melts. Let cool for 1 to 2 minutes, then whisk in the bourbon.

Pour the chocolate mixture over the crumb-nut mixture and stir well to combine. Place in the refrigerator to chill for 30 minutes. Form the mixture into balls with a small melon baller (about 2 teaspoons), roll in coatings as desired, and arrange on a parchment-lined baking sheet. Store in an airtight container in a cool place for up to 1 week.

2

CHICKEN

IN PRAISE OF THE YARDBIRD

Fried, potpied, stewed, smothered, or otherwise,
chicken is its own food group in the South

JULIA REED

AT ONE POINT DURING MY LENGTHY COLLEGE CAREER, a period during which I took almost as many semesters off as I attended, *Washingtonian* magazine ran a short piece describing me as one of DC's most "talked about" young hostesses. A friend had planted the item partly as a joke, but my father was unamused by both the "talked about" and the "hostess" parts, and financial support was promptly withdrawn. Since my afternoon job at *Newsweek*'s Washington bureau paid a whopping $48 a week, I turned to the want ads for additional employment, which is how I ended up in a cubicle selling a volume titled *Poultry* over the phone for Time Life. The book was part of a new series called the *Good Cook*, overseen by the great Richard Olney and partially written by Jeremiah Tower, who is now a friend, but at the time I had no idea of either man's prowess or reputation. Still, such was the power of *Poultry* that I became an immediate acolyte—I sold so many copies in my first week it was given to me as a prize.

It was a decided victory in the parental dustup—not only did I earn enough to continue in my party-giving career, I was also awarded a tool that enhanced it (and still does). But I actually loved the work itself—it turns out that I was born to talk turkey or, in this case, mostly chicken.

I grew up in a region where cookbooks outsell everything but the Bible and where a great majority of them feature a wide-ranging section on the noble bird. My fellow Mississippi Deltan Craig Claiborne, the longtime food editor of the *New York Times*, wrote in his autobiography, *A Feast Made for Laughter,* that "throughout my career I have printed more recipes for chicken than any other meat," adding that "my appetite for it has never faltered." Like Claiborne, whose mother ran a boarding house in Indianola where chickens roamed freely in the backyard, I was raised on an almost daily chicken diet that included fried chicken, of course, but also smothered chicken, stewed chicken, stuffed chicken, chicken and rice, chicken potpie, and creamed chicken on toast. Until he died in 2000, Claiborne threw a famous annual party in the Hamptons at which he served enormous casseroles of his mother's chicken spaghetti. My own mother's "company chicken" repertoire included a creamy chicken curry much like the one served at the late, great Memphis restaurant Justine's that bore almost zero resemblance to those of India or Thailand (but that was served accompanied by lovely little bowls of mashed bananas and crumbled bacon and a half dozen other condiments I adored). Like Country Captain, it is the much-loved "Southernized" version of exotic fare that I still feature at dinner parties to great acclaim.

Chickens had a 3,500-year history as domesticated animals before Columbus toted them to our shores, but I am confident that we embraced them with a fervor they hadn't previously known. From the get go, Southerners, especially, showed them particular deference, if not unabashed love, in the pot. In *Albion's Seed*, David Hackett Fischer's seminal book about the early British settlers in America, he writes that "among both high born and humble folk, eating was a more sensual experience in Virginia than in Massachusetts." To illustrate his point, he compares "the relentless austerity of New England's 'canonical dish' of cold beans" to the luxurious chicken fricassees of Virginia made with "a pint of claret, a pint of oysters, and a dozen egg yolks." It's an easy game, this: which would you rather eat?

A similar early recipe is found in my tattered Time Life volume along with one for Erskine Caldwell's Genuine Fried Chicken (which makes the dubious substitution of fine breadcrumbs for flour) as well as Southern Fried Chicken with

Cream Gravy. I've never been a gravy girl, but I've rarely met a piece of fried chicken I didn't like. On Saturdays, our cook Lottie made it for lunch with mashed potatoes and on Sundays we picked up a bucket from the Colonel after church. Kentucky Fried Chicken was the first fast food I ever ate, and I still have a soft spot for Harland Sanders's "original recipe" of eleven herbs and spices. KFC is now available pretty much worldwide, and when I lived in New York, Popeye's (founded in New Orleans in 1972) was an exotic staple on my dining table.

These days in Manhattan, fried chicken is an increasingly un-exotic staple at white tablecloth establishments all over town. On the West coast, no less an eminence than three-starred Michelin chef Thomas Keller serves it at his Ad Hoc and Bouchon restaurants and even markets a fried chicken kit. I've tried both the chicken and the kit, and they're surprisingly good, but the benchmark for most Southerners is almost invariably the first version made for them by a beloved family member or cook. I'll go to my grave knowing that I will never taste the likes of Lottie Martin's chicken again, but for the life of me I cannot tell you why. Like biscuits, great fried chicken has everything to do with the cook's hand, which is why, in the words of Calvin Trillin, "A fried chicken cook with a deep fryer is a sculptor working with mittens."

Trillin did not need to add "Black skillet is preferred." That goes without saying, and anyway, my friend (and yet another Mississippi Delta) Jimmy Phillips already recorded a song containing that lyric, along with some other stellar lines including:

When we sat down at the table it was
  glorious to see
All that knuckle-sucking goodness just
  looking back at me.
And:
If you have not been enlightened
May I venture to explain,
Full awareness is heightened
When the grease goes to your brain.

I could go on—"Fried Chicken" is a fine song, and there are plenty more gems within it. Every time I hear Jimmy play it, which is a lot, I am struck by the reverence with which he approaches his subject. But then it's something we've all long possessed. Even now, *Poultry* (in print and in pan) has a prized place in my kitchen. The mighty chicken—to borrow Jimmy's sentiments—is "a most delightful, quite exciteful bird."

FRIED CHICKEN THREE WAYS

Let's get this out of the way right off the bat: if you are one of the fortunate ones whose grandmother showed you how to conjure crisp, golden delicious fried chicken from a cast-iron skillet and a can of Crisco, say a prayer of thanks. And please invite us over for dinner. But if you're not, one of these three recipes should do the trick.

Each follows a three-step process: brine, dip, dredge. It's the way chicken has been fried in the South since there have been chickens to fry. Why brine? A soak in salt water helps liquefy compounds in the muscle, which plumps up the cells and results in extra-moist chicken. Herbed and spiced, the brine is also a vehicle for infusing the meat with flavor. Next comes the dip, usually buttermilk, which adds sweetness and tang but mostly is the glue to which the final element, the dredge, sticks.

The only place where we break with tradition is using a hefty Dutch oven instead of a cast-iron skillet. The Dutch oven—usually made of cast-iron, by the way, if it's a good one— is deeper, so there's less spatter. It's heavier too, so it's less likely to slide around if you have one of those modern smooth ceramic electric cooktops, which must have been invented by somebody who never fried an egg, much less a whole chicken in a skillet of molten fat. We think grandmother would understand.

FRIED CHICKEN: CLASSIC

SERVES 4 TO 6

GOLDEN, CRISP BUT NOT CRUNCHY, AND LIGHTLY SEASONED WITH A LITTLE cayenne kick, this is fried chicken in its most fundamental form. Let the dredged chicken rest in the refrigerator for 45 minutes to 1 hour so the crust will fully adhere and stay put when frying.

INGREDIENTS

1   (3½- to 4-pound) whole chicken, with neck, liver, and gizzard removed, cut into 10 pieces (wings, legs, thighs, and quarter breasts)

FOR THE BRINE

1   gallon water

¾   cup kosher salt

1   tablespoon herbs or spices, such as poultry seasoning (optional)

FOR THE DIP

1   quart buttermilk

2   tablespoons hot sauce

FOR THE DREDGE

3   cups all-purpose flour

1½   tablespoons kosher salt

1½   tablespoons freshly ground black pepper

½   teaspoon cayenne pepper

Peanut oil for frying

2   tablespoons bacon grease (optional, for flavor)

PREPARATION

To make the brine, in a stockpot, bring 4 cups of the water to a boil over high heat and whisk in the salt until dissolved and herbs, if using. Remove the pan from the heat, add the remaining water, and let cool to room temperature. Place the chicken pieces in the stockpot or divide the chicken and brine between large zip-top bags and refrigerate for at least 4 hours or overnight. When you're ready to fry, drain and rinse the chicken pieces thoroughly, then pat them dry with paper towels.

To dredge the chicken, set a wire rack over a baking sheet. Combine the buttermilk and hot sauce in a shallow pan or bowl. Mix the flour, salt, pepper, and cayenne in a second shallow pan or bowl. Dip the chicken pieces into the buttermilk mixture, then into the seasoned flour, shaking off excess. Set the breaded chicken pieces on the rack, transfer the baking sheet to the refrigerator, and let the chicken rest for at least 30 minutes or up to 1 hour to set the crust.

To fry the chicken, fill a Dutch oven or a large, deep-sided cast-iron skillet with 1 inch of oil and the bacon grease, if using. Clip a frying thermometer to the side of the pot, place over medium-high heat, and bring the oil to 350°F. (The temperature will drop considerably when the chicken is added; you'll want to regulate the heat to maintain a temperature of about 325°F as you fry the chicken.) Remove the chicken from the refrigerator and fry skin-side down in batches of no more than 4 pieces at a time for 8 minutes per side, until the meat registers 165°F on an instant-read thermometer. Remove the chicken with tongs to a wire rack set over a paper towel–lined baking sheet. Repeat until all the chicken is fried. Let the chicken cool for 20 minutes before serving.

FRYING BASICS

- Do not overcrowd the pan. The oil needs to circulate evenly around each piece of chicken.
- Moderate the heat so the oil fluctuates no more than 10 degrees in either direction.
- Do not reuse the oil after a frying session; other foods just won't taste as good.
- Save your taste buds: Let fried chicken cool for 20 minutes before taking a bite.
- If the chicken has been out of the frying pan for an hour, chill it.

FRIED CHICKEN: EXTRA-CRISPY

SERVES 4 TO 6

SOUTHERNERS ARE NOT THE ONLY PEOPLE ON THE PLANET WHO FRY CHICKENS. Koreans know their way around a bird and bubbling vat of oil too, as anyone who has visited Korean-American enclaves outside of Montgomery, Houston, or northeastern Atlanta knows well. Korean fried chicken is coated with rice flour or cornstarch, which creates a delicate, shell-like crust with an audible crunch. Enjoy it as is or toss with a blend of sweet chili sauce cut with soy sauce and Sriracha for a crisp-sticky-sweet spin on a Southern classic.

INGREDIENTS

- 1 (3½- to 4-pound) whole chicken, with neck, liver, and gizzard removed, cut into 10 pieces (wings, legs, thighs, and quarter breasts)

FOR THE BRINE
- 1 gallon water
- ¾ cup kosher salt
- 1 tablespoon herbs or spices, such as poultry seasoning (optional)

FOR THE DREDGE
- ½ cup cornstarch
- ½ teaspoon kosher salt
- ½ teaspoon freshly ground black pepper

FOR THE DIP
- 1 cup cornstarch
- ½ teaspoon kosher salt
- ½ teaspoon finely ground black pepper
- ¾ cup water

  Peanut oil for frying
- 2 tablespoons bacon grease (optional, for flavor)

FOR THE TOSS
- ⅓ cup sweet chili sauce
- 2 tablespoons soy sauce
- 1 tablespoon Sriracha
- 3 scallions, sliced

PREPARATION

To make the brine, in a stockpot, bring 4 cups of the water to a boil over high heat and whisk in salt until dissolved and herbs, if using. Remove the pan from the heat, add the remaining water, and let cool to room temperature. Place the chicken pieces in the stockpot or divide the chicken and brine between large zip-top bags and refrigerate for at least 4 hours or overnight. When you're ready to fry, drain and rinse the chicken pieces thoroughly, then pat them dry with paper towels.

To dredge the chicken, mix the dredge ingredients—the cornstarch, salt, and pepper—together in a large bowl. Toss the chicken in the mixture, coating each piece completely. In a second bowl, mix the dip ingredients—the cornstarch, salt, pepper, and water, whisking to form a thin slurry. Toss the chicken in the dip, shaking off excess.

To fry the chicken, fill a Dutch oven or a large, deep-sided cast-iron skillet with 2 inches of oil and the bacon grease, if using. Clip a frying thermometer to the side of the pot, place over medium-high heat, and bring the oil to 350°F. (The temperature will drop considerably when the chicken is added; you'll want to regulate the heat to maintain a temperature of about 325°F as you fry the chicken.) Fry the chicken in batches of no more than 4 pieces at a time for 16 minutes, until the meat registers 165°F on an instant-read thermometer, agitating the pieces frequently with tongs or a spider so they don't stick together. Remove the chicken to a wire rack set over a paper towel–lined baking sheet. Repeat until all the pieces are cooked. Let the chicken cool for 20 minutes while you make the toss.

To make the toss, combine the chili sauce, soy sauce, Sriracha, and scallions in a large bowl. Add the chicken, toss, and serve.

FRIED CHICKEN: NASHVILLE-HOT

SERVES 4 TO 6

SOME LIKE IT HOT, AND THAT'S ESPECIALLY TRUE IN MUSIC CITY, WHERE A particularly piquant variation of fried chicken has become its own genre. John Lasater, executive chef of the famed Hattie B's Hot Chicken, admits that cooks keep their recipes tight under the toque, but he was willing to share a version of his with us. Cayenne pepper figures in every step, including the final one: when the chicken comes out of the fryer, brush it or dunk it in a blend of the hot oil mixed with cayenne, garlic, and onion powder. "It's critical to whisk the hot oil well because all the spices naturally fall to the bottom," Lasater says. Serve the chicken with a loaf of white bread and pickles—and a fire extinguisher.

INGREDIENTS

- 1 (3½- to 4-pound) whole chicken, with neck, liver, and gizzard removed, cut into 10 pieces (wings, legs, thighs, and quarter breasts)
- Peanut oil for frying

FOR THE BRINE

- 1 quart buttermilk
- ¼ cup vinegar-based hot pepper sauce
- 3 tablespoons kosher salt
- 1 tablespoon cayenne pepper
- 2 tablespoons dark corn syrup

FOR THE DREDGE

- 2 cups self-rising flour
- 3 tablespoons cayenne pepper
- 2 tablespoons paprika
- 2 tablespoons onion powder
- 2 tablespoons garlic powder
- 2 tablespoons brown sugar

FOR THE DIP

- 2 large eggs
- ½ cup buttermilk

FOR THE NASHVILLE HOT BASTE

- ½ cup hot frying oil
- 2 tablespoons cayenne pepper
- 1 tablespoon onion powder
- 1 tablespoon brown sugar
- 2 teaspoons kosher salt
- 1 teaspoon garlic powder

PREPARATION

To brine the chicken, whisk the buttermilk, pepper sauce, salt, cayenne, and corn syrup in a large bowl to combine. Place the chicken pieces and buttermilk brine in a stockpot or divide the chicken and brine between large zip-top bags and refrigerate for at least 4 hours or up to 8 hours. Drain the chicken in a colander, but do not rinse.

Set a wire rack over a baking sheet. To make the dredge, combine the flour, cayenne, paprika, onion powder, garlic powder, and brown sugar in a large bowl and divide between two shallow dishes. Prepare the egg wash by beating the eggs with the buttermilk in another shallow dish. Dip the chicken pieces into the seasoned flour, shaking off excess, then into egg wash, then into the second dish of seasoned flour. Set the breaded chicken pieces on the rack, transfer the baking sheet to the refrigerator, and let the chicken rest for at least 30 minutes or up to 1 hour to set the crust.

To fry the chicken, fill a Dutch oven or a large, deep-sided cast-iron skillet with 1 inch of oil. Clip a frying thermometer to the side of the pot, place over medium-high heat, and bring the oil to 350°F. (The temperature will drop considerably when the chicken is added; you'll want to regulate the heat to maintain a temperature of about 325°F as you fry.) Remove the chicken from the refrigerator and fry skin-side down in batches of no more than 4 pieces at a time for 8 minutes per side, until the meat registers 165°F on an instant-read thermometer. Remove the chicken pieces with tongs to a wire rack set over a paper towel–lined baking sheet. Repeat until all the pieces are cooked. Let the chicken cool for 20 minutes while you make the hot baste.

To prepare the hot baste, carefully ladle ½ cup of hot frying oil into a small bowl. Whisk in the cayenne, onion powder, brown sugar, salt, and garlic powder to combine. Brush over the hot chicken and serve.

KING RANCH CHICKEN

SERVES 10 TO 12

SINCE EVERYTHING'S BIGGER IN TEXAS, WHY NOT BIGGER, BOLDER FLAVOR in one of the Lone Star State's classic recipes? A creamy mushroom mixture provides the base for this enchilada-like casserole, so extend a little extra effort there and swap canned condensed soup for a simple buttery béchamel sauce amped up with Tex-Mex seasonings. Brighten the Ro*Tel and canned chile mix with a few freshly roasted poblanos. Then unearth the biggest casserole dish you can find (you'll want a 9- by 13-incher at least 3 to 4 inches deep, with plenty of clearance so the cheese doesn't bubble over). And speaking of clearance, stand back when bringing this to the table. There's likely to be a stampede.

INGREDIENTS

8 tablespoons (1 stick) unsalted butter, plus 1 tablespoon for buttering the casserole dish

4 garlic cloves, minced

½ teaspoon ground cumin

½ teaspoon chili powder

1 teaspoon onion powder

¼ teaspoon cayenne pepper

½ cup all-purpose flour

2 cups whole milk, at room temperature

2 cups chicken stock

2 (4.5-ounce) cans chopped green chiles, drained

1 (28-ounce) can diced Original Ro*Tel tomatoes, well drained

4 poblano chiles, roasted, peeled, seeded, and chopped (see Tip)

Kosher salt and freshly ground black pepper

2 small white onions, diced

1 red bell pepper, diced

8 ounces sliced mushrooms

3 cooked boneless skinless chicken breasts, shredded

12 corn tortillas

3 cups shredded Monterey Jack or pepper Jack cheese

¼ cup chopped fresh cilantro, plus 2 tablespoons for garnish

PREPARATION

Preheat the oven to 350°F. Butter the baking dish and set aside.

To make the sauce, melt 5 tablespoons of the butter in a large saucepan over medium heat. Add the garlic, cumin, chili powder, onion powder, and cayenne and cook, stirring, for 1 minute. Whisk in the flour and cook, whisking constantly, for 1 minute. Slowly pour in the milk and stock, whisking to avoid lumps. Cook for about 10 minutes, stirring constantly, until the sauce becomes thick and coats the back of a spoon. Remove from the heat and stir in the green chiles, tomatoes, and poblanos. Taste and season with salt and pepper if needed; set aside.

To prepare the filling, melt the remaining 3 tablespoons butter in a large skillet over medium-high heat. Add the onions, bell pepper, and mushrooms and sauté for 10 minutes, until the onions are soft and the mushrooms have given up their moisture. Remove from the heat and stir in the shredded chicken, tossing to combine.

To assemble, spoon ½ cup of the sauce over the bottom of the prepared dish. Arrange 6 tortillas on top of the sauce to cover the bottom evenly. Top with half of the chicken mixture, followed by the remaining sauce. Sprinkle on half of the cheese and half of the cilantro. Top with the remaining 6 corn tortillas to cover the surface evenly. Repeat the layering with the remaining ingredients, ending with the cheese and cilantro. Bake for 30 to 45 minutes, until heated through and bubbly. Allow the dish to sit for 5 to 10 minutes before serving.

TIP: **To roast poblano chiles: Place the chiles on a baking sheet and set it 4 inches beneath the flame of a preheated broiler; broil for 6 minutes on each side, or until charred. Alternatively, place the chiles directly on the flame of a gas stove and, using tongs, turn to char on all sides. Seal the hot charred chiles in a plastic zip-top bag; let stand for 10 minutes to loosen the skins, then peel and seed the chiles.**

COUNTRY CAPTAIN

SERVES 4 TO 6

A LITTLE BIT EXOTIC, A LITTLE BIT FAMILIAR, COUNTRY CAPTAIN IS PERFUMED with history. This aromatic one-pot stew is most often associated with Savannah. "It was on the menu at the restaurant where I started my cooking career, and I fell in love," says Steven Satterfield, chef/owner of Miller Union in Atlanta. As a historically significant seaport, Savannah was a cross-cultural capital, and Country Captain's distinctive curry base speaks to the influence of the British spice trade. "It is the complex range of India-influenced spices that distinguishes this dish," Satterfield says. "So I stay true to that and make my own curry mix." He likes to serve the dish surrounded by bowls of colorful condiments, so the final flavor depends upon who adds what—the very essence of regional Southern cooking.

INGREDIENTS

- 4 tablespoons (½ stick) unsalted butter
- 4 tablespoons bacon grease
- 1 (3½- to 4-pound) whole chicken, with neck, liver, and gizzard removed, cut into 10 pieces (wings, legs, thighs, and quarter breasts)
- Kosher salt and freshly ground black pepper
- 2 cups diced yellow onion (about 1 onion)
- 2 cups diced celery (about 4 stalks)
- 2 cups diced green bell pepper (about 1½ peppers)
- 1 jalapeño, seeded and minced
- 1 teaspoon chopped garlic
- ¼ cup homemade curry powder (see Note)
- 2 cups chopped canned tomatoes, with 1 cup tomato juice reserved from the can
- 1 cup chicken stock
- 2 bay leaves
- ½ cup seedless raisins
- 2 scallions, sliced

CONDIMENTS

Toasted grated fresh coconut, crushed roasted peanuts, green tomato or apple chutney, pickled hot peppers, pickled okra

PREPARATION

Place a large braiser or Dutch oven over medium heat, add 2 tablespoons of the butter and 2 tablespoons of the bacon grease, and heat until slightly foaming, 3 to 5 minutes. Pat chicken dry with paper towels, then season with salt and pepper. Raise the heat to medium-high, add the chicken in batches, and brown it well on all sides, removing the browned pieces to a platter as they're done.

Reduce the heat to low and add the remaining 2 tablespoons butter and 2 tablespoons bacon fat. Add the onions and a pinch of salt and sauté until translucent, 3 to 4 minutes. Add the celery, bell peppers, jalapeño, and a pinch of salt and sauté until tender, 3 to 4 minutes. Add the garlic and stir until fragrant, about 30 seconds. Slowly add the curry powder, stirring well to evenly coat the vegetables, and cook until they are tender, 7 to 10 minutes, stirring frequently to keep the curry from burning. Add the tomatoes and their juices, the chicken stock, and bay leaves and stir well to combine. Increase the heat, bring the liquid to a simmer, and return the chicken to the pot.

Cover, reduce the heat to medium-low, and cook until the chicken reaches an internal temperature of 165°F, 35 to 45 minutes. Stir in the raisins, season with salt and pepper and remove the bay leaves.

Garnish with scallions. Serve with rice and the various condiments.

NOTE: **To make your own curry powder, mix together 1 tablespoon ground ginger, 2 teaspoons ground cumin, 2 teaspoons ground cardamom, ½ teaspoon ground turmeric, 2 teaspoons Hungarian paprika, 2 teaspoons ground coriander, 2 teaspoons ground cinnamon, ¼ teaspoon ground cloves, 1 pinch cayenne pepper, 1 pinch Colman's mustard powder, and 1 pinch dried thyme.**

CHICKEN BOG

SERVES 6 TO 8

CHICKEN BOG FALLS SOMEWHERE BETWEEN TOAD IN THE HOLE AND BLOOD pudding on the spectrum of unfortunate culinary names, but don't let that stop you from discovering the pleasures of this classic Lowcountry comfort food. Chicken bog is named for its soupy, porridge-like quality in which chunks of tender, pulled chicken are "bogged down" in rich broth. It's like the love child of chicken-rice soup and Italian risotto, with the addition of the signature smoky flavor good-quality sausage delivers.

INGREDIENTS

- 1 (3½- to 4-pound) whole chicken
- 1 carrot, cut into chunks
- 1 celery stalk, cut into chunks
- 1 large Vidalia onion, cut in half
- 1 teaspoon black peppercorns
  Bouquet garni (1 sprig fresh thyme, 1 sprig fresh flat-leaf parsley, and 1 fresh bay leaf, tied together with kitchen twine or a leek or green-onion skin)
- 3 tablespoons unsalted butter
- 6 ounces smoked sausage, diced
- 1 cup Carolina Gold rice, rinsed until the water runs clear
- 1 teaspoon paprika
- 1½ teaspoons kosher salt
- ½ teaspoon freshly ground black pepper

PREPARATION

Place the chicken and neck in a 4-quart saucepan or stockpot with the carrot and celery. (Discard liver and gizzard or reserve for another use.) Cut one onion half into chunks and add it to the pot. Add the peppercorns and bouquet garni and fill the pan with water to just cover chicken. Bring to a boil over high heat, then reduce the heat to low and simmer for 40 minutes, until the chicken is cooked through. Remove from the heat and, using tongs, transfer the chicken to a platter. Strain the broth and discard the solids. When the chicken is cool enough to handle, remove the meat from the carcass, shredding it with your fingers or two forks. Discard the bones and neck.

Dice the remaining onion half. Return the pan to the stovetop over medium-high heat. Add the butter, diced onion, and sausage, reduce the heat to medium, and sauté for 5 minutes, until the onion softens and the sausage begins to brown slightly. Add the rice and stir to coat it with the fat; cook, stirring, for 1 minute. Add 1 quart of the reserved broth, the paprika, salt, and pepper, and stir to scrape up the browned bits from the bottom of the pan. Add the shredded chicken and bring to a boil. Reduce the heat to low, cover, and cook for 30 minutes, until the rice is cooked through, stirring a few times. Remove from the heat. Remove the lid and stir the rice to separate the grains. Taste and adjust the seasoning if needed. Add additional warm broth ½ cup at a time for a moister dish if you like. Cool the remaining broth, then freeze it for another use.

CHICKEN THIGH POTPIE

SERVES 6

CHICKEN POTPIE IS A DISH MANY OF US CRAVE WHEN WE WANT TO CONJURE up the warmth of home and hearth, and chef Ashley Christensen, owner of Poole's Diner in Raleigh, North Carolina, is no different. "This potpie is inspired by my mother's kind of cooking: dishes that shout out to the classics, but with clean flavors and crisp textures," she says. Christensen grounds the pie in colder-month offerings of sweet potatoes and rutabagas and tender leaves of kale instead of the usual carrot and celery combo. Adding another bit of Southern flair, the chef uses a small amount of cornmeal in the crust, which provides a nutty, toasty flavor with an echo of sweetness to match the filling. "Though some potpies are encased in crust, I like the 'island' approach, letting the gravy bubble up around the pillow of crust," Christensen says. "Crust is potpie's defining moment, no matter how delicious the filling."

INGREDIENTS

FOR THE VEGETABLES

- 1 large rutabaga, peeled and diced
- 1 large sweet potato, peeled and diced
- 3 tablespoons olive oil
  Kosher salt and freshly ground black pepper
- 1 cup pearl onions
- 1 tablespoon balsamic vinegar
- ¾ cup oyster mushrooms, torn into pieces
- 1 cup chopped kale (about 5 large leaves)

FOR THE CHICKEN AND PAN GRAVY

- 4 large boneless skin-on chicken thighs
- 1 tablespoon all-purpose flour
  Kosher salt and freshly ground black pepper
- 1 tablespoon canola oil
- 1 tablespoon unsalted butter
- 1 sprig fresh thyme
- 1 sprig fresh rosemary
- 2 whole garlic cloves, peeled and crushed with the side of a knife
- 2 cups warm chicken stock

PREPARATION

FOR THE VEGETABLES Preheat the oven to 425°F.

In a large bowl, toss the rutabaga and sweet potato with 2 tablespoons of the oil and season with salt and pepper. Spread evenly over a baking sheet (or divide it between two baking sheets if needed) and roast for 25 to 30 minutes, until tender.

Meanwhile, toss the pearl onions with the vinegar and ½ tablespoon of the remaining oil and season with salt and pepper. Spread the onions evenly over a baking sheet and roast for 12 to 15 minutes, until tender.

Put the remaining ½ tablespoon oil in a medium skillet over medium heat. Add the mushrooms and sauté until tender, 5 to 7 minutes, then add the kale and wilt it slightly, about 2 minutes. Remove all the vegetables from the pans into one large bowl and set aside.

FOR THE CHICKEN Dust the chicken lightly with flour and season with salt and pepper. Place a large cast-iron skillet over medium heat and add the oil. Pan-fry the chicken until browned and cooked through, about 30 minutes, turning occasionally and adjusting the heat as needed. Remove from the skillet to a plate and set aside.

FOR THE PAN GRAVY Reduce the heat and add the butter. Add the thyme, rosemary, and garlic and sauté until the garlic is browned and aromatic, 4 to 6 minutes. Slowly pour in the flour, whisking constantly to form a paste and taking care not to let it burn, about 2 minutes. Slowly pour in the warm chicken stock, whisking until the mixture is smooth and slightly thickened, about 3 minutes. Season with salt and pepper, remove the herbs and garlic, and set aside.

RECIPE CONTINUES ▶

FOR THE CORNMEAL CRUST

- 1¼ cups all-purpose flour
- ¼ cup fine-ground cornmeal
- 1 teaspoon kosher salt
- ½ cup (1 stick) unsalted butter, diced
- 6 tablespoons ice water

FOR THE CRUST In a large bowl, whisk together the flour, cornmeal, and salt. Toss in the butter and place in the freezer for 1 hour. Transfer to a food processor and pulse until the butter is the size of small peas. Still pulsing, drip in ice water until the mixture begins to cling together; do not overprocess. Remove and shape the dough into a disk. Wrap the dough in plastic wrap and let it rest in the refrigerator for at least 6 hours or overnight.

Remove the dough from the refrigerator. Lightly flour a work surface, and roll dough to ¼-inch thickness, tracing the outline of your baking dish on a piece of parchment paper and trimming the dough ½ inch smaller than the outline. (This is not a sealed potpie; the partially prebaked crust will not completely cover the dish, which lets the filling bubble up along the sides.) Score the dough, place it in the freezer, and chill for 1 hour.

TO ASSEMBLE AND BAKE THE DISH Preheat the oven to 350°F.

Cut each thigh into 6 pieces and add the chicken to the vegetable mixture along with the pan gravy, stirring to combine. Transfer the mixture to a 10-inch round baking dish.

With the dough still on the parchment paper, transfer to a cookie sheet and bake for 15 to 20 minutes, rotating the crust every 5 minutes so it browns evenly, until the crust begins to crisp and becomes lightly browned. Remove the crust from the pan and place it on top of the chicken and vegetable mixture. Return to the oven and bake until hot and bubbly, 15 to 20 minutes. Cool slightly and serve.

SPICY-PICKLE CHICKEN SALAD WITH CHICKEN SKIN CRACKERS

SERVES 4

WHETHER YOU PREFER WHITE MEAT OR DARK, WE CAN SURELY ALL AGREE that the skin is actually the best part of a chicken. Rendered golden crisp, it's like the world's most delicious cracker. Which is exactly what it becomes in this recipe, accompanying a spicy mayonnaise-swaddled chicken salad, with inspiration from McCrady's restaurant in Charleston, South Carolina, which has introduced many a happy diner to the pleasures of fried chicken skins via its chalkboard bar-snack menu.

INGREDIENTS

FOR THE CHICKEN SALAD

- 2 bone-in skin-on chicken breasts
- 2 garlic cloves, sliced
- 6 to 8 fresh basil leaves
- 1 tablespoon olive oil
  Kosher salt and freshly ground black pepper
- 2 celery stalks, trimmed and finely diced
- ½ small shallot, finely diced
- ½ cup spicy pickle chips (preferably Alabama-made Wickles), drained and diced
- 3 tablespoons diced pimentos, drained
- ⅓ cup roughly chopped toasted pecans
- ½ cup mayonnaise
- 2 tablespoons pickle juice
- 4 dashes of hot sauce
- ½ teaspoon kosher salt
- ½ teaspoon freshly ground black pepper
- ⅛ to ¼ teaspoon cayenne pepper
- 4 romaine lettuce leaves for garnish

FOR THE CRACKERS

- Skins from the roasted chicken breasts
- Cayenne pepper
- Kosher salt and freshly ground black pepper

PREPARATION

FOR THE CHICKEN SALAD Preheat the oven to 375°F.

Using your index finger, carefully lift a small piece of the chicken skin from each breast, running your finger between the skin and meat to create a pocket without tearing the skin. Stuff each breast evenly with garlic slices and basil leaves. Drizzle with the oil and season with salt and pepper. Place on a baking sheet and roast for 40 minutes. Remove from the oven and set aside to cool.

Carefully lift the skins from the cooled breasts, keeping the skin intact and trimming where necessary with a paring knife or kitchen shears. Scrape away the cooked basil leaves and garlic and discard. Set the skins aside.

Remove the chicken meat from the bone, dice it, and place it in a large bowl. Add the celery, shallot, pickle chips, pimentos, and pecans.

To make the dressing, whisk together the mayonnaise, pickle juice, hot sauce, salt, pepper, and cayenne in a separate bowl. Add to the chicken mixture and toss to thoroughly coat.

FOR THE CRACKERS Place a cast-iron skillet over medium-low heat. Add the skins to the skillet skin-side up and cook for 30 to 45 minutes, flipping and pressing them occasionally, until the fat has rendered and the skins are thoroughly crisp. Remove from the pan and dust with cayenne, salt, and pepper. Drain on paper towels.

3

PORK, BEEF, & LAMB

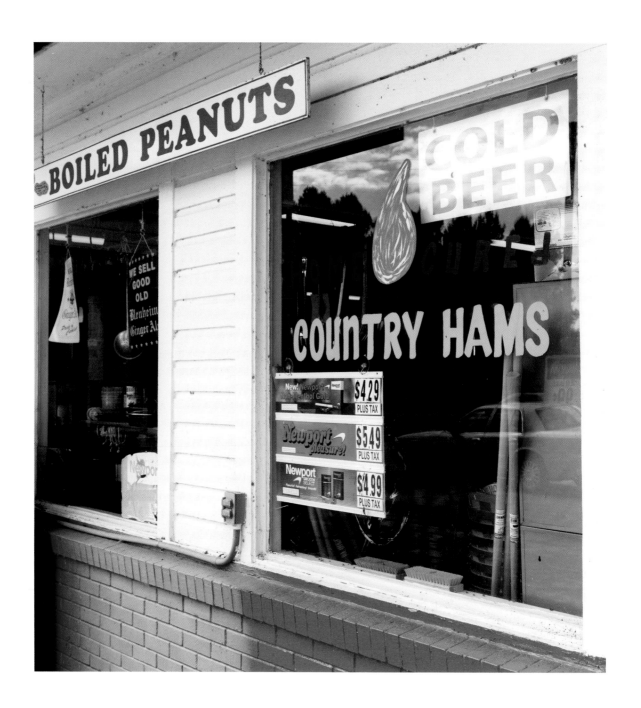

HOLDING ON TO THE HOG

Nothing brings people together like a slow-roasting pig

RANDALL KENAN

PRESIDENT ABRAHAM LINCOLN LIKED TO TELL A STORY about two naughty farm-boy brothers who one day let a prize hog loose from its pen. The hog treed one of the boys, then made a dash for the seat of the second boy's pants. The only way the boy could help himself was by grabbing on to the hog's tail and hanging on as it ran in circles. The boy called out, Lincoln liked to say, "Brother, brother, come down quick and help me let go of this hog!"

Country life in eastern North Carolina is similarly attached to pork. This situation was true long before the pork industry outstripped the tobacco industry. In many ways hogs have defined our community, black and white.

Hog-killing time, in the winter months, was a time for celebration. It may be difficult for suburbanites and urbanites to understand how an abattoir could be a happy place, but you must imagine a community converging on a single farm with a single purpose, a sharing that would come back to them. A general festival atmosphere out in the cold. Young boys and girls running about playing. Folk under trees and sheds, gossiping and telling bawdy lies. The corn-fed hogs were shot early in the morn, first thing, usually only three or four large ones. The bulk of the day was spent on butchery, cleaning chitlins, making liver pudding and sausage, and getting the hams ready to go into the smokehouse.

Generously salting them and hanging them up to dry and marinate in wood smoke, preparing the great heavy slabs of meat always rose to the level of art. When cured after many weeks, thinly sliced, and water-soaked for a long spell to leach out some of the salt before cooking, country ham would be the center of hawk-eye or red-eye gravy, breakfast staples created from ham drippings and coffee. The gravy was served over grits, along with the cooked salty ham, usually accompanied by scrambled eggs and fluffy light biscuits. My mother's legendary biscuits were good with anything: blueberries, strawberries, fried chicken, even black-eyed peas, but when accompanying ham, grits, and eggs they somehow seemed holy, just as the Good Lord intended.

And let's not forget the joy that is liver pudding and grits. Also sausage. Hocks became ubiquitous as a seasoning. As a boy I loved fishing a cooked ham hock from a long-simmered pot of butter beans.

With spring and summer and good-size shoats came that thing for which eastern North Carolina is probably best known (probably even more so than tobacco): barbecue, also a call for community and coming together.

When I was a kid, the fire and rescue squad in my small, unincorporated North Carolina hometown was all volunteer. Every other weekend— and almost every weekend during the summer months—the tradition was to have a benefit Saturday barbecue sale at the station. The station was white, two stories, and church-large, housing the fire truck and ambulance. The kitchen upstairs was restaurant quality, all white and stainless steel, and the women who looked after it kept the place spick-and-span.

Out back was the barbecue house, made of brick. There was an anteroom for storage stacked with cords upon cords of wood and a narrow, long room containing a brick-lined barbecue pit, able to hold at least four good-size hogs at once.

In eastern North Carolina, when a person says "barbecue" they mean, quite specifically, whole-hog barbecue. (Of course barbecued chicken was a thing, but the good people of the lowlands would never confuse the two.) The barbecue meat is then chopped into fine chunks and sauced with a vinegary, peppery mixture oft guarded by pit masters. Eastern North Carolinians like to think they invented barbecue and get mighty high-handed when it comes to thinking of cooking it any other way. Back in the day folk thought tomatoes were poison. We don't now, but we haven't adopted the sweet red stuff most Americans consider barbecue sauce.

Usually a deacon from our church, First Baptist Missionary Church, would show up with the donated hogs late on Friday afternoon. Most often it was my cousin Seymour, a well-regarded farmer who had also won high praise for his skills around a barbecue pit. His job was to get the fires going. His job was to supervise the laying-on of the hogs upon the metal screens suspended high over the coals. His job was to season and anoint the roasting meat with his secret sauce and to stay up all night, making sure there would be good and plenty pig meat to satisfy an entire community of about one thousand. The atmosphere was merry, even festive. And I loved it when my mother would allow me to spend the night at the firehouse "helping."

After staying up all night, sunrise brought taking the hogs from the fire. Sunrise brought witnessing Cousin Seymour disarticulate the meat from the bones—and by now it was so tender that it largely slid off like honey. Like a dog in a medieval kitchen, I got to munch on the boney parts, the meat seasoned to a fare-thee-well, robust, smoky, deeply satisfying. Witnessing the meat, now in white buckets, being taken upstairs, past the red-and-white-checkered serving tables, into the hospital-clean kitchen. The chopping. The seasoning. The tasting. The mounds of delectable pork made ready for the serving, for the sale, for the benefit, for the good, the good of us all.

And by noontime the people came, black, white, young, old. We all got heaping helpings of spicy goodness—along with coleslaw and potato salad and baked beans and hush puppies, that old, crunchy North Carolina classic. It was not fancy, but it was indeed fine. Community was an experienced thing, not simply an idea.

I doubt we'll ever let the hog go.

HOME-CURED SORGHUM BACON

MAKES 2½ POUNDS

THE THICK STRIPS OF BACON HAWKED BY THE LIKES OF PRODUCERS SUCH AS Allan Benton in Madisonville, Tennessee (Benton's Hickory Smoked Country Bacon) and Sam Edwards in Surry, Virginia (Edwards Hickory-Smoked Sliced Bacon) beat their grocery-store equivalents handily. Their only real competition is bacon made from scratch, which has one definite advantage: when you're the one starting with a slab of pork belly, you can customize the seasonings to suit yourself. Here sorghum syrup lends sweet nuance to the salt and grease of freshly crisped pork. You'll need some curing salt and—ideally—a smoker, though you can get by without one. This recipe does take a bit more time than just frying a skilletful of strips. But you know what comes to those who wait? Really good bacon.

INGREDIENTS

- 2½ pounds pork belly, skin removed
- ¼ cup dark brown sugar
- ½ cup kosher salt
- 2 tablespoons freshly ground black pepper
- 1½ teaspoons pink curing salt (see Note)
- ½ cup sorghum syrup
- Applewood chips

NOTE: **Pink curing salt is available at Williams-Sonoma stores and online from retailers like Weston Products. It is indeed pink and contains sodium nitrite and/or nitrate, which helps preserve the meat's color as it cures.**

TIP: **This recipe works without a smoker, although the result will skew more on the Canadian side of bacon—deliciously porky but lacking that depth of woodsy flavor true Southern smoked bacon delivers. Unwrap the cured pork belly, rinse and dry it, and place it on a wire rack set over a baking pan and bake at 175°F for 2 to 2½ hours, until it registers 150°F on an instant-read thermometer.**

PREPARATION

Rinse the pork belly and pat it thoroughly dry with paper towels. Mix the brown sugar, kosher salt, pepper, and curing salt in a small bowl. Sprinkle the mixture evenly on all sides of the pork belly, pressing with heel of your hand to help the salt mixture adhere.

Place a piece of plastic wrap twice the length of the pork belly on the countertop. Drizzle ¼ cup of the syrup evenly on top of the fatty side of the pork belly, then place the pork belly in the center of the plastic wrap syrup-side down. Drizzle the meaty side of the pork belly with the remaining ¼ cup syrup and bring the sides of the plastic wrap up and over the pork belly to wrap it tightly. Place in a zip-top bag and refrigerate for 1 week, turning halfway through the week.

When you're ready to smoke, remove the pork belly from the bag and rinse thoroughly to remove all traces of the salt mixture. Pat dry with paper towels, place on a wire rack set over a baking sheet, and return to the refrigerator unwrapped to air-dry for 24 hours.

Remove the pork belly from the refrigerator and let sit at room temperature for 30 minutes. Prepare a smoker with wood chips according to the manufacturer's instructions. Place the pork belly directly on the rack of the prepared smoker and smoke for 1½ to 2 hours, until the pork belly registers 150°F on an instant-read thermometer. Remove from the smoker and let cool. Refrigerate overnight before slicing lengthwise into strips. The bacon will keep, tightly wrapped, for 1 week in the refrigerator or 3 months in the freezer.

KNOW YOUR PORK
SALTY, SMOKY, & OTHERWISE

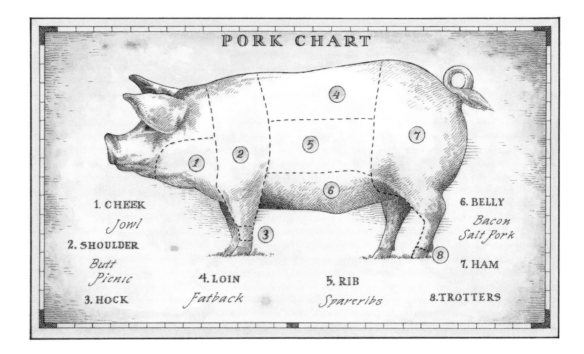

PORK CHART

1. CHEEK
   Jowl
2. SHOULDER
   Butt
   Picnic
3. HOCK

4. LOIN
   Fatback

5. RIB
   Spareribs

6. BELLY
   Bacon
   Salt Pork
7. HAM
8. TROTTERS

BACON: Pork belly—mostly meat with streaks of fat—cured and smoked. Beloved by all.

HOCK: The lower portion of a hog's leg—meat, fat, bone, and gristle—cut in a 3- to 4-inch cross-section. Sometimes cured, always smoked, and used to season broths, soups, stews, or any dishes cooked in similar low-and-slow fashion, such as collard greens or green beans.

JOWL: Cured and smoked pork cheeks, similar to bacon with an equal distribution of fat and meat.

FATBACK: The hard layer of pure white fat under a hog's back, sometimes fresh, sometimes salt-cured. Rendered from fresh, it makes lard. Any pieces with skin, meat, or membrane attached left behind after rendering are cracklins.

SALT PORK: Fat (often streaked with meat; see below) cut from the belly of a hog and heavily cured with salt, but not smoked. Sometimes sold sliced, but may also be found as a solid hunk. Used to season many dishes, it often starts a pot of greens or beans.

STREAK OF LEAN OR STREAK O' LEAN: Salt pork containing visible streaks of meat. Similar to bacon, but with the proportion of meat to fat reversed. Can be cooked just like bacon, but shrinks even more in cooking as the fat renders. What's left behind is deliciously golden and crisp but lacks bacon's smokiness.

SMOTHERED SKILLET PORK CHOPS

SERVES 4

LONG BEFORE WHISKEY EVEN TWINKLED IN ANYONE'S EYE, MUCH LESS tinkled in a glass, Madeira was the South's drink of choice. The sweet, brandy-spiked wine mellowed and matured on the long, hot voyage from its home, a Portuguese island off the coast of Morocco, to colonial port cities like New Orleans and Charleston. It died off after a blight decimated the vines in 1851, but in recent years it has seen a revival. To describe quality Madeira's flavor as caramel is an understatement—it's both sweet and savory with the added acid edge of ethanol. Those qualities are a natural pairing for pork, here amplified with buttery, golden chanterelles, freshly harvested from Southern woodlands in summer. This simple weeknight skillet dinner tastes like a long, Sunday-supper labor of culinary love.

INGREDIENTS

- 4 center-cut bone-in pork chops
- Kosher salt and freshly ground black pepper
- 2 tablespoons olive oil
- 1 tablespoon unsalted butter
- 1 small leek, white and light green parts only, diced (about ½ cup)
- 1 large shallot, diced
- 1 large garlic clove, minced
- 4 ounces chanterelle mushrooms, stemmed and sliced (if not available, you can substitute a medley of gourmet mushrooms)
- 1 cup Madeira
- 2 tablespoons red wine vinegar
- 3 sprigs fresh thyme

PREPARATION

Bring the pork to room temperature and season it lightly on both sides with salt and pepper. Place a large cast-iron skillet over high heat for 1 minute. Add 1 tablespoon of the oil and place the pork chops in the pan to sear for 2 to 3 minutes. Turn and cook for 1 to 2 minutes more to sear the other side. Transfer to a plate and reduce the heat to medium.

Add the remaining 1 tablespoon oil to the skillet along with the butter. As soon as the butter melts, add the leek and shallot and sauté for 1 minute. Add the garlic and mushrooms and sauté until lightly browned and the mushrooms have softened slightly, about 3 minutes. Add the Madeira, vinegar, and thyme sprigs. Bring to a boil, then reduce the heat to low and simmer for 5 minutes, until reduced slightly. Return the pork chops and any accumulated juices to the pan. Spoon the sauce and mushrooms over the pork and cook for 1 minute more to warm through.

SMOKY SOUP BEANS

SERVES 8 TO 12

SOUTHERN CUISINE OFTEN MAKES A LOT OUT OF A LITTLE, AND THERE'S NO better example than soup beans, which is just that: dried pinto beans and salt pork, bacon's backwoods cousin, set to simmer in water until the three ingredients combine to form a hearty, soulful soup much greater than the sum of its parts. There's not a thing in this world wrong with soup beans made the traditional way. But trading smoked ham hocks for salt pork stays true to the dish's humble spirit, while adding three things: firewood flavor, picked meat, and a bit of extra body. Diced aromatic vegetables and bay leaf elevate it just a bit more—but not above its raisin'.

INGREDIENTS

FOR THE SMOKED PORK STOCK

- 3 quarts water
- 1 small white onion, peeled and quartered
- 4 whole cloves
- 2 pounds smoked ham hocks

FOR THE SOUP BEANS

- 1 pound dried pinto beans
- 2 tablespoons unsalted butter
- 1½ cups diced white onion (about 1 medium onion), plus more for garnish
- 1 cup diced carrots (about 2 carrots)
- 1 cup diced celery (about 2 celery stalks)
- 3 garlic cloves, minced
- 1 bay leaf
- 2½ quarts smoked pork stock (recipe above)
- Picked ham hock meat (about 5 ounces)
- Kosher salt and freshly ground black pepper

PREPARATION

FOR THE SMOKED PORK STOCK Pour the water into a large stockpot or Dutch oven. Stud the onion quarters with the cloves and add to the pot with the ham hocks. Bring to a boil over high heat, then reduce the heat to low, cover, and simmer for 2 hours. Strain the stock, reserving the ham hocks and discarding the remaining solids; let cool.

When the ham hock is cool enough to handle, remove and discard the skin. Pull the meat from the bones and shred or dice it. Transfer the strained, cooled stock to the refrigerator. Once chilled, remove the fat that has solidified on the surface of the stock and discard it. Use the stock as instructed in the recipe below or freeze it for up to 3 months and thaw it when you're ready to complete the recipe.

FOR THE SOUP BEANS Rinse, drain, and pick through the beans. Transfer the beans to a stockpot or large bowl and add water to cover; soak overnight at room temperature to rehydrate. Drain the beans and leave them in the colander.

Melt the butter in a stockpot or Dutch oven over medium-high heat. Add the onion, carrots, and celery and sauté for 5 minutes, until softened, stirring occasionally. Add the garlic and bay leaf and cook, stirring, for 1 minute. Add the beans, smoked pork stock, and picked ham hock meat. Bring to a boil over high heat, then reduce the heat to low, cover, and simmer for 1½ hours, until the beans are tender. Season with salt and pepper. Taste and adjust the seasoning if needed. Ladle the soup into bowls and serve, topped with a scattering of diced raw onion.

SPICY BLACK-EYED PEA JAMBALAYA

SERVES 8

SCRIBBLED IN THE GUEST BOOK OF A WINDOWLESS RESTAURANT THAT WAS once a welding shop in Galliano, Louisiana, is a fervent message for the proprietor: "God loves Alzina!" The writer may be in a special position to know. After all, Alzina Toups, who attends mass just across Bayou Lafourche at St. Joseph Catholic Church, has cooked for countless priests, nuns, and bishops over the past thirty-five years at her reservation-only restaurant. Then again, maybe the note's author just figured that anybody who makes such a heavenly black-eyed pea jambalaya has got to be blessed. This recipe for jambalaya is one of her all-time most-requested. Like a traditional Creole jambalaya, it's a one-pot mix of rice, vegetables, and meat. Toups's deceptively simple version coaxes maximum flavor from a few well-chosen ingredients—bright bell pepper, two kinds of smoked sausage, and a double dose of jalapeño kick. "People love this one," she says. "They wipe out their dish."

INGREDIENTS

2 tablespoons vegetable oil

1 medium onion, chopped

1 medium green bell pepper, chopped

5 garlic cloves, minced

1 jalapeño, sliced

8 ounces mild smoked pork sausage, chopped or sliced

8 ounces hot smoked pork sausage, chopped or sliced

2 (15-ounce) cans black-eyed peas with jalapeños

2½ cups beef stock, plus more as necessary

½ cup chopped fresh parsley

⅓ cup chopped scallions

5 to 6 cups cooked long-grain rice prepared according to package directions

PREPARATION

Place a Dutch oven over medium heat and add the oil. Add the onion, bell pepper, garlic, and jalapeño and sauté, stirring occasionally, for 10 minutes, until the vegetables soften. Add the sausage and cook for 10 minutes, until browned, stirring occasionally. Add the black-eyed peas and broth and bring to a simmer. Reduce the heat to low and simmer uncovered for 1 hour. Just before serving, stir in the parsley, scallions, and rice, adding additional warm broth ¼ cup at a time if necessary to adjust consistency.

SWEET TEA–BRINED COUNTRY HAM

SERVES 28

(with plenty of leftovers for biscuits; see page 217)

THE COUNTRY HAMS OF THE SOUTH, LIKE THE FAMOUS SERRANO HAMS OF
Spain and prosciutto of Italy, rely on a salt cure that removes water from the meat until there's not enough moisture left for microbes to grow, a vital step in the days before refrigeration. With origins in Depression-era Savannah, this recipe takes inspiration from Harriet Ross Colquitt's *The Savannah Cook Book,* using tannins in tea to tame some—but not too much—of a country ham's saltiness and turn it into a holiday table centerpiece. Slowly braising the untrimmed ham in beer and molasses helps infuse moisture back into the meat, which is naturally basted by the thick fat cap before it's peeled away and replaced with a rind of sugar. The result blends the authentically rugged flavor of country ham with the sweetness and more-moist texture of city ham. "Fortunately," writes Colquitt, "this is not quite as complicated as it sounds." And it isn't, although it does take time. As for that, here's another pearl from Colquitt: "It would not be old-fashioned Southern cooking if time were an object or substitutes used."

INGREDIENTS

- 1 (14- to 16-pound) uncooked bone-in country ham, such as S. Wallace Edwards & Sons, hock end removed, rinsed and scrubbed to remove mold and excess salt
- 20 teaspoons loose black tea
- 1 (15-ounce) jar dark molasses (not blackstrap)
- About 6 (12-ounce) bottles Shiner Bock beer
- 1 cup dark brown sugar
- 24 to 32 whole cloves

TIP: **If you've ordered a quality whole ham for this recipe, it may still have the hock attached. Ask your favorite butcher to trim the hock so the ham will fit in a roasting pan before you start cooking.**

PREPARATION

In a large stockpot, bring 2 gallons of water to a boil over high heat. Stir in the tea leaves and half of the jar of molasses. Turn off the heat and let the mixture steep, about 1 hour. Pour 1 gallon of the mixture over the ham, and top with fresh cold water to cover (a spare cooler is the ideal vessel for this). Chill for 12 hours, then drain and cover with the remaining 1 gallon tea mixture and fresh cold water to cover. Chill for 12 hours more, then drain and rinse the ham, and prepare to cook it.

Preheat the oven to 400°F.

Place the ham fat-side down in a large roasting pan with a lid (or tent with foil). Add the remaining half jar of molasses and pour in enough beer so that the liquid comes about halfway up sides of the ham. Cover and bake for 30 minutes, then reduce the oven temperature to 325°F and continue to bake for 1½ hours. Remove the pan from the oven and carefully turn the ham fat-side up (spearing it with carving forks helps secure it for turning). Cover again and bake for 1½ to 2 hours more, until it comes to an internal temperature of 140°F. Remove from the oven and let the ham cool in the liquid. Raise the oven temperature back to 400°F.

Pour out the liquid from the roasting pan and discard it. Carefully carve the rind and most of the fat from the top of the ham, leaving about ⅛ inch of fat covering the exterior; discard the rind and excess fat. Cover the ham evenly with the brown sugar, pressing to help it adhere. Stud the ham evenly with cloves. Return the ham to the oven and bake uncovered for 15 minutes to allow the sugar to melt into the fat and form a flavorful dark brown crust. Remove from the oven and rest for at least 30 minutes. Thinly slice and serve warm or at room temperature.

COUNTRY HAM WITH THREE GRAVIES

The thing about country ham: you don't have to cook it much if you don't want to. The highest-end cured Southern country hams (sometimes aged as long as eighteen months) can be thinly sliced and eaten raw, like prosciutto. Even the inexpensive packaged slices of pre-cut country ham you can find in most grocery stores just need a few minutes in a hot skillet to develop a golden brown crust. What's left behind in that pan is where the cooking really begins. Use the rich, flavorful ham drippings as a base for a variety of gravies. The following are three of the most time-honored versions.

TRUE SAWMILL GRAVY

SERVES 4

⅓ cup per serving

THE FINELY MILLED FLOUR THAT THICKENS PASTY-WHITE "SAWMILL" SAUSAGE gravy today wasn't always an everyday ingredient for many Southerners. Certainly not the mountain men who worked logging camps in the late 1800s and early 1900s. Back then cornmeal did the job. This recipe adheres to that tradition, creating a thicker gravy that's more akin to grits. In fact, the lumbermen often joked that there was sawdust in their gravy, but they didn't complain about the flavor.

INGREDIENTS

- 1 tablespoon bacon grease or unsalted butter
- 4 cooked thick-cut country ham slices
- 3 tablespoons coarse-ground yellow cornmeal
- 1 teaspoon kosher salt
- 2 cups whole milk
- ¼ teaspoon freshly ground black pepper
- Dash of hot pepper sauce

PREPARATION

Melt the bacon grease in a large cast-iron skillet over medium heat. Fry the ham slices for 3 to 4 minutes per side depending on their thickness. Remove the ham slices from the pan and wrap them in foil to keep warm.

Reserve 1 tablespoon of the rendered fat in the skillet; discard the rest. Add the cornmeal and salt and cook, stirring regularly, until the cornmeal begins to brown, 2 to 3 minutes.

Slowly whisk in the milk, breaking up any lumps and scraping up any browned bits from the bottom of the pan. Cook, stirring often, for 5 minutes, until the gravy has thickened (it will thicken further upon standing). Season with pepper and the hot sauce. Serve with ham slices and warm biscuits.

RED-EYE GRAVY

SERVES 4

½ cup per serving

WHILE GRAVY SPIKED WITH COFFEE MAY WELL BE A POTENT WAKE-UP FOR the bleary-eyed at breakfast, this preparation most likely gets its name from the oily red-tinged "eye" that forms in the center of the pan as the coffee is stirred into the grease to make the gravy. That, or Andrew Jackson, who, in a dubious but delightful story related in John Egerton's classic *Southern Food*, may once have told a hung-over cook to prepare him a plate of ham and gravy "as red as your eyes."

INGREDIENTS

- 1 tablespoon bacon grease or unsalted butter
- 4 cooked thick-cut country ham slices
- 1½ cups strong brewed coffee
- 1½ teaspoons dark brown sugar or molasses
- Salt and freshly ground black pepper

PREPARATION

Melt the bacon grease in a large cast-iron skillet over medium heat. Fry the ham slices for 3 to 4 minutes per side depending on their thickness. Remove the ham slices from the pan and wrap them in foil to keep warm.

Reserve 1 tablespoon of the rendered fat in the skillet; discard the rest. Add the coffee and brown sugar, stirring to scrape up the browned bits from the bottom of the pan. Cook until reduced by half (about 1 minute). The gravy will be thin like *jus*. Season with salt (remembering that the ham is salty) and pepper. Serve with ham slices and warm biscuits.

TOMATO GRAVY

SERVES 4
¼ cup per serving

SIMILAR IN SPIRIT TO ITALIAN SUNDAY GRAVY (MARINARA), SOUTHERN tomato gravy likely has less to do with culinary cross-pollination than with industrious folks using meaty tomatoes, either put-up or fresh off the vine, to give the gravy body and supply a sweetness that complements the salty ham.

INGREDIENTS

- 2 tablespoons bacon grease or unsalted butter
- 4 cooked thick-cut country ham slices
- 1 Vidalia onion, diced
- 2 tablespoons all-purpose flour
- 1 (14-ounce) can diced tomatoes, drained
- ½ cup half-and-half
- ½ teaspoon kosher salt
- ½ teaspoon freshly ground black pepper

PREPARATION

Melt the bacon grease in a large cast-iron skillet over medium heat. Fry the ham slices for 3 to 4 minutes per side depending on their thickness. Remove the ham slices from the pan and wrap them in foil to keep warm.

Reserve 1 tablespoon of the rendered fat in the skillet; discard the rest. Add the onion and sauté for 5 minutes, until softened but not browned. Sprinkle with the flour and cook, stirring constantly, for 3 minutes, until the flour is incorporated. Stir in the tomatoes, half-and-half, salt, and pepper and simmer, stirring occasionally, for 3 to 5 minutes, until thickened. Serve with ham slices and warm biscuits.

HOW TO ROAST A WHOLE HOG

Thirty hours of whiskey, smoke, and pure pandemonium

JOHN CURRENCE

THE WHOLE-HOG ROAST IS THE TRUMP CARD OF FOOD EVENTS. NOTHING surpasses the reaction to rolling out a whole roasted swine to a gathering of hungry folks. And since most folks will never cook a whole hog themselves, there seems to be universal reverence not only for the result but also for the care and time it takes.

Thirty hours is the equivalent of a workweek, one and a quarter revolutions of the earth, ten college football games. And from start to finish, including the planning, prep, some light construction, steady consciousness, a rally, and a cleanup, it's also about how long it takes to cook a 175-pound pig. For my part, a chef and twenty-plus-year devotee of the pit, it encompasses everything I love: fire, knives, pig, drinking whiskey, telling lies, and staying up all night. Cooking a whole hog isn't that hard. The common misconception is that because you're dealing with the entire animal, the process is relegated to professionals or smoke-stained pit masters who have come by their knowledge as a result of Divine Providence. In reality, anyone who can take the time to complete the process should be able to do this.

Any number of variables play into the success of a whole-hog roast, but the one essential is having a second (and, sometimes, third) person to help with whom you really see eye-to-eye. You will, after all, spend almost a day and a half sweating and toiling together over a hot fire, medicating the occasional burn with libation, and fighting mild sleep deprivation, usually with extremely off-color humor. To be frank, the majority of the time is spent watching a fire burn—but you have to remain focused, as one. You are in a culinary foxhole together. You are brothers-in-arms.

Our experiences with friends are dispensed episodically these days, usually with metered sterility: a round of golf, a morning duck hunt, a long dinner. But a whole-hog roast surpasses them all. Only during the wee hours of the night stoking hot coals can you learn how intensely a friend is tortured by the characters in the book he is writing, or how deeply a friend's pride runs in his family's steel-working roots, or how meaningful a friend found his father's parting words the day he was dropped off at his freshman college dorm. These aren't things friends share around the card table. And that's why, no matter how hard it may be, I will find those thirty hours if the excuse arises to cook a hog. Every pig roast is, in its own way, sacred, never to be duplicated. RECIPE FOLLOWS ▶

The full list of items needed for a successful hog roast reads like the love child of Home Depot and *Joy of Cooking* (if only the Depot had a meat locker or *Joy of Cooking* called for power tools). For the sake of one's sanity, it's best to spend a leisurely afternoon gathering all the items on the list because beginning the following morning, and for a full 24 hours afterward, all attention will be on the pig. Pick it up the morning of or be prepared to keep it chilled overnight.

FROM THE HARDWARE OR HOME-IMPROVEMENT STORE

Cinder blocks (80)

Metal fence posts (3)

4 x 6-inch metal grates (2)

8 x 12-inch canvas painter's tarp

Shovel

Hoe

Gloves

Coat hangers, heavy wire, or rope

Half a cord of mixed seasoned cherry and hickory

FROM A DUMPSTER BEHIND A MAMMOTH DISCOUNT FURNITURE STORE

Giant cardboard box

FROM THE BEST LOCAL MEAT MARKET

Pig (whole, minus head, feet, innards, and hair)

FROM THE GROCERY STORE

Heavy-duty aluminum foil

Dry rub (½ gallon—heavy with salt, brown sugar, and red pepper flakes)

Barbecue sauce (1½ gallons)

THE FIRE Arrange the cinder blocks, which are the pit's structure, in a rectangle, about four blocks by five, three blocks high. Lay the fence posts across the short length of the pit, evenly spaced with the smooth side facing up. The grate goes on top of the slats of the post. Because the smooth side is up, you'll be able to slide the pig around some when need be. Place a final row of blocks around the top—they'll hold the cardboard off the pig.

Start the fire to preheat the pit walls so the pig doesn't go into a cold pit. Get about 10 pieces of hickory, each 18 to 20 inches long, to burn down to coals. These will be the first coals to see the hog. While the pit is preheating, bring the pig out and roll it open onto its back before seasoning it with the rub.

Cover one of the metal grates with foil and place the hog belly-down on the foil (the foil should keep the belly from scorching). Once the fire has burned down to coals, spread the coals around the bottom of the pit, going a little heavier in the corners where the coals will be under the hindquarters and shoulders.

Remove the top cinder block supports on one long side of the pit so you can slide the pig onto the fence-post rails. Then once the cinder blocks are replaced, cover the top of the pit with the cardboard box and drape the dropcloth over the entire thing to help retain most of the pit's smoke and heat. Now the waiting begins.

Outside the pit, start a second fire with another 8 to 10 pieces of wood. That fire will be rolled and massaged for the next hour or so, and once it has burned down, those coals will be spread along the floor of the pit. This routine will be repeated and performed hourly for the next 8 hours, which is, arguably, the most critical part of the cooking process.

The pit needs to be watched carefully during this time for three things:

1 *Flare-up.* It is absolutely critical that there be no flare-up in the pit. This occurs if rendered fat runs off the pig and reignites the coals in the bottom of the pit, making an extremely hot fat-fueled fire. If fat catches fire in the pit, you can end up with a scorched hog.

2 *Even heat.* With the cinder blocks stacked three high, there is about 30 inches of clearance between the coals and the pig. Each time you pull the tarp back and spread your coals, place your hand immediately underneath each of the quarters. The temperature should be very warm but not hot enough that you can't keep your hand near the pig for 10 or 15 seconds.

3 *Cool pit.* If the pit remains too cool for too long, the pig can end up spoiling. If you have ever smelled a bad refrigerator . . . well, we'll leave it at that. But the odds of this happening are relatively slim because you're restoking the fire every hour or so.

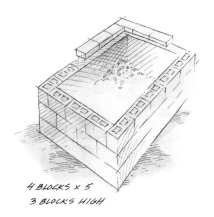

4 BLOCKS × 5
3 BLOCKS HIGH

SECOND FIRE
OUTSIDE THE PIT

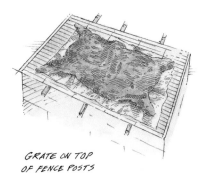

GRATE ON TOP
OF FENCE POSTS

SECURE THE 2ND GRATE
WITH COAT HANGERS

THE FLIP If you started all this at 8:30 a.m., by 6 p.m., the pig has cooked, belly-side down, for about 8 hours. Around the third or fourth time you pull the tarp and cardboard back, the pig should have started to turn from its cadaver-esque pink to a Thanksgiving-turkey golden brown. The fat in the pig skin and muscle will have begun to render (convert from fat solid and water to pure liquid fat) and slowly make its way deep into the meat of the pig. The exterior layer of skin will have dried out and have drawn tightly up. Now, flip the pig onto its back, where it will spend the rest of its time simmering in its personally tailored sauté pan—its own skin.

To flip the pig, remove the tarp, cardboard, and top row of cinder blocks on one long side of the pit. Then take the second metal grate and lay it on top of the pig. On one long side, secure the grates in three places with coat hangers (heavy wire or rope will also do).

Once the first side is secured, tie the second together. It takes two people to lift the pig from the rails and stand it on one long side. (You will want to wear a pair of work gloves while doing this.) Slowly lower the pig back to the rails and slide it back to the center. The (now) top grate and foil are removed and the belly is exposed. The exposed meat should be caramelized and tender.

At this point, bathe the entire cavity of the pig in your favorite barbecue sauce, dry rub, beer, whatever you like. From this point forward, repeat every time you uncover the hog and restoke the coals (once every hour to hour and 15 minutes). For about the next twelve hours, the heavy work is done.

THE FINISH Eight hours later, the cavity should be a simmering cauldron of fat and barbecue sauce. For all intents and purposes, the pig is actually finished cooking, but the last few hours will completely tenderize the hams. At this point, cut the size of the hot-coal load slightly every time you stoke the fire and bank the coals to the side of the pit. Again, this concentrates the little direct heat onto the hams and keeps the pit warm. Continue this for the next 4 or 5 hours until the hog is completely finished.

The unveiling is one of those moments like at the end of a college all-nighter, when sunrise evokes feelings of both elation and shame. Everything is ridiculously funny, but the pig is serious business. There is a momentary hush that gives way to interested whispers. Everyone is curious. It is like the first viewing of a child. Everyone *oohs* and *aahs* until *that* uncle finally breaks the ice and pinches a cheek. Then the glorious feeding frenzy begins.

CANE SYRUP & SPICE-RUBBED BEEF TENDERLOIN

SERVES 6

CANE SYRUP IS TRADITIONALLY MADE BY BOILING DOWN SUGAR CANE JUICE in a cast-iron cauldron over a fire for five hours. Thankfully for the time-pressed and cauldron-less, it's also available at local farmers' markets or online from producers like Steen's. The first cook of sugar cane juice (molasses is the second, blackstrap molasses is the third), cane syrup is naturally thin and only mildly sweet. Its slightly smoky edge is a natural for grilled meats. Here the syrup anchors a rub that's paired with the king of beef cuts: tenderloin. The syrup holds the rub onto the tenderloin so that a hairline crust forms, redolent of coffee and spices combined with a distant hint of smoke.

INGREDIENTS

- 1 (2½-pound) beef tenderloin, trimmed and tied
- 3 tablespoons cane syrup
- 1 tablespoon canola oil or peanut oil
- ½ teaspoon finely ground espresso
- ½ teaspoon chili powder
- ½ teaspoon smoked paprika
- ½ teaspoon dry mustard
- ½ teaspoon ground ginger
- 1 teaspoon garlic powder
- 1 tablespoon kosher salt
- ½ teaspoon freshly ground black pepper
- Pecan hulls for smoking

PREPARATION

Remove the tenderloin from the refrigerator and let it come to room temperature (20 to 30 minutes).

In a small bowl, whisk together the cane syrup, oil, espresso, chili powder, paprika, mustard, ground ginger, and garlic powder to form a thin paste. Pat the tenderloin dry with paper towels. Rub the cane syrup–spice mixture evenly onto the tenderloin, turning to coat it completely. Season evenly with the salt and pepper.

Heat a charcoal grill to medium-high with the coals banked on one side for direct and indirect cooking.

Sear the tenderloin for 2 to 3 minutes per side on the direct side of the grill. Add a handful of pecan hulls to the charcoal, transfer the tenderloin to the indirect cooking side of the grill, and cover the grill so the tenderloin roasts and smokes at the same time, 10 to 15 minutes. Uncover the grill, add more pecan hulls if necessary to maintain the smoke, and turn the tenderloin. Grill for 10 to 15 minutes more, until an instant-read thermometer inserted into the center registers 125°F for medium-rare.

Remove the tenderloin from the grill to a platter, tent with foil, and let rest for 15 to 20 minutes before untying and slicing.

CHICKEN-FRIED SHORT RIBS

SERVES 4

AT UNDERBELLY IN HOUSTON, JAMES BEARD AWARD–WINNING CHEF CHRIS Shepherd and his full-time butcher go to work on an entire cow every single week. Which means that they have to find creative uses for each part of the animal—including the ribs, which carry a whole lot of meat. "One day, we had ribs left over," Shepherd says, "and we said, 'Let's just braise and fry these damn things. It'll be delicious!'" Indeed they were. In a state where diners take chicken-fried steak very seriously, these ribs are a nod to tradition, but with more beef flavor than the customary eye of round. "It's chicken-fried steak, but it's also not," Shepherd says. "When you bite into it, it's meaty, tender, and thick."

INGREDIENTS

FOR THE SHORT RIBS

- 8 beef short ribs
- Kosher salt and freshly ground black pepper
- 4 tablespoons olive oil
- 6 cups beef stock
- ½ bottle dry red wine (about 2 cups)
- 10 garlic cloves
- 1 carrot, cut into quarters
- 1 white onion, cut into quarters
- 4 stalks celery, cut into large pieces

FOR THE SEASONED FLOUR

- 1 cup all-purpose flour
- 1 tablespoon plus 1 teaspoon kosher salt
- 1 tablespoon freshly ground black pepper
- 1 teaspoon paprika

- 2 large eggs
- ¼ cup whole milk
- Peanut oil for frying

PREPARATION

FOR THE SHORT RIBS Preheat the oven to 325°F.

Season the short ribs generously with salt and pepper. Place a large cast-iron skillet over high heat and add the oil. Sear the ribs for 1 to 2 minutes per side, working in batches if necessary to prevent crowding. Place the ribs in a deep pan and add the stock, wine, garlic, carrot, onion, and celery. Make sure the ribs are submerged in the liquid, then cover with foil and braise in the oven for 6 hours, carefully turning them in the liquid halfway through cooking (you want the braised meat to stay attached to the rib bone if possible). Carefully remove the ribs to a plate, cool to room temperature, then refrigerate. The ribs can be braised and cooled the day before frying. (Strain and save the stock for another use—it makes delicious gravy.)

TO DREDGE THE RIBS Combine all the seasoned flour ingredients in a large bowl. In a separate bowl, whisk together the eggs and milk to make an egg wash. Dredge the cooled ribs in the seasoned flour, then dip them in the egg wash and dredge again.

FOR FRYING THE RIBS Pour ½ inch of oil into a Dutch oven or a large, deep-sided cast-iron skillet and clip a frying thermometer to side of the pan. Bring the oil to 325 to 350°F over medium-high heat (the temperature will drop when the ribs are added, so you want to make sure to regulate the heat to maintain a temperature right around 325 to 350°F as you fry).

Working in batches, shake off excess flour and carefully add the ribs to the pan, adjusting the heat as needed to ensure the oil maintains an even temperature. Fry each side for 2 to 3 minutes, until golden brown. Drain on a paper towel–lined plate and serve.

MEAT-AND-THREE-STYLE HAMBURGER STEAK WITH ONION GRAVY

SERVES 6

ONE OF THE SOUTH'S MOST HALLOWED RESTAURANT STYLES, THE MEAT-AND-three is so simple it's confusing. Visit one, such as Puckett's in Nashville or Niki's West in Birmingham, and you'll see a bounteous steam-table spread of dozens of down-home foods served cafeteria-style. The confusing part comes when you have to start making decisions: one meat and three sides. Hamburger steak, made from inexpensive ground beef, smothered in gravy, and usually served with creamy mashed potatoes, is a staple of the genre. This recipe riffs off that classic but elevates it more than a few notches—mixing richer ground chuck with the sirloin and splashing some red wine into the onion-gravy base. It's still country at heart, just come to town.

INGREDIENTS

- 12 ounces ground sirloin
- 12 ounces ground chuck
- 1½ teaspoons Worcestershire sauce
- 1 teaspoon freshly ground black pepper
- ½ teaspoon kosher salt
- ½ teaspoon onion powder
- ¼ teaspoon cayenne pepper
- 1 tablespoon canola oil
- 1 tablespoon unsalted butter, plus more for serving
- 1 medium Vidalia onion, thinly sliced
- 3 tablespoons all-purpose flour
- 2 cups beef stock
- ⅔ cup red wine
- Chopped fresh parsley for garnish

PREPARATION

Mix the ground meats, ½ teaspoon of the Worcestershire sauce, the pepper, salt, onion powder, and cayenne in a large bowl using clean hands just to combine. Don't overwork the meat mixture or the patties will turn out tough. Divide into 6 equal portions and form them into oval patties about ½ inch thick. Depress the center of each patty slightly with your thumb so they cook evenly without puffing.

Heat 2 teaspoons of the oil in a large cast-iron skillet over medium-high heat until hot but not smoking. Add 3 patties and cook undisturbed for 6 minutes, then flip and cook for 4 to 5 minutes on second side for medium-rare, or until desired doneness. Transfer to a plate and keep warm by tenting loosely with foil. Cook the remaining patties in the same way and transfer to the plate.

Add the remaining 1 teaspoon oil and the butter to the hot skillet and swirl to melt. Add the onion and sauté for 7 to 10 minutes, scraping up the browned bits from the bottom of the pan. Add the flour and stir for 1 minute. Slowly pour in the stock, wine, juices that have collected from the meat on the plate, and the remaining 1 teaspoon Worcestershire sauce. Stir to scrape up any remaining bits from the bottom of the pan and simmer for 5 minutes to reduce and slightly thicken the gravy.

Return the patties to the skillet to warm through. Serve the patties topped with gravy and a tangle of onions. Garnish each serving with a pat of butter for added richness and a sprinkling of parsley. Serve with mashed potatoes.

KENTUCKY-STYLE SMOKED LAMB

SERVES 8 TO 10

TO MOST SOUTHERNERS, BARBECUE MEANS PORK OR BEEF, MAYBE CHICKEN.
To residents of Owensboro, Kentucky, barbecue means only one thing: mutton. Raising sheep for
wool was big business for the Dutch who settled this area; when sheep aged out of wool production,
they moved on to the dinner table. And so the tradition of pit-smoked mutton barbecue began, and
it continues to this day at places like Old Hickory Bar-B-Que and Moonlite Bar-B-Q Inn. Mutton
barbecue usually comes dressed with another strong flavor—a tangy Worcestershire-heavy "dip" that is
a dark cousin to the more traditional pepper-and-vinegar concoctions. For cooks outside of Kentucky,
lamb makes a fine substitute—its tenderness is only amplified by a low-and-slow smoke, but the meat
still has a deliciously gamey edge.

INGREDIENTS

FOR THE LAMB

- 1 (6-pound) boneless leg of lamb, trimmed and tied
- 2 tablespoons vegetable oil
- 2 tablespoons Worcestershire sauce
- 3 garlic cloves, minced
- 2 tablespoons molasses
- 1 tablespoon kosher salt
- 2 tablespoons freshly ground black pepper
- 1 teaspoon onion powder
- ¼ teaspoon ground allspice

FOR THE KENTUCKY BLACK BARBECUE DIP

- 2 cups water
- ¼ cup cider vinegar
- ¼ cup freshly squeezed lemon juice
- ¼ cup ketchup
- ⅓ cup Worcestershire sauce
- 1 tablespoon dark brown sugar
- 1 teaspoon freshly ground black pepper
- ½ teaspoon kosher salt
- ½ teaspoon onion powder
- ½ teaspoon garlic powder
- ¼ teaspoon ground allspice

  Soaked hickory or applewood chips

PREPARATION

FOR THE LAMB Place the lamb in a large zip-top bag. Whisk together the
oil, Worcestershire sauce, garlic, molasses, salt, pepper, onion powder,
and allspice and add to the bag with the lamb. Remove the air from
the bag, seal it, and massage the meat with the marinade, turning to
evenly coat. Refrigerate for at least 8 hours or up to 24 hours, turning
occasionally, before smoking.

FOR THE DIP Prepare the dip by combining all the ingredients in a medium
nonreactive saucepan over medium-low heat. Bring to a simmer,
whisking regularly, and cook for 15 minutes, until slightly thickened.
Remove from the heat and cool. Transfer half of the mixture to a
bowl to use for basting the meat on the grill; reserve the other half for
saucing the cooked lamb.

Prepare a smoker with soaked hickory or applewood chips according
to the manufacturer's instructions. Fill a drip pan with boiling water.
When the temperature reaches 250 to 275°F, place the lamb fat-side
up in the center of the rack above the drip pan. Smoke for 6 to 8
hours (about 1½ hours per pound of meat), basting with sauce every
30 minutes after the first hour, until the meat registers an internal
temperature of 125 to 135°F (rare to medium), replenishing the wood
chips if necessary. Remove the meat from the smoker and let rest for
30 minutes before slicing or chopping. Serve with the reserved barbecue
dip for saucing at the table.

NATCHITOCHES MEAT PIES

SERVES 12

THE SAVORY HAND PIES FROM NATCHITOCHES (THAT'S "NACK-A-TUSH"),
Louisiana—perhaps best known as the setting for the movie *Steel Magnolias*—are not unlike the empanadas of Spain and Latin America. Filled with ground beef sautéed with the holy trinity of Cajun and Creole cuisine—bell pepper, onion, and celery—they're one of Louisiana's official state foods. The hearty pies are typically deep-fried, but here we've taken a cue from Louisiana chef John Folse of Lafitte's Landing Restaurant in Donaldsonville, Louisiana, who bakes his version for a more flaky pie-like crust. If you'd rather fry your meat pies, pour about 2 inches of peanut oil in a Dutch oven, heat it to 360°F, then drop the pies in two or three at a time and fry for 1 to 2 minutes per side.

INGREDIENTS

FOR THE FILLING

- 1 teaspoon vegetable oil
- 8 ounces ground sirloin
- 8 ounces ground pork
- ½ cup finely diced green bell pepper
- ½ cup finely diced red onion
- ⅓ cup finely diced celery
- 2 garlic cloves, minced
- ½ teaspoon kosher salt
- ¼ teaspoon freshly ground black pepper
- Pinch of cayenne pepper
- 1 bay leaf
- 1 cup beef stock
- ½ teaspoon Worcestershire sauce
- 2 teaspoons all-purpose flour

FOR THE PASTRY

- 2¼ cups all-purpose flour
- 1½ teaspoons kosher salt
- ½ teaspoon baking powder
- ½ cup cold lard or ½ cup (1 stick) unsalted butter, cut into small pieces
- 1 large egg
- ⅓ cup ice water
- 2 teaspoons distilled vinegar
- 1 large egg whisked with 1 tablespoon water for the egg wash

---

TIP: **These pies can be assembled and frozen before baking. Place them on a parchment-lined baking sheet and freeze for 3 to 5 hours, until frozen solid, then place them in freezer bags. Pull out as many as you need when you have a hankering; thaw them in the refrigerator for an hour or two before baking.**

PREPARATION

FOR THE FILLING Place a large cast-iron skillet over medium-high heat and add the oil. Add the sirloin and pork and cook, breaking up the chunks with the back of a spoon, for about 10 minutes, until browned and all the moisture has evaporated.

Reduce the heat to medium and add the bell pepper, onion, celery, and garlic; sauté for 10 minutes, or until the vegetables have softened. Stir in the salt, pepper, cayenne, and bay leaf. In a measuring cup, whisk the Worcestershire sauce into the stock. Pour half of the stock mixture into the pan, stirring to scrape up the browned bits from the bottom of pan and cook, stirring often, until the liquid has evaporated (3 to 4 minutes). Whisk the flour into the remaining beef stock mixture, stir it into the meat, and cook for 5 minutes more. Remove the skillet from the heat and transfer the meat to a bowl to cool while you prepare the pastry.

FOR THE PASTRY Pulse the flour, salt, and baking powder together in the bowl of a food processor a few times to combine. Scatter small spoonfuls of lard or pieces of butter into the dry ingredients and pulse again until the mixture comes together into pea-size bits. In a small bowl, beat together the egg, ice water, and vinegar, add it to the flour mixture, and pulse just until it forms a shaggy dough. Transfer the dough to a square of plastic wrap and knead a few times. Form the dough into a disk, wrap tightly, and refrigerate for at least 1 hour or overnight.

Remove the chilled dough from the refrigerator and divide it into 12 equal portions. Roll each into rounds about 6 inches in diameter and ⅛ to ¼ inch thick.

TO ASSEMBLE AND BAKE THE MEAT PIES Preheat the oven to 400°F.

Place 2 heaping tablespoons of the cooled meat mixture in the bottom half of each dough round. Dip a finger into the egg wash and trace around the edges of the dough circle to coat. Fold the dough in half over the meat and press to seal the edges. Crimp by pinching with your fingers or using the tines of a fork. Cut two or three slits in the top of each pie, brush with the remaining egg wash, and transfer to a parchment-lined baking sheet. Bake for 30 minutes, or until golden and flaky. Cool slightly and serve warm.

GRILLADES & GRITS

SERVES 4 TO 6

TO THE FRENCH, *GRILLADES* ARE THIN PIECES OF GRILLED OR BROILED MEAT. But to anyone from Creole country or nearby environs, grillades have nothing whatsoever to do with a grill. They're thin-pounded pieces of tender, milky veal (or eye of round or even pork chops if you prefer), coated in seasoned flour, browned in oil, butter, or bacon grease, then set to simmer in a rich tomato-based sauce. Here the flour from the browned meat helps thicken the sauce as it cooks, although you can certainly play around with filé powder too. It's dried, pulverized sassafras root that, along with okra, helps give extra body to many Creole and Cajun dishes. If the sauce doesn't look thick enough to your liking, stir in half a teaspoon of filé before adding the mushrooms and parsley. There is one other important distinction to note about Creole grillades: Served over grits, grillades are typically a breakfast or brunch meal. Over rice, they're dinner.

INGREDIENTS

- 1½ pounds veal or eye of round cutlets
- ¼ cup all-purpose flour
- 1½ teaspoons Creole seasoning, such as Tony Chachere's
- ½ teaspoon kosher salt
- ¼ teaspoon freshly ground black pepper
- ¼ teaspoon garlic powder
- 2 tablespoons bacon grease or unsalted butter
- 1 tablespoon unsalted butter
- 1 white onion, diced
- 1 green bell pepper, seeded and chopped
- ½ cup chopped celery with leaves
- 3 garlic cloves, minced
- 1 (28-ounce) can whole peeled tomatoes, drained
- 2 bay leaves
- 1 cup veal, beef, or pork stock
- 1 tablespoon Worcestershire sauce
- 8 ounces cremini mushrooms, sliced
- ⅓ cup chopped fresh parsley
- 4 cups hot cooked grits, prepared according to package instructions

PREPARATION

Pat the meat with paper towels to thoroughly dry it. Pound to ½-inch thickness with the smooth side of a meat mallet, then cut into 3-inch-wide strips. Combine the flour, Creole seasoning, salt, pepper, and garlic powder in a large zip-top bag. Add the pieces of meat and shake well to coat.

Melt 1 tablespoon of the bacon grease in a large cast-iron skillet or Dutch oven over medium-high heat. Brown half of the meat for 2 minutes per side; remove from the pan and set aside. Add the remaining tablespoon of bacon grease to the pan and repeat with the remaining pieces. Set the meat aside and keep warm by tenting loosely with foil.

Reduce the heat to medium and add the butter to the pan along with the onion, bell pepper, celery, and garlic. Sauté for 5 minutes, or until softened, stirring often. Crush the tomatoes with your hands over the vegetables and add them to the pan with the bay leaves, stock, and Worcestershire sauce and stir well. Slip the meat back into the pan, reduce the heat to low, and simmer for 30 minutes, stirring occasionally. Add the mushrooms and parsley, cover, and cook for 10 minutes more, until mushrooms are cooked through. Taste and adjust the seasoning if needed. Serve over the grits.

YAKAMEIN

SERVES 10

RAMEN-LIKE YAKAMEIN HAS BECOME THE SALTY, PROTEIN-RICH HANGOVER cure of choice in a city that often needs one—New Orleans. The dish, most likely brought to the Crescent City by Chinese immigrants in the nineteenth century, consists of noodles and strips of beef in a hearty, Cajun-spiced broth, topped with hard-boiled egg and scallions. You can find both upscale versions made with expensive meats and homemade noodles and corner-store bowls of stew meat with beef bouillon and cheap spaghetti—far more common and, many would argue, just as tasty. The master of this nourishing form is Linda Green, a frequent vendor at parades and festivals, who calls herself "the Ya-Ka-Mein Lady." Green learned how to make yakamein from her mother and grandmother. While she has never written down the family recipe, she did agree to share a version with us.

INGREDIENTS

- 1 (2½- to 3-pound) boneless chuck or eye of round roast
- 8 to 9 cups water
- 2 teaspoons Creole seasoning, such as Tony Chachere's
- ½ to ⅔ cup soy sauce, plus more to taste
- 1 tablespoon ketchup, plus more for topping if you like
- 1 tablespoon Worcestershire sauce
- 1½ tablespoons hot sauce, plus more to taste
- 1 (1-pound) package spaghetti, cooked according to package directions
- 1 bunch scallions, trimmed and sliced
- 5 hard-boiled eggs, cut in half (See Devilish Eggs on page 29 for cooking instructions)

PREPARATION

Place the beef roast in a large stockpot. Cover with water, and then add the Creole seasoning. Place over medium-high heat, bring to a simmer, then reduce the heat to low and simmer for 3 to 4 hours, until the beef is tender. Remove the beef to a large bowl and allow the beef and stock to cool for 20 to 30 minutes.

Shred or chop cooled beef, removing and discarding any large chunks of fat. Skim the fat from the top of the stock. Add the soy sauce, ketchup, Worcestershire sauce, and hot sauce to the stock, tasting as you go and adjusting the seasonings if needed.

When you're ready to serve, reheat the skimmed stock over medium heat until simmering.

To serve, divide the spaghetti and meat among 10 bowls. Top each with scallions and half an egg and ladle some stock over the top. Serve with hot sauce or ketchup.

TIP: Use chuck and your broth will have more fat and smaller bits of meat swimming in it; use eye of round and you can peel away long strips of tender beef to swirl with the spaghetti.

4

FISH
&
SHELLFISH

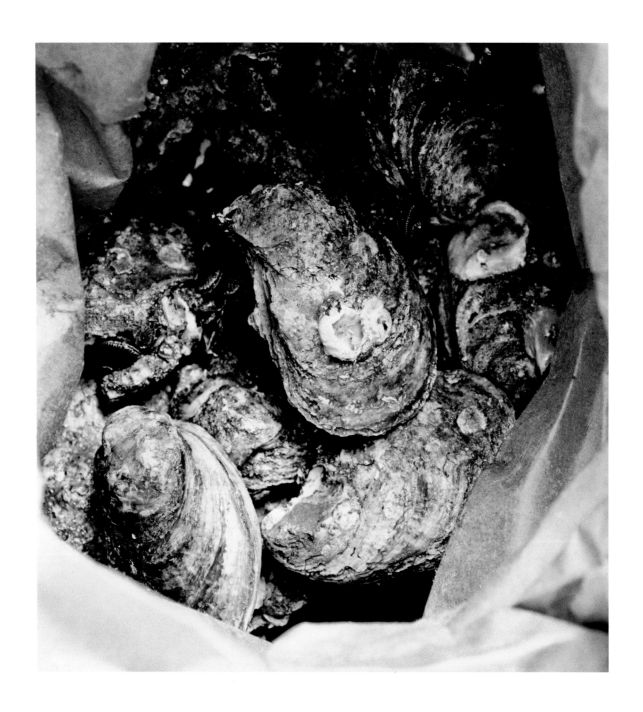

YOUR FIRST OYSTER

It's usually not love at first sight, but then you understand what all the fuss is about

RICK BRAGG

THE FIRST ONE I ATE TASTED LIKE RIVER MUD.

It was not that earthy, pungent, *essence du monde* that well-traveled people like to go on about over their *quenelles aux huîtres*. It tasted like wet dirt, only slicker, fishier, like what a tadpole would taste like if you sucked it right out of the ditch, or a wet hoof print.

Of course, I was not a gourmand then. I was a sun-scorched boy in a dockside restaurant in Panama City, intoxicated by the aroma of coconut butter suntan lotion and piña colada lip balm, and flabbergasted by ten thousand teenage Baptists in tiny two-piece bathing suits. I wanted to eat oysters because it seemed like a thing a man of the world would do in 1971, like being a spy against the Communists or owning an MGB. But that taste, and that horrible consistency—somewhere among raw chicken liver, Jell-O, beef tripe, and Dippity-do—haunted me for years.

"What does one look like?" one of my brothers asked me at the time.

"Well," I said, "it's gray-lookin'."

"What does it taste like?" he asked.

"Well," I said, "it's . . . it's . . ." but it was just beyond me then.

How could people eat something I could not even say? Maybe, I remember thinking, they might not be so damn awful if they were cooked. I mean, I suspect that a pork chop would be pretty grim if you had to eat it while the hog was still kicking. But later, in high school, one of my mean girl cousins gave me a fried one from her seafood platter, and even though it was entombed in batter and well and truly dead, it still tasted like tadpole, but crunchier this time.

I spit that one out. At least back then, I did not have to pretend to like them to fit in. That came later, when I became a writer.

There are just some things that male writers of a certain ilk feel they have to do. I call it the Curse of Hemingway. We have to like to fish. We have to be proficient in blowing birds from the sky with shotguns. And we have to love oysters. We have to sit around a table in some sun-blasted shack on some desolate, mosquito-infested cay and slurp 'em right out of the shell. Or they take our vowels away.

I love to fish. I am not good at it, but I love it. In my youth, I slaughtered some birds, though it seemed like a lot of firepower to get a few mouthfuls of meat—and I still think quail hunting is just an excuse for biscuits and gravy. Then my wife put a dozen bird feeders in our backyard, cooed over finches, hummingbirds, and cardinals, and made me deeply ashamed.

But even as I got a more sophisticated palate, I could only tolerate oysters. Oh, I put up a good front. Any real man can eat one oyster, two, even three. He just bellies up to it, chews, and gulps. There were worse things. Snails, I guess. Sushi. Turkey bacon.

But I could not make myself like them in my first forty years. I thought moving to Florida, twice, would at least break down my resistance. But that too had no real impact, and the young, oyster-hating man I was vanished into old age.

The change, when it did come, almost made me believe in magic. And like most magic, here in my South, it happened in New Orleans.

I remember the moment. I believe I was sitting in a cool, dark place in the French Quarter, one of those places that Katrina would drown and remove forever from all but fond memory. It was fall, which means it was only eighty-nine in the shade, and as I recall I was mildly drunk on brown whiskey, though it could have been some fruity rum drink and I am just embarrassed to say.

I went in for some crawfish bisque, not the creamy kind but a gumbo-like concoction that was redolent with onions, peppers, and little bitty crawfish heads stuffed with, well, stuffing. It was a reason to live.

I do not know why I ordered the oysters—maybe because I saw the words half dozen and thought this might be my chance to try them again and not be so wasteful. I did not try to slurp them from the shell, but carefully prepared them in the fashion I was told my grandfather ate them when he drifted down to the Florida Gulf coast in the 1950s to roof houses, fish, sleep on the sand, and eat things he could not find in the foothills of the Appalachians.

I took a saltine, plopped down an oyster, forked on some cocktail sauce, daubed on a fingernail-size spot of horseradish, squeezed a lemon over the whole mess, and popped it in my mouth.

Like I said, it had to be magic. One minute you hate, the next you love. But it was *good*.

I know that oyster purists will say I did not truly taste the oyster, that I am a commoner, but they can kiss my ass.

The cocktail sauce and horseradish did not mask the oyster, only provided a little misdirection, a little sleight of hand, and I chewed and liked it. They say you can taste the sea in it, and I think that is true. I even ate the last one naked, with just a little lemon, and it was pretty fine. It had to be New Orleans, I believed. In New Orleans, you walk on roads flecked with crushed oyster shells, and there is a whole culture of oysters, a mystique. Oyster recipes and oyster lore naturally pooled there, some of them indigenous, some trickling down from other places.

"One time my mother bit down on one and there was a pearl in it," says Jim Davis, director of the Center for the Book at the State Library of Louisiana. "My daddy took it and made her a ring out of it. We don't know if the fact that it was cooked made it any less valuable."

In New Orleans, oysters are almost an art form. You eat them covered in spinach and garlic and bacon and cheese; you eat them roasted, baked, even grilled over an open flame in their shells.

And I came to like them all. At Upperline, one of the great restaurants of this world, I ate them in oyster stew, in heavy cream, but you could have dropped a coaster in there instead and it probably still would have tasted pretty good.

In a half dozen kitchens around town, I had them in oyster dressing, which I consumed in such quantities I wanted to die, and in gumbo so good you would pray, quietly, that the cook would say, "Babe, you want me to put this in some Tupperware, so you can take some home?" And of course, all over town, I ate them in po' boys and oyster loaves, dripping with hot sauce and tartar sauce, with cold root beer on the side. I was not just eating food, I was consuming culture, and as I came to love the city, I came to love its oysters.

But it was not just the place, as it turned out. Once my resistance was broken, I ate them in Florida, I ate them on the Alabama coast, and I loved them there too. Maybe there is no magic to it at all. Maybe—as my momma always told me—as I get older I come to appreciate more of the world around me. Someday, she told me, I will even like butter beans.

A few years ago I got to eat dinner with one of the great writers of our time at one of the great restaurants of our time, Highlands Bar and Grill in Birmingham. Pat Conroy ate about ten oysters, with nothing but a smile.

I ate four, four of the best oysters I've ever had, and prepared one more—in the way my grandfather ate them—for my fifteen-year-old stepson, Jake. He gasped and choked only slightly, and fought it down.

"I know, son," I said, and gave him a pat.

"It will," I said, "get better."

OYSTERS BIENVILLE

MAKES 1 DOZEN

CREATED AT ARNAUD'S RESTAURANT IN THE FRENCH QUARTER (AND NAMED for Jean-Baptiste Le Moyne, Sieur de Bienville, the second colonial governor of Louisiana), this baked oyster dish is straight-up New Orleans—about as decadent as any food that's not a dessert can be. Traditionally, briny oysters are swaddled in a creamy béchamel sauce with sautéed chopped shrimp, shallots, and garlic. Instead of shrimp in the topping, New Orleans chef Justin Devillier of La Petite Grocery goes even more rich and sensuous with applewood-smoked bacon and swaps out the nutmeg used in classic béchamel for aromatic Angostura bitters. This recipe is for a dozen oysters, but it's easy to multiply upward for any amount of folks you need to feed. They go down quick.

INGREDIENTS

FOR THE SAUCE

- 1 tablespoon vegetable oil
- 1 garlic clove, minced
- 1 jalapeño, seeded and minced
- ¼ cup finely chopped red bell pepper
- ¼ cup finely chopped celery heart (about 1 rib)
- ½ cup finely chopped shallots (about 4 shallots)
- 2 tablespoons unsalted butter
- 3 tablespoons all-purpose flour
- ½ cup oyster liquor (supplement with water if necessary)
- ½ cup heavy cream
- 1 teaspoon Angostura bitters
- 2 tablespoons fresh thyme leaves
- 2 tablespoons sliced fresh chives
- 2 tablespoons finely chopped flat-leaf parsley
- Coarse salt and freshly ground white pepper

FOR THE BREADCRUMB TOPPING

- ⅓ cup finely chopped cooked applewood-smoked bacon
- ⅔ cup freshly grated Parmesan cheese
- ⅔ cup panko breadcrumbs
- 3 tablespoons unsalted butter, melted

OYSTERS

- 12 Gulf oysters, shucked, liquor reserved (arrange the oysters on an open bottom shell and discard the top shell)
- Rock salt

PREPARATION

Preheat the oven to 475°F.

FOR THE SAUCE Place a medium saucepan over medium-high heat and add the oil. Add the garlic, jalapeño, bell pepper, celery, and shallots, reduce the heat to medium, and cook, stirring occasionally, until the vegetables start to release their moisture but don't brown, 4 to 6 minutes. Add the butter and melt it in, stirring occasionally. Slowly add the flour, whisking constantly, until it is incorporated and cook for 2 minutes, continuing to whisk constantly. Slowly add the oyster liquor and cream, whisking until smooth. Increase the heat to high and bring to just under a boil, whisking constantly, until sauce thickens, about 1 minute. (If needed, you can adjust the thickness with water. This is the trickiest part. You need to use enough water to thin the sauce and prevent scorching, but not so much that the sauce gets too thin.) Reduce the heat to low and simmer, stirring occasionally, until the sauce coats the back of a spoon, about 2 minutes. Remove from the heat, add the bitters, thyme, chives, and parsley, and season with salt and pepper. Stir to incorporate.

FOR THE BREADCRUMB TOPPING Combine the bacon, cheese, and panko in a medium bowl and slowly add the melted butter, folding lightly with a spoon.

TO ASSEMBLE AND BAKE Fill an oven-safe baking dish halfway with rock salt as a bed for the oysters and place it in the oven to preheat for 10 to 12 minutes, until the salt becomes hot. Nestle oysters in the salt. Top each oyster with 1 tablespoon or more of sauce and sprinkle with a generous amount of the breadcrumb mixture. Transfer to the prepared pan and bake until golden brown and slightly bubbling, 7 to 10 minutes.

Line 2 shallow bowls or rimmed serving plates with rock salt. Using tongs, transfer the oysters to the prepared plates and serve with cocktail forks.

FROGMORE STEW

SERVES 8 TO 10

IF YOU CAN BOIL WATER, YOU CAN MAKE FROGMORE STEW, WHICH YOU MIGHT know better by its more common name: Lowcountry boil. It's a one-pot mix—a "boil"—of coastal Carolina and Georgia's peak summer offerings. "You can't do much more than find the best ingredients and make them sing," says Mike Lata, chef and co-owner of FIG and the Ordinary in Charleston, South Carolina, who trades traditional blue crab for easier-to-eat stone crab claws in this recipe. You don't even need utensils to eat it. Unlike the one-pots of some great port cities—bouillabaisse in Marseille or cioppino in San Francisco—Frogmore Stew is drained from its cooking liquid and transferred to a platter or sometimes just spread out on a newspaper-covered picnic table and eaten with your hands.

INGREDIENTS

9 to 10 quarts water

At least ½ cup Old Bay Seasoning

16 small new potatoes (about 12 ounces), about 1 inch in diameter, rinsed but not peeled

8 ounces kielbasa, sliced into ½-inch-thick rounds

2 medium Vidalia onions, peeled and quartered lengthwise

3 ears fresh corn, shucked and cut into thirds

16 fresh shrimp, preferably white Carolina shrimp with head on (you may want more depending on size of shrimp)

8 stone crab claws (about 2 pounds)

GARNISHES

Soft butter (for the potatoes and corn), sea salt, lemon wedges, Tabasco sauce, and cocktail sauce

PREPARATION

Fill a large (at least 12-quart) stockpot two-thirds of the way with water and bring to a simmer over medium-high heat. Reduce the heat to maintain a simmer, add the Old Bay, and simmer for 5 minutes to infuse (the water should be abundantly seasoned and aromatic).

Add the potatoes, kielbasa, and onions and adjust the heat to maintain simmer; cook until the potatoes are fork tender, 15 to 18 minutes. Add the corn and simmer until the kernels are slightly softened, about 3 minutes. Add the shrimp and crab claws and cook until the shrimp becomes pink, and both the shrimp and crab are lightly fragrant, 5 to 6 minutes. Strain the solids from the cooking liquid and transfer them to an oversize platter or paper-lined table.

MARYLAND CRAB CAKES

SERVES 4

IN MARYLAND, CRAB CAKES ARE PRACTICALLY A RELIGION. THAT'S WHY SPIKE Gjerde, chef and co-owner of Baltimore's Woodberry Kitchen, doesn't make concessions when it comes to their quality, serving them only when crabs are in season. "We get fresh Chesapeake Bay crab from April to early November," he says. Different picking houses may produce crab that is more or less "clean," but the meat still needs a final check, and the chef is particular about the process. "The hallmark of a great crab cake is that it's devoid of shell but with the lumps intact," he says. At the restaurant, Gjerde uses a black light to illuminate any remaining bits of shell. But for the home cook, his advice is simple: take your time. The effort, we can assure you, will be well worth it.

INGREDIENTS

- 1 pound jumbo lump crabmeat, picked over
- 1 large egg
- 3 tablespoons mayonnaise
- 1 cup fresh breadcrumbs (see Tip)
- ¼ teaspoon ground moderately hot red pepper, such as Aleppo or Marash, or ½ teaspoon sweet paprika
- Scant 1 teaspoon ground black pepper
- Pinch of cayenne pepper
- Scant 1 teaspoon freshly squeezed lemon juice
- ½ teaspoon kosher salt
- Canola oil or grapeseed oil for frying

PREPARATION

Place the crabmeat in a bowl and keep it cold. In a separate bowl, whisk the egg with the mayonnaise, then add ¼ cup of the breadcrumbs and add remaining ingredients except the oil, mixing well. Scrape the egg mixture over the crab and fold it in gently with a wooden spoon or your hands. Let the mixture rest in the refrigerator for 10 minutes.

Sprinkle the remaining ¾ cup breadcrumbs on a plate. Divide the crab mixture into quarters; gently form each portion into a loose ball and gently press onto a plate to form a disheveled patty. Repeat with the remaining crab.

Place a large skillet over medium heat and add about ½ inch of oil. Heat until the oil is shimmering but not smoking. Carefully add the crab cakes and cook until nicely browned on the bottom, 3 to 4 minutes. Flip and cook until the second side is golden brown, about 2 minutes. Remove from the pan and serve immediately.

TIP: **Fresh-made breadcrumbs (day-old bread with crusts removed, pulsed 5 or 6 times in a food processor) are crucial for crab-cake success; they soak up the egg mixture and gently hold everything together. Don't use canned crumbs unless you want a gritty cake.**

FRIED CORNMEAL-CRUSTED CATFISH

SERVES 4 TO 6

SURE, THE COASTAL SOUTH HAS ITS MANY SEAFOOD DELICACIES, BUT AS YOU move inland, the catfish reigns supreme. With good reason. A properly farmed catfish—preferably from a Southern producer and not from overseas—has a clean, mildly sweet taste. More than any food except, perhaps, chicken or potatoes, catfish cries out for a dip in hot oil. A coarse cornmeal batter does something magical. First, its sweetness is a just-right match for the fish's flavor. Here a touch of crab- or shrimp-boil seasoning does a little flavor voodoo, too. And then there's the contrast—big, soft flakes of pure white moist fish against cornmeal's grittiness and heft. You'll know each piece is perfectly done the moment it does something catfish doesn't ordinarily do: floats to the top.

INGREDIENTS

Peanut oil for frying

2 pounds catfish fillets

Kosher salt and freshly ground black pepper

2 cups all-purpose flour

2 tablespoons crab boil seasoning, such as Zatarain's

2 large eggs

½ cup half-and-half

1 tablespoon hot sauce

2 cups coarse-ground yellow cornmeal

Tartar sauce (page 240)

PREPARATION

Heat 1 inch of oil in a Dutch oven or large, deep-sided cast-iron skillet fitted with a frying thermometer to 375°F.

Rinse the catfish fillets and pat thoroughly dry with paper towels. Cut the fillets in half lengthwise (if very large, halve them crosswise too). Season lightly with salt and pepper and set aside.

Set up a dredging station. Combine the flour and crab boil seasoning in a small shallow dish. Beat the eggs with the half-and-half and hot sauce in a second shallow dish. Place the cornmeal in a third shallow dish. Dip a piece of catfish in the flour, shaking off excess, then into egg wash, letting excess drip away. Finally, roll the fish in cornmeal and slip it carefully into the hot oil 3 pieces at a time. Fry the fish for 3 minutes, carefully turn them, and continue to fry for 3 minutes more, until golden brown. Transfer to a wire rack set over a baking sheet and place in a 200°F oven to keep warm while you continue to fry batches of fish.

When all the fish is fried, serve immediately with tartar sauce on the side.

SHRIMP & RICE GRITS

SERVES 4

SHRIMP AND GRITS MAY HAVE BEEN INVENTED IN CHARLESTON, SOUTH Carolina, but many would agree the combination, originally a workingman's breakfast, was perfected in Chapel Hill, North Carolina, at Crook's Corner restaurant by the late chef Bill Neal. And although cheese, bacon, and meaty mushrooms all figure in Neal's recipe, Crook's Corner shrimp and grits are actually quite light, thanks to the brightness of lemon juice and the freshness of scallions and parsley. Our version keeps that character but steers the dish back toward its Lowcountry roots. First, by incorporating tomatoes, a staple of Charleston's style, gently blistered in a skillet to add roasty depth. Second, by using grits made from rice, another Lowcountry staple. Rice grits cook up every bit as creamy as the corn kind but have a toasted, nutty quality. The result is a standout dish no matter where—or what time of day—you eat it.

INGREDIENTS

- 4 cups chicken stock
- 1 tablespoon unsalted butter
- 1 cup Anson Mills Carolina Gold rice grits
- ½ cup finely grated Parmesan cheese
- Kosher salt and freshly ground black pepper
- 1 tablespoon olive oil
- 6 garlic cloves, minced
- 1 pint grape tomatoes
- 1 ounce applewood smoked bacon, finely diced
- 1½ cups sliced cremini mushrooms
- 1 cup sliced scallions
- 1 pound shrimp, peeled and deveined
- ⅛ teaspoon cayenne pepper
- Juice of 1 lemon
- Hot sauce
- 2 tablespoons chopped fresh parsley

TIP: **If you have a high-powered blender, such as a Vitamix, you can make your own rice grits by blending 1 cup long-grain rice on high speed for 10 seconds to break the grains into small pieces.**

PREPARATION

In a large saucepan, bring 3½ cups of the stock to a boil over high heat. Add the butter, then slowly add the rice grits, whisking to incorporate. Reduce the heat to low, cover, and cook for 20 minutes. Stir in the cheese and season with salt and pepper. Keep warm.

Place a large cast-iron skillet over medium-high heat. Add the oil and swirl it around the pan. Add half of the garlic and stir constantly for 30 seconds to toast it and flavor the oil, watching carefully so the garlic doesn't burn. Using a slotted spoon, remove the garlic to a paper towel–lined plate to drain, leaving as much oil in the pan as possible. Add the tomatoes to the skillet and leave undisturbed for 1 minute. Stir, then leave undisturbed for 1 to 2 minutes more, until blistered and spotted black; transfer to a bowl.

Add the bacon to the skillet and reduce the heat to medium. Cook until browned and crisp, 3 to 5 minutes, then remove it with a slotted spoon to another paper towel–lined plate to drain. Add the mushrooms to the rendered fat and cook, stirring, until they release their moisture, about 5 minutes. Stir in the scallions.

While mushrooms cook, sprinkle shrimp with ¼ teaspoon salt and the cayenne. Add the shrimp and the remaining garlic to the pan with the mushrooms and scallions and cook until the shrimp begin to turn bright pink and opaque, about 3 minutes. Add the remaining ½ cup stock, the lemon juice, and hot sauce and cook for 1 to 2 minutes, until warmed through. Taste and season with salt, pepper, and hot sauce if needed. Stir in the reserved tomatoes just to warm through.

Spoon the hot rice grits onto serving plates and top with the shrimp mixture. Garnish each serving with parsley and a bit of the reserved toasted garlic and crisped bacon.

RAMP-STUFFED TROUT

SERVES 2

IF YOU'RE FLY-FISHING FOR TROUT IN THE WATERS OF THE SOUTHERN Appalachians in April, another tasty quarry may lie not far from the banks of the stream: ramps. These wild mountain leeks are a springtime delicacy from North Georgia to West Virginia and beyond. Ramps have what is politely called a pungent, garlicky odor (and if you eat them raw, you will too). Slicing and sautéing the bulbs helps smooth the sharp edge off their flavor. Even so, a little goes a long way, which is a good thing, as ramps can cost $30 a pound at gourmet markets—all the more reason to pay close attention when you're out in the woods.

INGREDIENTS

- 8 to 10 ramps with bulbs and leaves attached
- 1 lemon
- ½ teaspoon Dijon mustard
- ¼ teaspoon kosher salt
- ¼ teaspoon freshly ground black pepper
- 1 tablespoon unsalted butter
- 2 (12-ounce) trout, cleaned and gutted
- 4 hickory-smoked bacon slices
- 1 tablespoon olive oil
  Lemon wedges for serving

PREPARATION

Cut the white ramp bulbs away from the green tops and cut the tops diagonally into 1-inch pieces. Finely mince 1 ramp bulb and place it in a small bowl. Finely grate the zest of the lemon and transfer it to the bowl with the minced ramp bulb. Slice half of the zested lemon into rounds. Squeeze the juice from other half over the minced ramps and lemon zest. Add the mustard, salt, and pepper and set aside.

Mince the remaining ramp bulbs. Melt the butter in a medium sauté pan over medium heat until foamy. Add the ramp bulbs and a pinch of salt and sauté for 2 minutes, until softened, then add the ramp tops and sauté for 2 minutes. Remove the pan from the heat and stir in the macerated lemon–ramp bulb mixture; set aside.

Rinse the trout and pat it thoroughly dry with paper towels. Open each trout and season the flesh lightly with salt and pepper. Spoon half of the ramps into the cavities along with 2 or 3 lemon slices. Arrange the bacon slices on a board and lay the stuffed trout on top; wrap the bacon around each trout.

Place a large cast-iron skillet over medium-high heat. Add the oil and swirl it around the pan. Add the trout and cook for 6 minutes, then turn and cook for 6 minutes more, or until the bacon is crisp and the trout is cooked through. Remove the trout from the pan and serve immediately with lemon wedges.

TIP: When ramps aren't available, you can substitute a medley of onions. Substitute ½ small shallot for the lemon-macerated minced ramp bulb, and for sautéing use 1 diced leek (white and light green parts only), ¼ cup snipped chives, ½ cup thinly sliced scallions, and 1 small minced garlic clove, adding several minutes to the sauté time to soften the leeks thoroughly.

APALACHICOLA OYSTER STEW

SERVES 4 AS AN ENTRÉE,
or 6 as an appetizer

TO TRACE THE TRAJECTORY OF OYSTER STEW IN THE SOUTH, PICK YOUR
possible thread—Irish immigrants to the Chesapeake and the hills beyond reproducing a creamy
dried-fish stew of their European homeland with abundant North American ingredients, or German
immigrants bringing their dairy-based traditions to Louisiana's Creole country. This version meets
roughly in the geographic middle, taking inspiration from Florida's Panhandle region, where the rich
stew is made with plump Apalachicola Bay oysters, although you can use any variety of quality fresh
oysters you like. Add them just before serving to gently heat through. Concentrated oyster liquor
and clam juice lend an extra element of brine, while Conecuh sausage from the just-inland town of
Evergreen, Alabama, delivers smoke and spice.

INGREDIENTS

- 1 tablespoon unsalted butter
- 2 teaspoons vegetable oil
- 2 ounces smoked sausage, such as Alabama-made Conecuh, diced (about ¼ cup)
- ½ cup diced leeks, white and light green parts only
- 1 carrot, peeled and diced
- ½ celery stalk, diced
- ½ cup finely diced new potatoes (2 or 3 potatoes)
- 1 fresh thyme sprig
- ½ teaspoon kosher salt
- ¼ teaspoon freshly ground black pepper
- 2 pints freshly shucked oysters with liquor
- ¼ to ⅓ cup dry white wine
- 1 (8-ounce) bottle clam juice
- 2 cups half-and-half
- ½ teaspoon Worcestershire sauce
- ½ teaspoon hot sauce, plus more for serving
- Chopped fresh parsley or chives for garnish

PREPARATION

Melt the butter in the oil in a Dutch oven over medium-high heat. Add
the sausage and cook, stirring, until browned, about 3 minutes. Add
the leeks, carrot, celery, potatoes, thyme, salt, and pepper and cook,
stirring occasionally, for 5 minutes to soften the vegetables.

Drain the oysters in a fine-mesh sieve set over a glass measuring cup to
collect their liquor. Add an equal amount of wine to oyster liquor. Pour
the liquor mixture into a small saucepan, place over medium-high heat,
and reduce by half, about 2 minutes. Transfer the reduction to the pan
with the vegetables.

Reduce the heat to medium-low and add the clam juice, half-and-half,
Worcestershire sauce, and hot sauce to the pan. Simmer for 10 to 15
minutes, until the potatoes are tender, watching the pan carefully to
make sure the liquid doesn't boil, which would cause the half-and-half
to break. Slip the oysters into the liquid and cook for 1 to 2 minutes
more, until barely warmed through. Remove thyme stem. Ladle into
bowls and serve garnished with parsley and hot sauce.

SAUTÉED SHRIMP & OKRA

SERVES 4 TO 6

"I EAT OKRA EVERY WEEK—SOME WAY, SOMEHOW," SAYS CHARLESTON, SOUTH Carolina, chef BJ Dennis. "I'll make a gumbo. I'll eat okra by itself, just sautéed. I'll deep-fry it, too. It's my favorite vegetable." It's also a powerful symbol of history and place for Dennis, who has deep roots in the Gullah/Geechee culture of coastal South Carolina and Georgia, where freed West Africans lived in often-isolated island communities after the Civil War. Not only has Dennis been eating okra his entire life, but the crop has been a part of his family history for much longer than that. "It came from Africa," he says. "Culturally, it's in my DNA." Shrimp, abundant in South Carolina waters, is another Lowcountry staple and a natural companion to the chopped okra and other garden-fresh vegetables in this one-skillet meal.

INGREDIENTS

- 1 tablespoon vegetable oil, plus more if needed
- 1½ pounds okra, trimmed and chopped
- 1 pound shrimp, peeled and deveined
- 2 to 3 teaspoons minced garlic
- 1 teaspoon minced jalapeño
- 1 teaspoon minced fresh ginger
- ½ cup diced onion
- 1 teaspoon kosher salt
- ½ teaspoon freshly ground black pepper
- 2 tablespoons minced fresh parsley
- ½ teaspoon minced fresh thyme leaves
- 1 cup diced tomato, with juices

PREPARATION

Place a cast-iron skillet over medium heat and add the oil. Add the okra and cook, stirring occasionally, until it begins to brown, about 5 minutes. If the okra starts to stick, add more oil. Add the shrimp, garlic, jalapeño, ginger, onion, salt, and pepper and cook for 5 minutes, until the onion softens and the shrimp begin to turn pink and opaque. Add the parsley, thyme, and tomato and cook until the shrimp is cooked through, 2 to 3 minutes more. Taste and adjust the seasonings with salt and pepper if needed.

GRILLED REDFISH ON THE HALF SHELL

SERVES 4

BLACKENED REDFISH MAY HAVE BEEN ALL THE RAGE IN THE 80s, BUT ANOTHER preparation reigns supreme among fishermen in the know thanks to redfish's thick scales. Keep them on the fillets and they'll form a protective cup (a shell, if you will) around the mild white flesh while the fish grills over an open flame. No fussing, no flipping, no sticking. Lay the fish skin-side down on the grates, close the grill, and about fifteen minutes later, you'll be ready to sit down to one of the best fish dinners you've ever made. When you return home with a fresh catch (hopefully), all you'll need to do is mash a few flavorful ingredients into softened butter, slice a few rounds of lemon, and you're good to grill.

INGREDIENTS

- ½ serrano chile, seeded and minced
- ½ small shallot, minced
- 1 garlic clove, minced
- 1 tablespoon chopped fresh cilantro
- 1 teaspoon hot sauce
- 1 teaspoon Cajun seasoning
- 6 tablespoons (¾ stick) unsalted butter, softened
- 4 redfish fillets, skin and scales left on (if unavailable, you can substitute snapper)
  Canola oil
  Kosher salt and freshly ground black pepper
- 1 lemon, sliced into thin rounds

PREPARATION

Heat a charcoal or gas grill to medium.

In a small bowl, mash the chile, shallot, garlic, cilantro, hot sauce, and Cajun seasoning into the softened butter with a fork until thoroughly combined.

Brush the skin side of the fish lightly with oil. Season the flesh side lightly with salt and pepper. Spread 1 tablespoon of the butter mixture on each fillet and top with 3 or 4 lemon rounds.

Place the fillets scale-side down on the grill. Close the lid and grill for 12 to 15 minutes, until the scales are blackened and the fish is cooked through. Remove from the grill, place on plates, and top each fillet with a bit of the remaining flavored butter.

GREEK-STYLE FLOUNDER

SERVES 4

SURPRISINGLY ENOUGH, BAKLAVA IS NEARLY AS COMMON AS BARBECUE IN and around Birmingham, Alabama, thanks to a wave of Greek immigrants who arrived in the early 1900s and brought the bright, sunny flavors of the Mediterranean with them. One of those immigrants, Tom Bonduris, opened the Bright Star restaurant in nearby Bessemer in 1907, and it's still owned by members of his family today. This recipe is based on a Bright Star favorite: the freshest Gulf fish—snapper, cobia, triggerfish, or, here, flounder—sautéed in fruity olive oil and bathed in a simple sauce that's loaded with lemony, herbal flavors.

INGREDIENTS

- 4 (6-ounce) flounder fillets
- 3 tablespoons unsalted butter, melted
- Kosher salt and freshly ground black pepper
- ¼ cup all-purpose flour
- Zest of 1 lemon
- Juice of 2 lemons
- 1 tablespoon chopped fresh oregano
- ½ cup plus 1 teaspoon extra-virgin olive oil
- Lemon wedges for serving

PREPARATION

Brush the flounder fillets with the melted butter and season lightly with salt and pepper. Spread the flour in a thin layer on a dinner plate and press both sides of the fillets in the flour, shaking off excess. Transfer to a wire rack and set aside.

Combine the lemon zest, lemon juice, oregano, ½ teaspoon salt, and ¼ teaspoon pepper in a small bowl. Slowly whisk in ½ cup of the oil to create an emulsified sauce.

Preheat a large, well-seasoned cast-iron skillet (or, to safely avoid sticking, a nonstick skillet) over medium heat and add the remaining 1 teaspoon oil. Add the fish and cook for 3 minutes, then flip and cook on the second side for 2 minutes, or until cooked through. Transfer to a platter and spoon the sauce over the fish. Serve with lemon wedges.

SMOKED TROUT HASH

SERVES 4 TO 6

CHEF JOHN FLEER IS A MASTER OF TRANSFORMING HUMBLE SOUTHERN Appalachian cuisine into haute plates—rising to prominence at Walland, Tennessee's, exclusive Blackberry Farm resort and now manning his own kitchen at Rhubarb in Asheville, North Carolina. Meat-and-vegetable hashes are a staple of his table year round, usually with bacon. But not always. "Using smoked trout is a way to keep the smoke in the dish while changing the flavor a little bit," Fleer says. Fleer uses Sunburst Trout Farms smoked-trout fillets, sourced from the nearby Pisgah National Forest, when he makes this winter-vegetable hash—a fresh take on a Southern standby that will do your cast-iron skillet proud.

INGREDIENTS

- 1 cup peeled and chopped celeriac (½-inch cubes)
- 6 tablespoons olive oil
- ½ teaspoon kosher salt
- ¼ teaspoon freshly ground black pepper
- 1 cup peeled and chopped butternut squash (½-inch cubes)
- 1 pound fingerling potatoes, peeled and sliced ¼ inch thick
- ½ cup diced onion
- ½ cup diced celery
- 1 garlic clove, sliced
- 1 tablespoon chopped fresh sage
- 1 tablespoon chopped fresh flat-leaf parsley
- 8 ounces smoked trout, such as North Carolina Sunburst Trout Farms, crumbled

PREPARATION

Preheat the oven to 375°F.

In a medium bowl, toss the celeriac with 1 tablespoon of the oil, season with ¼ teaspoon of the salt and ⅛ teaspoon of the pepper, and spread evenly on a baking sheet. Roast for 20 minutes. Meanwhile, toss the squash with 1 tablespoon of the remaining oil and the remaining ¼ teaspoon salt and ⅛ teaspoon remaining pepper. Add to the sheet with the celeriac and roast for an additional 40 minutes, or until both vegetables are tender.

Fill a large saucepan or stockpot halfway with water and bring to a boil. Place the potatoes in the water, boil for 3 to 4 minutes, until tender, then drain, cool, and slice.

Put the remaining 4 tablespoons oil in a large sauté pan or skillet over medium-high heat. Add the onion and celery and cook until softened, about 5 minutes. Add the garlic and half of the sage and cook for another 30 seconds. Add the cooked potatoes, celeriac, and squash, tossing to combine, and heat until all the ingredients are warmed through, 1 to 2 minutes. Add the remaining sage, the parsley, and the smoked trout and cook for an additional minute, until the trout is warmed through. Remove from the heat, taste, season with additional salt and pepper if needed, and serve.

PINEBARK STEW

SERVES 12

GIVEN THE ABUNDANCE OF PINE TREES IN THE SOUTH, YOU MAY NOT BE surprised to learn that they've been used as an ingredient in the region's cuisine for centuries—from pine-needle tea to sap-boiled potatoes. South Carolina pinebark stew is one of the most beloved coniferous concoctions. Don't worry, you won't actually be munching on bark. The stew is made with any freshwater fish, a tomato-curry broth with chunks of potatoes, and, yes, a hint of fresh pine. This interpretation, made with catfish, gets a gentle dose of pine flavor two ways: vegetables roasted in pine-needle smoke and a garnish of finely chopped pine needles—similar to a sprinkle of rosemary.

INGREDIENTS

- 1 large Vidalia onion, quartered
- 1½ pounds whole small yellow potatoes
- 6 garlic cloves, peeled
- 4 cooked hickory-smoked bacon slices, crumbled, with the fat reserved
- 4 to 5 handfuls clean fresh green pine needles, plus 2 tablespoons finely chopped for garnish
- 2 teaspoons kosher salt
- 1 teaspoon freshly ground black pepper
- 1 cup ketchup
- 2 tablespoons Worcestershire sauce
- 1 teaspoon hot curry powder
- 3 cups coarsely chopped tomatoes
- 1 pound catfish fillets or strips of other freshwater fish, such as crappie, trout, or bass, cut into chunks

PREPARATION

Preheat the oven to 450°F and turn on the vent hood if you've got one.

Toss the onion, potatoes, and garlic in a large bowl with the reserved bacon fat. Layer half of the pine needles in the bottom of a Dutch oven and set it over high heat. When the needles begin to smoke, add the onion, potatoes, and garlic, wrap tightly with foil and cover with the lid, and transfer to the oven. Let the vegetables roast and smoke for 25 minutes, then remove the pan from the oven and, using tongs, remove the vegetables from the pot. When the vegetables are cool enough to handle, chop the onion into bite-size pieces, halve or quarter the potatoes, and mince the garlic. (Discard the roasted pine needles.)

Return the vegetables to the pot and add water to cover, about 1½ quarts. Add the salt, pepper, ketchup, Worcestershire sauce, and curry powder and bring to a boil over high heat. Reduce the heat to low and simmer uncovered for 10 minutes. Add the tomatoes and fish and cook for 10 minutes more, until the fish is cooked through.

Ladle the soup into bowls and serve garnished with the bacon crumbles and a sprinkle of finely chopped pine needles.

5

GAME

A TASTE FOR THE HUNT

The greatest meal of my life involved a Triscuit

JONATHAN MILES

AT THE AGE OF ELEVEN, YOU SEE, I CAME INTO POSSESSION of a .177-caliber Crosman air rifle. The rifle shot mushroom-shaped lead pellets, and if you pumped the rifle a dozen times or so, to the point that a pneumatic/mechanical explosion felt dangerously imminent, it shot them pretty hard. One afternoon, bored with plinking cans, I took lazy, purposeless aim at a mourning dove perched upon a branch in the next-door neighbor's yard. Perhaps I meant to scare it, to startle it skyward, I don't know. In any case I felt certain I couldn't hit it.

I hit it. The way the dove dropped, in an awful flutter of wings, mirrored the state of my insides; my heart collapsed in free-fall panic. As a boy of the suburbs, I'd never killed anything before, or even considered it; my imaginary targets had always been Nazi infantrymen. I leaped the concrete-block wall dividing our yard from the neighbor's and dashed across his backyard to where the fallen dove was flailing in the shade. Desperate to end its misery, I pumped the rifle to its airy maximum and shot the dove point-blank in the head. The stillness that followed didn't console me. My eyes soaked, I shot it again, and then again, sobbing, and then again and again until I was finally out of pellets.

I could have left it or buried it. But something inside me, with a wise and moral voice like Obi-Wan Kenobi's, said I had to eat it. Wasting it, said the voice, would only compound the sin. As a latchkey kid, as we were called in those days, I'd become proficient at making Triscuit pizzas in the broiler to feed myself after school, but that marked the beginning and end of my cooking chops. With a pocketknife, I cut the dove open, not knowing what to look for but finding a small wedge of purple breast meat from which I carved a few mangled slices. I heaped them atop some Triscuits and watched them sizzle under the red electric coil, my tear-smeared face staring back at me from the oven glass. And then, alone at the breakfast counter, I ate them.

I don't wish to overstate the moment, but the greater risk, it seems to me, lies in understatement. With each sniffling, tentative bite came an ever more profound understanding of the natural world, an epiphanic realization of what it meant to eat meat, to eat flesh, to eat animals, of the way death begets life, the way death feeds and nurtures life, of the cruel and beautiful order under which we all operate, boy and dove alike. If design, as the teleological argument goes, is how God makes His presence known, then here at the breakfast counter was God, speaking to me from a Triscuit pulpit. And though I wept in hot shame and terror, something else occurred to me as well, a sensation at once irreconcilable but undeniable: the dove breast, seared from the broiler, unadorned with even salt and pepper, was . . . delicious. Here was pain, at seeing the world's dark heart revealed, but here too was a new and riveting pleasure.

For almost thirty years now I've been trying to re-create that meal. With doves, of course, shot over sunflower and millet fields in Mississippi and Georgia, but with ducks too, lifted gently from the mouths of wet Labrador retrievers in the Arkansas Delta and elsewhere, and with wild turkeys, and with squirrels, and with a musky-flavored wild boar I shot in the Tennessee mountains, and plenty of deer as well: all in the service of a single memory. Not too long ago I read about Facebook founder Mark Zuckerberg's vow to only eat the meat of animals he's killed himself, which he's been doing on a California farm. This is commendable, if a bit unwieldy, but may just be the next logical frontier in the locavore and ethical-eating movements that have been blessedly spreading throughout the nation. For hunters, however, this is no frontier.

It's something every hunter comes to understand, whether by shooting his or her first squirrel under grandfatherly tutelage (as my son did with his pop), or accidentally shooting a dove over a concrete wall: that only by killing, by enacting (or at least observing) the transformation of animal to meat, can we own up to our appetites with anything like honesty. "Man is a fugitive from Nature," wrote the Spanish philosopher José Ortega y Gasset, and, as we all know, the fugitive's life is necessarily constructed upon lies. Meat is not an abstract protein; that's the lie, subconscious but toxic all the same. It's the lie we abet every time we toss out a cellophane-wrapped package of meat that went neglected in the refrigerator's way-back, stung by the waste of money if stung at all. For the thoughtful hunter there is no such blitheness. Grandiose though it may sound, the hunter afield is stalking more than game; he's stalking truth.

But why wild truth? This is where pleasure bleeds in, admittedly, but also something deeper. It's become fashionable of late for restaurateurs to extol the provenance of the meat on their menus—what farm the pig came from, who fed it—in order to tell a story of how that pork shank made its way onto your plate. These have become the dinnertime equivalent of bedtime stories, designed to lull you into virtuous enjoyment. And while they're a necessary corrective after decades of industrial storylessness, these stories are inevitably about the farmer, not the animal. What we hear about the animal is what was or wasn't done to it. With wild animals, it's different. The story belongs to the animal, except for the ending, when the story turns briefly to the hunter.

At a deer-hunting camp I used to frequent near Crystal Springs, Mississippi, we used to perform something we called the "autopsy." The idea was to determine just how the deer had died—where the bullet had hit, what precisely it had done—but, out in that low-ceilinged tin shed, gathered around a pendent whitetail carcass, our whiskey breath visible in the autumn-chilled air, we'd learn a whole lot about its life too: what it'd been eating, what the scars on its hide revealed, how that hairline fracture on its hind leg was what had prevented it from springing away fast enough to beat a clumsy shooter. This is not to suggest we lounged about the deer camp telling stories about our deer in the sacred manner of movie Indians. Of course not; we told dirty jokes like everyone else. But it is to say that the deer were present, not as mere meat, commodities, or, God forbid, trophies, but as wild and sentient creatures whose lives we had deigned to take—hungrily, but respectfully.

The flavor of game, like its story, belongs to the animal, not to any farmer, and not to the hunter. It's contingent on its diet, its age, its sex, its life, and it's owing to this that the flavors can vary so widely, so maddeningly. Yet there's an elemental magic to those free-ranging and often untamable flavors, a direct link to the natural chaos that lies within that grand design I happened upon as a weepy eleven-year-old boy. For a cook, this can be challenging: it took me months to devise methods of making that ancient boar edible, and despite valiant efforts I have yet to charm guests with a bite of Canada goose. Yet this is somehow part of the allure too. Into the kitchen with game comes wildness, with its infinite degrees of complexity, and its infinite mine of stories. This is why the oxymoronic farm-raised game is such a wan replica of the genuine article: its life and death are predetermined, its story not its own. "Poetry," said the French critic Denis Diderot, "must have something in it that is barbaric, vast and wild." As a Triscuit once taught me, the same goes for eating.

SLICED DOVE BREASTS ON CORNBREAD CROSTINI WITH GREEN TOMATO MARMALADE

SERVES 6

THIS IS A GROWN-UP VERSION OF JONATHAN MILES'S DOVE BREAST TRISCUIT. (See "A Taste for the Hunt," page 124.) Because they're so tiny—about two ounces—dove breasts go from just-done to overdone in seconds. You're going to want them no more than medium rare. Keep your eye on the skillet and flip smaller breasts after about two minutes, larger breasts about three minutes. Another trick to keep them tender is to let the breasts rest after cooking so what juices they contain redistribute back into the meat. Transfer them from the pan to a plate, loosely tent with foil, and then wait—ten minutes minimum, fifteen if you can stand it—before slicing.

INGREDIENTS

FOR THE GREEN TOMATO MARMALADE

- 1 pound green tomatoes, finely chopped
- ½ cup sugar
- 3 tablespoons freshly squeezed lemon juice
  Kosher salt and freshly ground black pepper

FOR THE CORNBREAD CROSTINI

- 2 cups coarse-ground yellow or white cornmeal
- 2 teaspoons baking powder
- ½ cup all-purpose flour
- ¼ teaspoon kosher salt
- 2 tablespoons sugar
- 2 cups buttermilk
- 2 large eggs, lightly beaten
- ¼ cup neutral oil, such as canola
- ½ cup corn kernels

FOR THE DOVE BREASTS

- 6 dove breasts
- 3 tablespoons unsalted butter
  Kosher salt and freshly ground black pepper
- 2 tablespoons very finely chopped fresh mint

PREPARATION

FOR THE GREEN TOMATO MARMALADE Combine the green tomatoes, sugar, and lemon juice in a container, cover, and refrigerate overnight. Transfer the mixture to a medium saucepan and bring to a boil over high heat. Reduce the heat to low and simmer for about 1 hour, stirring frequently, until the mixture has thickened. Season with salt and pepper.

FOR THE CORNBREAD CROSTINI Preheat the oven to 400°F. Line a baking sheet with foil and grease with nonstick cooking spray or oil.

In a large bowl, combine the cornmeal, baking powder, flour, salt, and sugar. Add the buttermilk, eggs, and oil and stir until the mixture is just moistened. Fold in the corn kernels. Pour the batter onto the prepared baking sheet and bake until golden brown, about 20 minutes. Allow the cornbread to cool for about 5 minutes, loosen the edges with a knife, and invert onto a large cutting board. Cut into 4-inch squares, then cut each square in half diagonally to form triangles.

FOR THE DOVE BREASTS Melt the butter in a large sauté pan over medium-high heat. Season the dove breasts lightly with salt and pepper, then add the breasts to the skillet skin-side down and sear for 2 to 3 minutes depending on the size of the breasts. Flip the breasts and continue to cook for 1 minute longer. Transfer to a plate, loosely tent with foil, and leave to rest for 5 to 10 minutes, then slice.

TO ASSEMBLE THE DISH Arrange the cornbread triangles on a platter and top each with a few slices of breast, then drizzle each with a spoonful of green tomato marmalade and garnish with the mint.

GRILLED QUAIL WITH CHOCOLATE GRAVY

SERVES 4

IT'S TIME TO TALK ABOUT QUAIL AND CHOCOLATE. WAIT—DON'T STOP READING. There is a reason these two ingredients should be married, and chef Robert Newton has figured it out. It's not a far leap if you take a moment to consider classic Mexican moles built with a touch of bitter chocolate and usually spooned over poultry. Newton, who grew up in Arkansas and now feeds New Yorkers' fried-chicken fixation at his restaurant Wilma Jean, has a particular fondness for chocolate gravy, a slurry of cocoa powder, sugar, flour, and milk that he remembers seeing cooling on stoves in countless kitchens in the Ozarks. "Chocolate gravy is one of those lost things," he says. The birds are given an aggressive spice rub, then grilled quickly over a hot flame. Pool the gravy on a plate, add a bird, drizzle with a little more gravy, and then shave some Virginia peanuts on top. It's a beautiful marriage, Southern style.

INGREDIENTS

FOR THE QUAIL

- 1 tablespoon coriander seeds
- 1 teaspoon cumin seeds
- 5 allspice berries
- 3 tablespoons smoked paprika
- 1 tablespoon benne seeds
- 1 large garlic clove
- ½ teaspoon kosher salt
- ¼ cup canola or other neutral oil
- ¼ cup orange juice
- 8 quail, semi-boneless (breastbone and backbone removed, with legs and wings intact)
- 6 to 8 large peanuts

FOR THE GRAVY

- ¼ cup cocoa powder
- 2 tablespoons all-purpose flour
- 1¼ cups whole milk
- 2½ tablespoons sugar
- 2 teaspoons sea salt or kosher salt
- ¼ teaspoon cayenne pepper
- 2 tablespoons unsalted butter

PREPARATION

FOR THE QUAIL Toast the coriander seeds, cumin seeds, and allspice berries in a small skillet over medium heat until fragrant, about 1 to 2 minutes. Remove to a plate and cool for 2 to 3 minutes, then grind in a spice grinder to a powder. Place the ground spices in a small bowl and add the paprika and benne seeds. Mix well.

Chop the garlic, sprinkle it with salt, and mash into a paste on the cutting board using the side of a knife. Add the garlic, oil, and orange juice to the spices and mix thoroughly.

Snip the wing tips off the quail. Place quail in a shallow baking dish, pour the rub over the quail, turning to coat, then cover the dish with plastic wrap and place in the refrigerator, and marinate for at least 1 hour but no longer than 6 hours.

Prepare a medium-hot grill and cook each bird for 7 to 9 minutes, turning once, until medium-rare.

FOR THE GRAVY Combine the cocoa powder, flour, milk, sugar, salt, and cayenne in a saucepan over medium heat. Cook until thickened, 5 to 7 minutes, whisking often to eliminate lumps. Remove from the heat and stir in the butter. The sauce can be reserved while the quail cooks; just loosen with a few tablespoons of water as you reheat it.

TO ASSEMBLE THE DISH Pool a ladleful of gravy on a plate, top each with 2 quail, drizzle with chocolate gravy, and then, using a Microplane grater, shave peanuts over each bird.

BRAISED QUAIL WITH LEEKS, DATES, & CIDER

SERVES 4

ANYONE WHO HAS EVER SWUNG A SHOTGUN AT QUAIL KNOWS THE DIMINUTIVE birds are prone to sudden bursts of flight. To be successful, you need to be a quick shot. Speed counts when it comes to cooking them too. "By virtue of their size, quicker methods work best for quail," says James Beard Award–winning Georgia chef Hugh Acheson. "And unlike larger game birds, the white and dark meat will cook at about the same time." The key to keeping the quail meat moist and tender is in the preliminary sear, which not only deepens the flavor but also creates a crust that prevents the birds from steaming in the cooking liquid. "You want the skin to get good and crisp," the chef says. "Although it will soften again during the braising, the birds will retain that browned goodness." Stock is mixed with hard cider for a lighter, crisper braising liquid, grounded by the earthiness of the leeks and the natural sweetness of Medjool dates. "All it takes is one pot and simple ingredients," Acheson says. "The quail are up to you."

INGREDIENTS

- 8 quail, semi-boneless (breastbone and backbone removed) with legs and wings intact
- Sea salt or kosher salt and freshly ground black pepper
- 4 shallots, peeled and cut in half
- 2 tablespoons olive oil
- 1½ cups hard apple cider
- 2 medium leeks, white and pale green parts only, cut into ½-inch pieces (about 2 cups)
- ½ cup Medjool dates, pitted and chopped (about 6 dates)
- Bouquet garni (4 sprigs fresh thyme, 4 sprigs fresh flat-leaf parsley, and 1 fresh bay leaf, tied together with kitchen twine or a leek or green-onion skin)
- 1½ cups chicken stock

PREPARATION

Rinse the quail under cool running water, dry on paper towels, and season liberally with salt and pepper. Stuff a shallot half into the cavity of each bird and truss it by simply tying together the drumsticks with kitchen twine.

Place a Dutch oven over medium-high heat and add 1 tablespoon of the oil. Heat until just below smoking (the oil should shimmer, almost as though it is moving across the surface in waves). Working in batches if necessary, gently add the quail and brown on each breast side, about 2 minutes per side, then flip and brown on the second side. Remove the quail from the pan to a plate. Deglaze the pot with a splash of cider, using a wooden spoon to scrape up any browned bits from the bottom, and pour the juices over the reserved quail.

Reduce the heat to medium, add the remaining 1 tablespoon oil, then add the leeks and cook for about 5 minutes, until softened. Add the dates, bouquet garni, and the remaining cider and cook for 3 minutes, then add the stock and quail. Raise the heat to medium-high, let the liquid come almost to a boil, cover, and reduce the heat to low. Simmer for 15 to 20 minutes, then remove the quail and reduce the cooking liquid until slightly thickened, 3 to 5 minutes. Remove and discard the bouquet garni. Place the quail on serving dishes, spooning the liquid over the top, and serve.

DUCK & OYSTER GUMBO

SERVES 8 TO 10

WHEN FAMED NEW ORLEANS CHEF JOHN BESH AND HIS FRIENDS HEAD DOWN to their camp in Cameron Parish each winter, duck hunting may be the reason, but gumbo is the sport. "If we're not competing with each other over it, we're cooking it together," Besh says. There's always a stop at Black's Oyster Bar in Abbeville for oysters, ready to drop into the pot at the last moment. Then it's gun to duck; duck to gumbo. But before the bird comes the very soul of the gumbo: roux. Born of a classical French culinary technique, roux is a cooked mixture of fat and flour used to thicken a sauce. Since a roux is impossible to taste while it's cooking—way too hot—there's always some debating about when it's done. Here's where experience comes in. The mix for Besh's gumbo takes about an hour to make, or in the words of his friend Blake, it's a "three-beer roux." Budweiser, Budweiser, Budweiser, and you're good to go.

INGREDIENTS

- 2 wild ducks (2½ to 3 pounds each), or 1 (5- to 6-pound store-bought duck), quartered
  Kosher salt and freshly ground black pepper
- 2 tablespoons herbes de Provence
- 1 cup rendered duck fat or lard (or vegetable oil if you must)
- 1 cup all-purpose flour
- 2 onions, diced
- 2 celery stalks, chopped
- 1 pound andouille sausage, diced
- 8 ounces smoked pork sausage, chopped
- 1 tablespoon minced garlic
- 3 quarts chicken or duck stock
- 2 cups oyster liquor
- 1 tablespoon Worcestershire sauce
- 2 tablespoons Creole seasoning
- 2 bay leaves
- 2 cups sliced okra
- 3 cups oysters
  Tabasco sauce
- 4 cups cooked jasmine rice, prepared according to package instructions
- ½ cup chopped scallions

PREPARATION

Preheat the oven to 450°F.

If using a store-bought duck, remove the neck and giblets and reserve for another use. Dry the duck and, using a two-prong fork, pierce the fat of the skin all over without hitting the meat beneath. Liberally season the duck with salt and pepper, and add the herbes de Provence. Roast until the fat has rendered and the skin is crisp, about 2 hours, or until the duck reaches an internal temperature of 165°F. Remove from the oven and pour the fat into a heatproof container. Once the duck is cool enough to handle, pick all the meat and skin from bone and cut into roughly 1½-inch pieces. Set aside.

To make the roux, place a large Dutch oven over medium heat and add 1 cup of the reserved duck fat (if your ducks did not yield this much fat, top it off with melted lard). Add the flour and cook, stirring often, until it takes on a deep chocolate color, about 35 minutes, adjusting the heat if it's cooking too fast. Stir in the onions and cook another 5 to 10 minutes. Add the duck, celery, sausages, and garlic and cook for 5 minutes, stirring frequently.

Add the stock, oyster liquor, Worcestershire sauce, Creole seasoning, bay leaves, and okra, raise the heat to high, and bring the mixture to a boil. Reduce the heat and simmer to marry the flavors, occasionally skimming fat that rises to the top, about 1½ hours.

Add the oysters and continue to simmer for another 5 minutes. Season the gumbo with salt, pepper, and Tabasco sauce. Serve over rice and garnish with chopped scallions.

DUCK WITH SATSUMA SAUCE

SERVES 4

DUCK AND ORANGE MAKE FOR A NATURAL PAIRING. ACROSS THE SOUTH, DUCK season starts in late November, almost the exact same time sweet satsumas are ripening from north Florida to east Texas. The two combine here in a centerpiece dish that can upstage any Thanksgiving turkey. If you've never tasted a satsuma, expect flavor that's sweet like an orange but even more floral and fragrant, with a slight limey tang. If you can't find satsumas, substitute clementines; they're not as juicy, so plan to buy more if using them for this recipe. Since the meat is the main event, bigger birds like mallards work best for whole roasting, although there's nothing wrong with a store-bought duck either. Using the neck to make a rich stock enhances every bite of the dish. This is a complicated recipe, but the results are worth the effort. You can make things easier by parboiling the duck and making the stock and sauce (minus the butter, which you'll stir in at the end) the day before you plan to roast the bird.

INGREDIENTS

- 1 (4- to 5-pound) duck, thawed if frozen
- 3 celery stalks, chopped
- 1 carrot, cut into chunks
- 6 small shallots
- ½ cup white wine
- 4 scallions, thinly sliced
- 1 bunch fresh parsley, stems and leaves separate
- 2-inch knob fresh ginger, peeled and sliced into coins
- 10 whole black peppercorns
- 10 whole coriander seeds
- 12 to 14 satsumas
- 2 teaspoons grated satsuma zest
- ¼ cup Bayou rum, Bayou Satsuma Rum Liqueur, or Cointreau Noir
- 2 tablespoons unsalted butter
- 1 tablespoon kosher salt
- 2 teaspoons freshly ground black pepper
- 1½ teaspoons paprika
- 1 teaspoon ground coriander
- 4 cups cooked long-grain rice, prepared according to package instructions

PREPARATION

Preheat the oven to 425°F.

Remove the neck and giblets from the duck; discard the giblets or reserve for another use. Rinse and pat the duck dry thoroughly with paper towels and chop the neck into 1-inch pieces with a cleaver. Put the neck pieces in a small roasting pan with half of the celery, the carrot, and 1 halved shallot. Roast for 20 to 25 minutes, shaking the pan halfway through, until the neck pieces and vegetables have browned.

While the bones and vegetables are roasting, bring a large stockpot of water to a boil. Prick the skin of the duck all over with sharp fork tines almost parallel to the surface so as not to pierce the meat. Carefully slip the duck into the boiling water to submerge it and cook for 10 minutes. Remove with tongs to a plate, let cool, and pat thoroughly dry.

Remove the roasting pan from the oven and pour the wine into the pan, scraping with tongs or a spatula to remove any browned bits. Transfer the liquid and solids to a small saucepan and place over high heat. Thinly slice the remaining 5 shallots and set 2 of them aside. To the saucepan, add the 3 sliced shallots, 3 cups water, 3 scallions, parsley stems, half of the ginger, the peppercorns, and the coriander seeds. Bring to a boil, then reduce the heat to medium-low and cook until the liquid is reduced by half, about 30 minutes. Strain the liquid through a fine-mesh sieve into a heatproof bowl, pressing on the solids with the back of a spoon, and return the liquid to the saucepan. You should have about 1½ cups liquid.

RECIPE CONTINUES ▶

Zest 2 to 3 of the satsumas so you have 2 teaspoons zest. Reserving 1 satsuma for the duck, juice the remaining satsumas until you have 1½ cups of juice. Add the juice to the saucepan with the strained stock and stir in the liqueur and 1 teaspoon of the zest. Simmer until reduced by half, about 10 minutes. Set aside and keep warm.

Preheat the oven to 450°F.

In a small bowl, combine the remaining 1 teaspoon zest with the salt, ground pepper, paprika, and ground coriander. Sprinkle all over the bird and inside its cavity. Cut the remaining satsuma in half and stuff it in the duck cavity with the remaining celery, shallots, and ginger, and half of the parsley leaves.

Place the stuffed bird breast-side up on a wire rack set in a roasting pan and roast for 15 minutes. Lower the oven temperature to 350°F and roast for 45 minutes more. Remove the duck from the oven, pour off any fat, and carefully turn breast-side down. Return to the oven and roast for 20 to 30 minutes more. Remove the duck from the oven, pour off any accumulated fat, and carefully turn the duck breast-side up. Increase the oven temperature to 450°F, return the pan to the oven, and roast for 15 to 20 minutes more, until an instant-read thermometer inserted in the meaty portion of the thigh registers 175°F and the duck skin is golden brown and crispy. Let the duck rest for 15 minutes before carving to allow the juices to redistribute.

Reheat the sauce over medium-low. Whisk in the butter and add the remaining scallion. Taste and adjust the seasonings if needed.

Spoon the rice onto a platter and arrange the duck pieces in the center. Spoon the sauce over the meat. Chop some of the remaining parsley and sprinkle it over the top. Serve with the remaining sauce on the side.

PERFECT POPPERS

MAKES 24 POPPERS;
serves 6 to 8

THERE'S NOTHING WRONG WITH THE STANDARD GRILLED POPPER—A SLICE of wild game bird breast stuffed into a jalapeño with cheese, then wrapped in bacon. That said, a little experimentation can pay tasty dividends. First, the cheese. Too often the standard spoonful of Philly oozes out, disappearing between the grill grates. Soft, creamy goat cheese melts too, but not as fast. Next comes the duck—or dove or pheasant or even venison. Lightly press the slice of meat on top of the cheese-stuffed pepper; aim to seal the cheese inside. Then, the bacon. This is the rare instance where thin-sliced is best; too thick, and what's inside the popper will get done long before the bacon does. A final drizzle of cane syrup is like that little bit of maple syrup that strays off the pancakes and over into the sausage—a deliciously sweet counterpoint to heat and smoke.

INGREDIENTS

- 12 jalapeños, stems removed, halved, and seeded
  - About ½ (3-ounce) log herbed goat cheese
  - Granulated garlic
- 1 duck breast half, trimmed and sliced into 24 thin pieces
- 1 teaspoon kosher salt
- 1 teaspoon freshly ground black pepper
- 24 thin-sliced center-cut bacon strips (about 1 pound)
- 24 wooden picks (presoaked in water for 15 minutes)
  - Cane syrup

PREPARATION

Heat a charcoal grill to medium (or a gas grill to medium-low). Let the coals burn down until ashy and glowing.

While the grill comes to temperature, arrange the jalapeño halves on a board. Place 1 teaspoon of the cheese inside each. Dust lightly with granulated garlic. Place strips of duck on top of the cheese-stuffed peppers, pressing lightly to seal in the cheese. Season with salt and pepper.

Lay the bacon flat on the board, one slice at time. Use two-thirds (the wider end, if the slice is uneven) of each slice of bacon to roll a popper diagonally, encasing the popper from bottom to top. Twist the remaining third over the popper's top (further insurance on keeping the ingredients inside). Push a pick diagonally through this final strip to hold the bacon in place.

Place the poppers on the grill grate, pepper-side down. As the bacon crisps (in 2 to 3 minutes), roll each popper on its side and cook for about 2 minutes per side, then finally turn the popper so the top cooks for about 2 minutes more. If the poppers are different sizes, place larger ones over the hottest spots on the grill, and smaller ones, which will cook faster, over cooler spots.

Remove the poppers to a plate and drizzle lightly with cane syrup. Serve immediately.

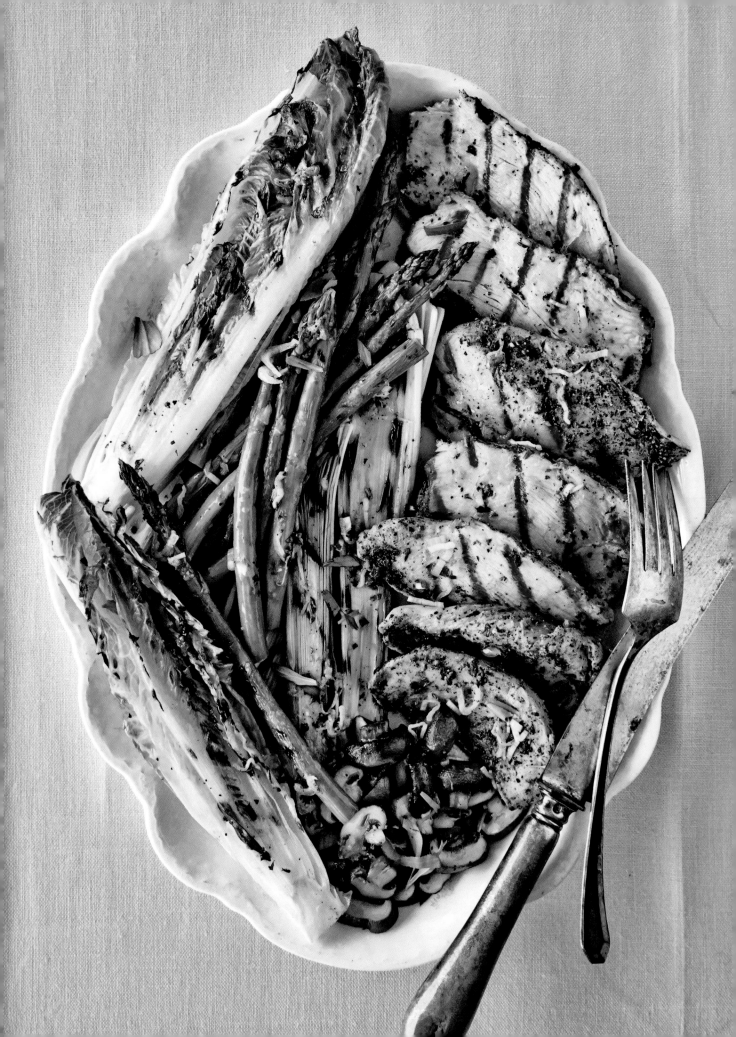

GRILLED WILD TURKEY BREAST
& SPRING VEGETABLE SALAD

SERVES 4

FOR ALL ITS NOBILITY AND CRAFTINESS, A WILD TURKEY DOESN'T EXACTLY taste like its Butterball cousin. The meat is generally gamier and drier, but treat it right and it's a sublime pleasure. This is where brining comes in. This recipe uses a dry brine, a salt-heavy mixture of seasonings that helps the meat retain moisture, just like the more familiar wet brine. The turkey can dry brine in the refrigerator overnight or up to twenty-four hours before you slice the meat. If you plan to try this with store-bought turkey breast instead, cut the salt in the brine by at least half. Most supermarket poultry comes already injected with a sodium solution to help preserve, tenderize, and moisten the meat.

INGREDIENTS

FOR THE TURKEY AND DRY BRINE

- 1 boneless turkey breast half (about 1½ pounds)
- 1 tablespoon kosher salt
  Grated zest of 1 lemon
- 1 teaspoon finely chopped fresh thyme leaves
- 1 teaspoon finely chopped fresh tarragon leaves
- 1 teaspoon freshly ground black pepper
- ½ teaspoon granulated garlic

FOR THE SALAD

- 1 bunch asparagus
- 1 leek, white and light green parts only, cut in half lengthwise and rinsed
- 1 large shallot, cut in half lengthwise and peeled
- 5 large cremini, button, or morel mushrooms
- 2 tablespoons plus ½ cup olive oil
- 2 large romaine lettuce heads, outer leaves removed, cut in half
- ¼ cup tarragon vinegar
  Grated zest of 1 lemon
  Chopped fresh tarragon for garnish

PREPARATION

FOR THE TURKEY AND DRY BRINE Rinse the turkey breast and pat it dry with paper towels. Combine the remaining ingredients in a bowl or zip-top bag; reserve ½ teaspoon of the dry brine mixture for later use. Place the turkey in the zip-top bag, remove as much air as possible, and seal. Massage the dry brine into the turkey breast to evenly coat it on all sides. Refrigerate for at least 8 hours or up to 24 hours. Remove the turkey breast and slice it diagonally into 8 thin portions.

FOR THE SALAD Heat a charcoal grill to medium-high. Toss the asparagus, leek, shallot, and mushrooms with 1 tablespoon of the oil and grill them in batches, starting with the asparagus, then the leek, then the shallot, and then the mushrooms. Grill for 3 minutes per side, or until the vegetables are tender and have grill marks. Transfer to a bowl and cover with plastic wrap to keep warm.

Grill the turkey slices for 3 to 4 minutes per side. Transfer to a platter. Drizzle the romaine with 1 tablespoon of the oil and grill for 1 to 2 minutes on each side to develop grill marks and wilt slightly. Transfer the romaine to individual plates. Divide the turkey, asparagus, and mushrooms among the plates.

Prepare a dressing: Thinly slice the grilled shallot and leek and put them in a small zip-top bag with the reserved ½ teaspoon dry brine, the vinegar, the remaining ½ cup oil, and the lemon zest. Seal and shake vigorously to thoroughly combine. Spoon the dressing over the turkey and vegetables. Garnish with tarragon, if desired, and serve warm.

RABBIT & CORNMEAL DUMPLINGS

SERVES 6

IF YOU'VE NEVER COOKED RABBIT BEFORE, THIS RECIPE IS A GOOD STARTING point. First, there's the cooking method. Rabbit meat is lean, like all game, so cooking low and slow in liquid makes it tender. But the combination of flavors is what will put this dish into regular rotation on your Sunday dinner menu—dumplings sweetened with cornmeal and cream cheese join the meat in a hearty mustard-wine sauce. The amazing thing about a slowly simmered braise is how those flavors will evolve, fully coming together a day or two after the dish is made. You can prepare this recipe all at once or chip away at it in stages. Braise the rabbit and strain and skim the cooking liquid a few days before you plan to serve the dish. Then make the dumpling dough and wrap and chill it until you're ready to roll.

INGREDIENTS

FOR THE RABBIT

1   (3-pound) rabbit, cut into frontquarters, hindquarters, and saddle

    Kosher salt and freshly ground black pepper

2   tablespoons olive oil

1   thick-cut applewood-smoked bacon slice, halved

1   large Vidalia onion, chopped (about 1½ cups)

2   carrots, peeled and cut into chunks

2   celery stalks, cut into chunks

3   garlic cloves, minced

1   cup dry red wine

1   fresh rosemary sprig

1   (28-ounce) can whole peeled tomatoes, drained

½   teaspoon red pepper flakes

4   cups chicken stock

PREPARATION

FOR THE RABBIT Preheat the oven to 325°F. Season the rabbit pieces liberally with salt and pepper. Put the oil and 1 bacon slice half in a large Dutch oven over medium-high and cook until the bacon is crisp and the fat is rendered (about 3 minutes per side). Remove the bacon and set aside. Sear the rabbit pieces in the pot on all sides until golden brown, about 3 minutes per side. Remove the rabbit and set aside.

Add the remaining bacon slice half, the onion, carrots, and celery to the pot and sauté for 10 minutes, or until the vegetables have softened and begun to turn golden; add the garlic and cook for 1 minute more. Add the wine and deglaze the pot, scraping up any browned bits from the bottom. Add the rosemary sprig, tomatoes, red pepper flakes, and 2 cups of the stock. Nestle the rabbit pieces in the pot on top of the vegetables. Cover and transfer to the oven; bake for 2 hours.

Remove from the oven and transfer the rabbit pieces to a plate to cool. In a large bowl, strain the braising liquid through a fine-mesh sieve, pressing the solids with the back of a spoon to extract all their liquid. Discard the solids. (You should have 2 to 2½ cups of strained braising liquid.) Skim any fat from the surface, then return the liquid to the pot, along with the remaining 2 cups stock. Place over high heat and bring to a boil, then reduce the heat to low and simmer for 30 minutes, uncovered. Pick the rabbit meat from the bones (being careful to remove any small bones) and set the meat aside.

FOR THE DUMPLINGS

1 pound cream cheese, softened

1 large egg

1 large egg yolk

¼ cup all-purpose flour

2 teaspoons kosher salt

1 tablespoon freshly ground black pepper

2 teaspoon chopped fresh thyme

2 cups soft cornbread crumbs (see cornbread recipe, page 215)

TO FINISH

1½ teaspoons grainy mustard

½ cup heavy cream

Chopped fresh flat-leaf parsley

FOR THE DUMPLINGS Beat the cream cheese with an electric mixer until fluffy. Add the whole egg and egg yolk, beating until combined. Add the flour, salt, pepper, and thyme and beat until incorporated. Fold in the cornbread crumbs with a rubber spatula. Divide the dough in half. Tightly wrap one half and freeze it to make dumplings another day. Wrap and refrigerate the other half for at least 1 hour before proceeding.

Roll the chilled dumpling dough into a 1-inch-thick log on a generously floured surface. Cut the dough log into 1-inch pieces, like gnocchi. (You should have about 30 dumplings.)

Whisk the mustard and cream into the simmering liquid and slip the dumplings into the pot. Cook for 5 minutes. Add the rabbit meat and cook to warm through, about 1 minute. Serve the dumplings and rabbit in shallow bowls with a ladleful of braising liquid. Garnish each serving with parsley. Serve immediately.

APPLEWOOD BACON–WRAPPED VENISON LOIN

SERVES 4

THERE ARE CERTAINLY A FEW PURISTS WHO WILL ARGUE THAT WRAPPING venison in bacon is a culinary white lie because it masks the true flavor of the meat. Fair enough. But for the rest of us, there's no denying it sure is tasty. Not to mention a great way to introduce uninitiated game eaters to the pleasures of venison. This recipe, from chef Walter Bundy, of Lemaire in Richmond, Virginia, keeps things simple. A soak in milk made mildly aromatic with garlic, pepper, and woodsy rosemary helps tenderize the meat. A wrapper of bacon infuses it with smoke-kissed flavor. And a butter baste adds richness.

INGREDIENTS

- 1 venison loin, silverskin removed
- 1 cup whole milk
- 3 to 4 garlic cloves, crushed
- Small handful of whole black peppercorns
- 2 sprigs fresh rosemary, needles picked off the stem and chopped
- Kosher salt and freshly ground black pepper
- 1 pound sliced applewood-smoked bacon
- 1 tablespoon vegetable oil
- 2 tablespoons unsalted butter

PREPARATION

Cut the venison loin in half crosswise and put in a container with the milk, crushed garlic, peppercorns, and rosemary; refrigerate overnight.

Drain the venison, discarding the milk and other ingredients, and pat dry with paper towels. Season with salt and pepper.

Lay the bacon strips on a cutting board, with pieces overlapping slightly, forming two large bacon sheets. Place one loin half across one bacon sheet and gently roll to cover it with the bacon. Repeat with the other loin half.

Place a large cast-iron skillet over medium-high heat. Add the oil, swirling to coat the pan. Place the loins in the skillet, seam-side down. Sear for 4 to 5 minutes, until the bacon is crispy. Add the butter to the skillet, occasionally spooning it over the venison to baste it. Using tongs, turn the loins and sear for 4 to 5 minutes more, continuing to baste with butter, until the bacon is cooked through on all sides and the venison reaches an internal temperature of about 130°F. Remove the loins from the pan and let rest for 5 minutes. Slice into medallions and serve.

CHILI CON VENISON

SERVES 6 TO 8

WE SIDE WITH TEXAS WHEN IT COMES TO CHILI. NO BEANS, THANKS. JUST meat, and lots of it. And if it's venison, even better. Also nice? Plenty of kick, which, here, comes from smoked chipotle chiles in adobo sauce, an ingredient you can find in most grocery stores. Be sure to thoroughly pat the meat dry before browning to ensure good caramelization, which sears the essence of its flavor into the entire pot. That's especially important here to help the flavor of the venison stand up against the spices.

INGREDIENTS

- 2½ pounds venison loin, silverskin removed, cut into cubes
- Kosher salt and freshly ground black pepper
- ¼ cup all-purpose flour
- 3 tablespoons canola oil
- 3 tablespoons unsalted butter
- 1 large red onion, diced
- 4 garlic cloves, minced
- 1 tablespoon chili powder
- 1½ teaspoons ground cumin
- 1 teaspoon ground allspice
- 1 cinnamon stick
- 12 ounces dark beer, such as Lazy Magnolia Southern Pecan Nut Brown Ale
- 2 (12-ounce) cans Ro*Tel diced tomatoes with green chiles, drained
- 2 cups beef stock
- 3 tablespoons dark brown sugar
- 1 canned chipotle chile in adobo sauce, minced
- 2 teaspoons dried oregano
- ⅓ cup chopped fresh cilantro

GARNISHES

- Tortilla chips, sour cream, fresh cilantro leaves, grated sharp cheddar cheese, chopped scallions, jalapeños, lime wedges

PREPARATION

Toss the venison in a bowl with a generous sprinkling of salt and pepper. Put the flour in a wide shallow bowl and add half of the venison, tossing to coat. Place a Dutch oven over medium-high heat and add 1 tablespoon of the oil and 1 tablespoon of the butter. Put the floured venison in the pot and cook for 2 minutes per side to develop a rich brown crust. (Be careful not to overcrowd the pot or you will steam the meat; work in batches if necessary.) With a slotted spoon, remove the meat to a plate and set aside. Repeat with the remaining venison.

Reduce the heat to medium and add the remaining 2 tablespoons oil and 2 tablespoons butter. Add the onion and sauté for 5 minutes, or until softened, stirring occasionally. Add the garlic, chili powder, cumin, allspice, and cinnamon stick. Sauté for 1 minute. Add the beer and deglaze the pot, scraping up any browned bits from the bottom. Return the venison to the pot and add the tomatoes, stock, brown sugar, chipotle, and oregano. Cover and simmer over low heat for 1½ hours. Remove from the heat and stir in the cilantro.

To serve, arrange garnishes on the table. Ladle chili into serving bowls and let each person top the chili to their liking.

SOUTHERN SOUL BRUNSWICK STEW

SERVES 15 TO 18

ON A PEDESTAL IN BRUNSWICK, GEORGIA, SITS A TWENTY-FIVE-GALLON
cast-iron stew pot in which, according to local legend, the residents of nearby St. Simons Island made
the first-ever batch of Brunswick stew. Residents of Brunswick County, Virginia, which also lays claim
to the dish, might have a few words to say about that. But there's no argument that the folks at Southern
Soul Barbeque, on St. Simons Island, cook up an outstanding version of the stew, which began as a hot
pot of game meat—squirrel, traditionally—and vegetables. Co-owners Griffin Bufkin and Harrison
Sapp developed their recipe over years of local research. While they use a variety of their own smoked
meats (pork, chicken, turkey, and brisket) in the dish, feel free to substitute venison, wild hog, or, yes,
squirrel, if you're so inclined.

INGREDIENTS

- 1 cup (2 sticks) salted butter
- 3 cups sweet onions, finely diced (about 2 large onions)
- 2 tablespoons minced garlic
- 2 teaspoons cayenne pepper
- 1 tablespoon freshly ground black pepper
- 1 tablespoon sea salt
- ¼ cup Worcestershire sauce
- ½ cup North Carolina vinegar barbecue sauce
- 1 cup sweet mustard-based barbecue sauce
- 3 pounds meat of your choosing (preferably smoked)
- 2 quarts crushed fresh tomatoes or good-quality canned tomatoes
- 2 cups coarsely chopped tomatoes
- 1 quart fresh sweet yellow or white corn kernels (frozen in a pinch)
- 1 quart fresh baby butter beans (frozen in a pinch)
- 2 quarts chicken stock
  Hot sauce for serving

PREPARATION

In a large Dutch oven or stockpot, melt the butter over medium-high
heat. Add the diced onion, then the garlic, and sauté until the onions
are translucent, about 15 minutes. Stir in the cayenne, black pepper,
salt, and Worcestershire sauce. Simmer for 6 to 8 minutes, then add
the barbecue sauces and meat and cook for another 10 minutes. Add the
crushed and chopped tomatoes, the corn, beans, and stock. Reduce
the heat to low and simmer for 2 to 3 hours, adding more stock to thin
if needed. Serve with hot sauce.

6

VEGETABLES & SIDES

HEAD OF THE TABLE

The enduring appeal of Southern sides

ALLISON GLOCK

WHEN I WAS GROWING UP, IT WAS COMPULSORY for every plate my mother served to offer "something green." Not literally, of course. "Something green" meant something vegetable-based. Often, something from our yard, at least until we moved to Florida, where the bugs plagued the tomatoes and cukes so tenaciously that Mother would return from the garden, hands thrown up in despair, muttering in colorful language about grubs and DDT and how back in West Virginia she could drop a seed from her pocket and it would grow a Mortgage Lifter tomato as big as a house.

Nonetheless, something green remained a mandate, and on a good day, that something was creamed corn as sweet as pudding, or lima beans that dissolved in your mouth like cotton candy, or scalloped potatoes crisped in the oven by rafts of butter floating in a heavy shake of cream. It is and has always been a particularly Southern gift to make the vegetable as seductive as the meat. Say what you will about fried chicken, pulled pork, meat loaf, country ham, ribs, and the rest—when Southern folks come together around a table, it is the sides they covet most. Perhaps this is because we do such astonishing things with our vegetables.

What Yankee visitors have misguidedly described as "draining the life from," Southerners see as reducing to a profound essence. Take my mother's pole beans. My sisters and I would snap them at the table, their interior seeds popping out like lost teeth. The cleaned beans would join a boiling pot stuffed with ham hocks and white onion and bacon fat from our tin under the sink, and there they would simmer until their stringiness relented and they became as slick and soft as briny tapioca, tearing like tissue under the weight of your fork. I used to sink my beans into the mashed potatoes inevitably plunked by their side, the salt of the seductively limp bean a boon to the cream of the mash. I'm sure there was protein on my plate, too. I just don't remember it.

The Atlanta-based chef Steven Satterfield, known among his peers as the Vegetable Whisperer, recalls how during childhood visits to his grandmother Ducky's house in Asheville, North Carolina, meals were often served sans meat. "One of Ducky's talents was the ability to gently coax the flavors out of vegetables with very little manipulation," he says. "She was a produce queen." At Satterfield's farm-centric Miller Union restaurant, he serves Ducky's icebox pickles and chowchow, among other recipes. "I think of her when I cook and picture her guiding me. I hold the vegetables, think about how they were grown and cared for. I feel like if you pay attention, the produce will almost tell you what it wants to be and how it should be cooked."

It is of no small import that vegetables can be handled. They are not cheese or sauce or delicate berries in need of onerous, precious containers. Vegetables are hardy, stable, tactile wonders that you can gather in your arms or heap into your apron, food you can nibble plucked straight from the earth, or toss into brown paper sacks and lug home to spill atop your counter in a riot of possibilities. Vegetables define organic connection. When you watch your meal evolve from seed to sprout to plate, it transcends craving. It becomes a relationship. One that in the South we are fortunate to cultivate more months of the year than not.

At home, my daughters clamor as much for hoppin' John and butter beans as for dessert. When they think of home-cooked meals, they are not imagining the main course. Unless the main course is macaroni and cheese. Which, as any Southerner will tell you, counts as a vegetable too.

HOPPIN' JOHN

RESOLUTIONS TEND TO COME AND GO, BUT SOUTHERNERS HAVE A MORE enduring New Year's ritual—a bowl of hoppin' John. While folklore varies about the origins of this West African–influenced dish, a pork-flavored pot of rice and black-eyed peas, the symbolism stays the same: the beans represent coins, and the pork conveys optimism, because pigs forage forward and don't look back. "During the years my family moved around the South, I had many versions of hoppin' John," says Stephen Stryjewski, an Army brat and now co-owner and chef of Cochon in New Orleans. "But it was living in the Carolina lowlands, where black-eyed peas and rice were historically grown in abundance, that I learned to love the complexities of the dish." He sticks to a traditional recipe, but with two Louisiana twists—Cajun Grain rice, a brown jasmine variety flecked with bits of wild red rice, and the local pork specialty, tasso ham, letting its spicy, smoky flavor seep into the pot.

INGREDIENTS

FOR THE BLACK-EYED PEAS

- 1 pound dried black-eyed peas, rinsed and picked over
- 12 ounces tasso ham, diced
- 1 onion, halved
- 3 garlic cloves
- 3 bay leaves

FOR THE RICE

- 8 ounces bacon, diced
- 1 onion, diced
- 3 celery stalks, diced
- 1 bell pepper, diced
- 1 small jalapeño, seeded and minced
- ½ teaspoon fresh thyme
- 1 cup Cajun Grain rice (or a good-quality long grain rice)
- 6 scallions, sliced
- ½ bunch fresh parsley, chopped
- 1 teaspoon kosher salt
- ½ teaspoon freshly ground black pepper

PREPARATION

FOR THE BLACK-EYED PEAS In a large Dutch oven or kettle, combine the peas, ham, onion, garlic, and bay leaves with 2 quarts water. Bring to a boil, reduce the heat to medium-low, and simmer gently until the peas are tender but not mushy, about 45 minutes, adding up to ½ quart more water if needed. Drain the peas and ham, reserving the cooking liquid. Set aside. Remove and discard the onion, garlic, and bay leaves.

FOR THE RICE Wipe out the pot with paper towels and place over medium-high heat. Add the bacon and cook until golden, about 10 minutes, then add the onion, celery, bell pepper, and jalapeño. Using a wooden spoon, stir occasionally, cooking until the onions are soft and translucent, 8 to 12 minutes. Add the thyme and 2½ cups water, increase the heat to high, and bring to a boil. Reduce the heat, stir in the rice, cover, and simmer until the rice is tender, 17 to 22 minutes.

Stir in the scallions, parsley, and black-eyed peas and ham, season with salt and pepper, and adjust the consistency with the reserved cooking liquid. The dish should be moist but not soupy. Serve hot.

SMOTHERED COUNTRY-STYLE GREEN BEANS

SERVES 10

CHEF KEVIN CALLAGHAN, OF ACME FOOD & BEVERAGE CO. IN CARRBORO,
North Carolina, remembers always seeing a banged-up can of bacon fat in his grandmother's refrigerator. "Right by the opened jars of jams and pickles," he says. And her green beans, enriched with that fat, were always on his family's Thanksgiving table. "We had the beans, Senator Russell's Sweet Potato Casserole, turkey, stuffing, and sliced canned cranberry sauce." Today the chef serves these green beans in his restaurant during the holiday, often getting help snapping the beans from his daughters. Then, into the pot they go, where their crisp vegetal freshness will be transformed into something almost meaty. "Sometimes during other seasons," he says, "I forget how good fresh green beans cooked to hell and back can taste."

INGREDIENTS

½ cup bacon grease

2 cups thinly sliced shallots or sweet onions

Kosher salt and freshly ground black pepper

3 pounds green beans, strings removed, snapped into 1½-inch pieces and well rinsed

1 quart chicken stock

PREPARATION

Melt the bacon grease in a Dutch oven over medium heat. Add the shallots, stirring to coat. Sprinkle with salt. Cook until almost translucent, 8 to 10 minutes. Add the beans and stock, making sure that the stock covers the beans. Bring to a boil, then reduce the heat to a simmer. Cook until the stock is almost completely evaporated, about 2 hours. Add salt and lots of pepper to taste and serve hot.

NOT-QUITE-SO-COOKED-TO-DEATH GREEN BEANS

SERVES 4 TO 6

LIKE THE SLOW-SIMMERED KIND OF GREEN BEANS WE ALL GREW UP EATING, this recipe benefits from bacon. But it's sautéed to lend a little crunch, just like the beans themselves, for a more modern—though still delicious—version. Instead of taking on a briny, meaty quality, quickly cooked green beans have a fresh, grassy flavor. They're tender, but still slightly crisp, and, yes, they'll squeak between your teeth when you take a bite. If you have ½ cup Cheerwine Onion Marmalade (page 242) on hand, you can warm it and use that instead of caramelizing the onion.

INGREDIENTS

Kosher salt

1½ pounds green beans, trimmed

2 tablespoons unsalted butter

3 thick-cut hickory-smoked bacon slices, cooked and crumbled (1 tablespoon rendered fat reserved)

1 medium white onion, thinly sliced

Freshly ground black pepper

Chopped toasted salt-roasted peanuts

PREPARATION

Bring a large stockpot of salted water to a boil over high heat. In a separate bowl, prepare an ice bath. Blanch the beans in the boiling water for 5 minutes, or until just tender. Drain and shock the beans in the ice bath. Drain again and blot the excess moisture with a clean kitchen towel; transfer to a large bowl. Set aside.

In a large cast-iron skillet, melt 1 tablespoon of the butter with the reserved bacon fat over medium heat. When it becomes foamy, in 2 to 3 minutes, reduce the heat to medium-low and stir in the onion. Cook for 10 to 15 minutes without browning the onion, stirring occasionally, until tender, then increase the heat to medium and cook, stirring often, until the onions are soft and brown, 10 to 15 minutes more.

Add the remaining 1 tablespoon butter to the pan and, when foamy, toss in the green beans and salt and pepper to taste. Serve garnished with the bacon and peanuts.

BUTTER BEAN SUCCOTASH

SERVES 8 TO 10

ELSEWHERE IN THE WORLD, *PHASEOLUS LUNATUS* **ARE KNOWN AS LIMA BEANS—** white, pale green, or multicolored. But in the South, petite varieties of limas are known as butter beans. Like any good nickname, it hits on a truth—butter beans are smoother, creamier, and more tender than ordinary limas. They're so good, you barely need to cook them at all. Pair them with fresh sweet corn and bell pepper in this simple fifteen-minute sauté, and it's easy to see why "butter bean" is a Southern term of endearment.

INGREDIENTS

- 1 tablespoon peanut oil or bacon grease
- 1 tablespoon unsalted butter
- 1 large red onion, chopped
- 3 garlic cloves, minced
- 1 large green bell pepper, diced
- 3 cups fresh corn kernels
- 1½ pounds (5 cups) fresh butter beans
- 1 teaspoon kosher salt
- ½ teaspoon freshly ground black pepper
- 1 tablespoon chopped fresh marjoram leaves
- 2 tablespoons snipped fresh chives
- ½ cup vegetable stock

PREPARATION

Warm the oil and butter in a large sauté pan or Dutch oven over medium heat. Add the onion and sauté for 5 minutes, until softened, then add the garlic and sauté for 1 minute more. Add the bell pepper, corn, butter beans, salt, black pepper, marjoram, chives, and stock. Simmer for 8 to 10 minutes, until the stock is evaporated and the beans are just tender. Serve hot.

HEIRLOOM TOMATO SALAD WITH GREEN GODDESS BUTTERMILK DRESSING

SERVES 6

THE SOUTH'S HEIRLOOM TOMATOES DON'T JUST HAVE GREAT NAMES—ARKANSAS Travelers, Spear's Tennessee Greens, Mortgage Lifters, Cherokee Purples—they also have amazing flavors, putting any standard supermarket hybrid to shame. This stunning salad lets the tomatoes shine, paired with corn and cucumber for refreshing crispness, and all enveloped in a tangy, herb-infused buttermilk dressing.

INGREDIENTS

- 6 ripe garden tomatoes, sliced ⅓ inch thick
- ½ cucumber, thinly sliced
  Kernels from 1 cooked ear Silver Queen corn
- 2 thick bacon slices, cooked and crumbled
- 1 tablespoon sliced fresh chives

PREPARATION

Arrange the tomato and cucumber slices artfully on a platter. Drizzle with half of the dressing. Sprinkle with the corn kernels and bacon. Garnish with the chives. Serve with extra dressing on the side. (Any remaining dressing will keep, refrigerated, for up to 1 week.)

GREEN GODDESS BUTTERMILK DRESSING

Makes about ¾ cup

INGREDIENTS

- ⅓ cup whole buttermilk
- ⅓ cup mayonnaise
- 2 tablespoons freshly squeezed lemon juice
- 1 teaspoon Worcestershire sauce
- ½ teaspoon kosher salt
- ¼ teaspoon freshly ground black pepper
- 1 tablespoon sliced fresh chives
- 1 tablespoon chopped fresh dill
- 2 teaspoons chopped fresh tarragon

PREPARATION

Combine the buttermilk, mayonnaise, lemon juice, Worcestershire sauce, salt, pepper, chives, dill, and tarragon in a blender. Blend until smooth.

SUMMER SQUASH CASSEROLE

SERVES 8 TO 10

IF SOMEONE ON YOUR BLOCK HAS A BACKYARD GARDEN, CHANCES ARE YOU'VE come home to find a bag of zucchini and summer squash with a friendly note on your porch. These prolific summer produce staples combine with another fundamental element of good neighbordom—the make-and-take casserole—in this classic recipe. Slicing the squash into half-inch-thick rounds, then parboiling, draining, and lightly pressing with paper towels helps absorb excess moisture, so the pieces hold their shape and texture while baking. It's a little extra effort that pays off—no slippery, slimy squash here. The slices are suspended in a custardy, eggy mixture that rises as it bakes, almost crossing into soufflé territory. Bake two, eat one with dinner, and deliver the other to that nice couple who just moved in down the street.

INGREDIENTS

- 3 zucchini
- 2 yellow summer squash
- 5 large eggs, beaten
- 1 cup half-and-half
- 3 tablespoons all-purpose flour
- ⅓ cup chopped scallions
- ½ cup shredded Italian-blend cheese
- ½ cup freshly grated Parmesan cheese
- 2 teaspoons Greek seasoning, such as Cavender's
- 2 tablespoons unsalted butter, melted, plus 1 tablespoon for buttering the baking dish
- 24 buttery crackers, such as Ritz, crushed

PREPARATION

Preheat the oven to 350°F. Butter a 2-quart (8-by-11½-inch) baking dish.

Slice the zucchini and squash into ½-inch-thick slices and place in a large sauté pan or Dutch oven with water to cover; bring to a simmer over medium heat and cook for 10 minutes. Drain in a colander. Arrange the slices in a single layer on a clean towel and top with another clean towel, pressing lightly to absorb excess moisture.

In a large bowl, whisk together the eggs, half-and-half, and flour. Stir in the scallions, ¼ cup of the Italian-blend cheese, ¼ cup of the Parmesan cheese, and the Greek seasoning. Add the squash slices and gently fold them into the wet ingredients. Spread the mixture in the prepared baking dish. Top with the remaining cheeses.

Stir the melted butter into the crushed crackers and sprinkle the crumbs evenly over the surface of the casserole. Bake for 25 to 30 minutes, until set. Serve hot.

SLOWLY SIMMERED FIELD PEAS

SERVES 6 TO 8

SILVER QUEEN FROM MARYLAND'S EASTERN SHORE IS NOW THE GOLD standard for sweet corn everywhere. Californians grow heirloom Cherokee Purple tomatoes sourced from Tennessee seed. Georgia's famed Vidalia onion is even on the menu at Applebee's. But field peas—crowders; black-, pink-, or yellow-eyed; purple-hulled; pale-green lady peas—are still something of a Southern secret. Each one has a slightly different flavor. Crowders and black-eyed peas are on the earthier end of the spectrum, ladies more delicate and creamy. Here, a constellation of other summer-garden stars complement the peas: tomato, jalapeño, and a medley of herbs. And whether you cook with fresh summer shellings or rehydrate from dry, field peas give off liquid as they simmer and soften, beanlikker that's every bit as tasty as the potlikker from a mess of greens.

INGREDIENTS

- 1 pound fresh shelled field peas
- 1 large carrot, peeled and diced
- 1 celery stalk, diced
- ¼ white onion, chopped
- ½ bacon slice, cut into 4 pieces
- 1 jalapeño, halved lengthwise and seeded
- 2 garlic cloves, smashed and peeled
- 1 fresh thyme sprig
- 1 bay leaf
  1-inch piece lemon zest
- 1 teaspoon kosher salt, plus more to taste
- ½ teaspoon freshly ground black pepper, plus more to taste
- 4 Roma tomatoes, seeded and diced
- 2 tablespoons olive oil
- 3 tablespoons chopped fresh flat-leaf parsley

PREPARATION

Rinse the peas under running water in a colander and pick out any bad ones. Drain the peas and put them in a large sauté pan or Dutch oven. Add the carrot, celery, and onion. Stir in the bacon, jalapeño, garlic, thyme sprig, bay leaf, lemon zest, salt, and black pepper. Add water to just cover the peas. Bring to a simmer over medium heat and cook for 15 minutes, stirring occasionally.

Add the tomatoes and cook for 10 minutes more. Remove and discard the jalapeño, garlic, thyme sprig, bay leaf, and zest. Stir in the oil and parsley. Season with salt and black pepper to taste. Serve warm.

TIP: **If you're using smaller, more delicate lady peas, they'll cook quicker than their stouter sisters, like crowders, which may need a little more time. Sample one or two peas 10 minutes into cooking, and go from there until you reach the desired texture.**

CUCUMBER PICKLES & PICKLED RADISHES

"It's a real treat if you make pickles for someone," says Andrea Reusing, the chef and owner of Lantern restaurant in Chapel Hill, North Carolina. Reusing's love affair with pickling and fermenting started with her grandmother, who had a basement operation from which poured all manner of sauerkraut, pickles, and brandied peaches. It clearly made an impression; the pickle plate, with five or more briny combinations, is a centerpiece of Reusing's menu today. Reusing keeps the process—and the flavors—interesting by layering surprising ingredients into the basic brine formula: adding shiso leaves to cucumber pickles and dropping all manner of vegetables into a bath of vinegar, Thai red chiles, and ginger. Beyond pickling's utility, it's also a great way to add some unexpected punch to the plate—perfect, as Reusing notes, for late summer, "when your family is sick of you and your CSA."

PICKLED CUCUMBERS WITH SHISO

MAKES ABOUT 5 QUARTS

INGREDIENTS

- ¼ cup plus 2 tablespoons kosher salt
- 10 whole black peppercorns
- 1 head of garlic, unpeeled and cut in half crosswise
- 3 quarts (about 2 pounds) small pickling cucumbers, any stems trimmed to ½ inch
- 5 purple shiso leaves

PREPARATION

Bring 2 cups of water to a boil in a small saucepan over high heat. Remove from the heat and add the salt, peppercorns, and garlic. Let cool, and then add the mixture to 2 quarts of cold water. Put the cucumbers and shiso leaves in a large sterilized jar, crock, or food-safe plastic container. Pour the brine mixture over the cucumbers, covering them completely. Place one or more small plates on top of the cucumbers to keep them completely submerged. Store in a cool (68 to 70°F is ideal), dark room for 3 to 7 days, checking every day or so and removing any mold or foam that rises to the top. The pickles are done when they are pleasantly sour and tangy but still firm. Store refrigerated for several weeks.

VARIATIONS Use the same salt-to-water ratio with the following pairings: sliced red cabbage and caraway seeds; whole baby carrots and sliced fresh fennel bulb; halved baby beets and fresh dill sprigs; sliced Japanese turnips and scallions.

PICKLED RADISHES WITH CHILES & GINGER

MAKES ABOUT 1½ QUARTS

INGREDIENTS

- 2 bunches of radishes
- 1 cup distilled white vinegar
- ½ cup sugar
- 2 tablespoons kosher salt
- 2 fresh Thai chiles, split lengthwise
- 4 garlic cloves
- 1 small piece of ginger, peeled and cut into thin rounds

PREPARATION

Wash and trim the radishes, leaving about ½ inch of stem. Cut the radishes in half lengthwise and put them in a heatproof 2-quart jar with a lid.

In a small nonreactive saucepan, combine the vinegar, sugar, and salt with 3 cups water and bring to a boil. Cook for 1 minute to dissolve the sugar and salt completely. Remove from the heat and let cool until warm. Add the chiles, garlic, and ginger to the jar and pour enough of the warm liquid over the radishes to completely cover them. Let cool, then cover and refrigerate for at least 24 hours and up to several weeks.

VARIATIONS Green tomato wedges (add whole coriander seed; omit the ginger); cauliflower florets (add ground turmeric; omit the ginger); halved ripe semi-hot red chiles, such as Fresno.

FRESH-CORN SPOONBREAD

SERVES 4

THE SAME HUMBLE INGREDIENTS—CORNMEAL, MILK, BUTTER, AND EGGS— that make a classic skillet of cornbread (see page 215) can also combine to create a timeless soufflé. Prepare it plain, and spoonbread serves as a supporting player for the meal—like rice or mashed potatoes. Gild it with fresh whole corn kernels or sliced scallions, and the spoonbread just might steal a little shine from other items on the plate.

INGREDIENTS

- 4   cups milk
- 1   cup fine yellow cornmeal
- 2   teaspoons sugar
- 1½ teaspoons kosher salt
- 1   tablespoon unsalted butter, plus 1 tablespoon for buttering the baking dish
- 2   large eggs
- 1   cup fresh corn kernels or ½ cup sliced scallions (optional)

PREPARATION

Put 3 cups of the milk in a saucepan over medium-high heat and cook, stirring constantly, until scalded—just below boiling. In a medium bowl, make a slurry by whisking the cornmeal, sugar, and salt with the remaining 1 cup milk. Whisk the slurry into the hot milk. Cook for 5 minutes, whisking frequently. Remove from the heat and pour the mixture back into the bowl. Whisk in the butter and let cool for 30 minutes, whisking from time to time to allow heat to dissipate and to keep a skin from forming on the surface.

Meanwhile, preheat the oven to 375°F. Butter a 1-quart baking dish.

Whisk the eggs into the cornmeal mixture, gently fold in the corn kernels or scallions, if using, and transfer the mixture to the prepared baking dish. Bake for 1 hour, or until cooked through and lightly browned on top. Serve warm.

TIP: **For even fluffier and more soufflé-like spoonbread, separate the eggs, then whisk the yolks into the cornmeal mixture. Beat the egg whites separately until stiff peaks form and gently fold them into the cornmeal mixture.**

CAST-IRON CHARRED CORN

SERVES 6

BUILDING LAYERS OF FLAVOR—COMPLEMENTARY AND CONTRASTING—IS A fundamental of good cooking, be it classic French or down-home Southern. From her first restaurant job at a little crêperie to stints in such leading Georgia kitchens as the Five & Ten, in Athens, chef Whitney Otawka has always specialized in bringing a touch of continental refinement to her cooking. Otawka's take on classic Southern creamed corn is a great example. She heightens corn's fresh flavor two ways—first, charring the kernels to add a layer of caramelized complexity, then extracting their milky remnants from the cob (the liquid corn "milk") to lend more sweetness to the heavy-cream base. Then comes the contrast—the mild bite of sautéed onion and crisp, smoky bacon.

INGREDIENTS

- 8 ears of corn, husks and silk removed
- ¼ cup finely diced bacon
- ½ tablespoon unsalted butter
- ½ cup minced Vidalia onion
- ½ cup heavy cream
- ½ teaspoon kosher salt
   Freshly ground black pepper
- 1 teaspoon minced fresh chives

PREPARATION

To remove the corn kernels, cut off the ends of each ear to make flat surfaces. One at a time, stand the ears in a wide casserole dish and carefully cut down the sides with a sharp knife. Next, hold each cob over a bowl and scrape with the back edge of the knife to remove the "milk." Discard the milked ears and set the liquid aside.

Place a cast-iron skillet over medium-high heat. Add the cut corn kernels to the pan and cook for 2 to 3 minutes, tossing occasionally. Add the bacon and continue to cook until the kernels are slightly charred and the bacon begins to crisp, about 5 minutes, stirring occasionally. Remove from the heat and set aside.

In a medium saucepan, melt the butter over medium-low heat. Add the onion and cook until softened, 3 to 5 minutes. Add the corn "milk," the charred corn and bacon mixture, and the cream. Reduce the heat to low and cook, stirring often, for 4 to 5 minutes. Season with salt and pepper. Sprinkle with the chives and serve hot.

KIL'T GREENS WITH BACON JAM

SERVES 6 TO 8

TRADITIONALLY, APPALACHIAN COOKS PREPARE KIL'T GREENS IN THE springtime, from tender garden lettuces and the nascent leaves of wild plants. When those delicate greens meet a hot dressing, they wilt and soften immediately. In other words, they're kil't. At Holly Hill Inn and her five other restaurants in and around Lexington, Kentucky, Ouita Michel gives her greens a sweet death, dousing them in a sumptuous bourbon-bacon jam. For maximum flavor, she says, use a variety of fresh greens. "If you do, say, young kale and mustard greens together, you get a blend of sweet and spicy," Michel says. "Then you get the skillet hot, add the bacon jam, add the greens, and toss, toss, toss until they *just* start to break down."

INGREDIENTS

- 2 pounds mixed young greens, such as mustard, chard, kale, and spinach
- ¼ cup Bacon Jam (recipe follows)

  Kosher salt and freshly ground black pepper

  Garnishes (optional): hot pepper vinegar, red onion, sliced hard-boiled egg

PREPARATION

Submerge the greens in a large container of water to rinse, remove any large stems, and rip leaves into bite-size pieces if necessary. Drain the greens and blot excess moisture with a clean kitchen towel. Place a large cast-iron skillet over medium-high heat, add the Bacon Jam, and cook until melted, 2 to 3 minutes. Add the greens, increase the heat to high, and toss frequently with tongs until the greens just start to wilt and before they release too much liquid. Season with salt and pepper to taste. Garnish as desired and serve immediately.

BACON JAM

Makes about 2 cups

Bacon. Bourbon. Need we say more?

INGREDIENTS

- 1 pound applewood-smoked bacon, diced
- 1½ cups diced onion
- ⅓ cup bourbon
- 1 cup apple cider vinegar
- 1 cup brown sugar
- ¼ cup grainy mustard

PREPARATION

Cook the bacon in a cast-iron skillet over medium-high heat, turning occasionally, until the fat has rendered and the bacon just starts to turn golden, 4 to 5 minutes. Add the onion, reduce the heat to low, and cook until the onion is tender, 8 to 10 minutes. Add the bourbon, vinegar, brown sugar, and mustard and simmer until thickened, about 20 minutes. Refrigerate until ready to use.

SWEET POTATO CASSEROLE WITH SORGHUM

SERVES 10 TO 12

"IN A SOUTHERN FAMILY, THERE'S ALWAYS SOMEONE WHO MAKES ONE DISH, one thing they're truly great at," says Tandy Wilson of City House, in Nashville, Tennessee. "These recipes tend to be 'talked,' passed down from cook to cook." That's the case with the chef's favorite sweet potato casserole, a dish inherited from his grandmother. Instead of the standard marshmallow topping, the recipe uses sorghum syrup for a rich, deep sweetness, and chopped roasted peanuts for a pleasing crunchy contrast. "Now every Thanksgiving," Wilson says, "it's my job to make Nana's sweet potato casserole."

INGREDIENTS

FOR THE SWEET POTATOES

- 7 pounds sweet potatoes (about 12 sweet potatoes)
- ¼ cup sorghum syrup
- 1 cup (2 sticks) unsalted butter, cut into small pieces while cold, then slightly softened at room temperature, plus 1 tablespoon for buttering the baking dish
- 1½ tablespoons kosher salt

FOR THE TOPPING

- ½ cup sugar
- ¾ cup all-purpose flour
- ½ cup (1 stick) cold unsalted butter, diced
- 2 cups peanuts, coarsely chopped
- 1 tablespoon kosher salt
- ⅔ cup sorghum syrup

PREPARATION

FOR THE SWEET POTATOES Preheat the oven to 350°F. Put the potatoes on a foil-lined baking sheet and roast until tender throughout, 1½ to 2 hours. When cool enough to handle, peel away the skin and put the pulp in a large mixing bowl. Using a potato masher, blend the sweet potato pulp together with the syrup, butter, and salt until smooth. Lightly butter a large (9-by-12-by-2½-inch) 3-quart baking dish and transfer the sweet potato mixture to the dish.

FOR THE TOPPING Preheat the oven to 350°F. In a medium bowl, using your hands, mix together the sugar, flour, butter, peanuts, and salt until the butter chunks are pea size. (You are looking for a streusel-like topping here.) Evenly distribute over the top of the sweet potato mixture. Bake until the topping is crisp and golden brown, about 30 minutes.

Transfer the baking dish to a cooling rack, and drizzle the casserole with the syrup, using a crosshatch pattern. Let the syrup sink into the topping for a few minutes before serving.

JEFFERSONIAN SPRING SALAD

SERVES 4

AT MONTICELLO, THOMAS JEFFERSON'S CHARLOTTESVILLE, VIRGINIA, ESTATE, the founding father kept fifty-eight years' worth of copious garden records, noting the plantings that flourished and those that floundered, along with the annual harvest dates of his favorite vegetables. Top among them: English peas and tender lettuces, such as reddish brown–tinged Brown Dutch, ruffled spinach, mâche, and cress. Dressings for Jefferson's salads were most often mustardy, egg-based vinaigrettes that used benne seed (a close relative of sesame) oil made from pressing seeds grown on-site. Use whatever combination of tender spring lettuces you enjoy—a few fresh pea tendrils would make a nice addition too—and raise a salad fork to the forebear of the farm-to-plate movement.

INGREDIENTS

- 1 head red Bibb lettuce, torn into bite-size pieces
- 2 cups baby spinach leaves
- 2 cups mâche (Lamb's Lettuce)
- ½ cup cooked fresh English peas or thawed frozen peas
- 1 cup sugar snap peas, halved diagonally
- 3 hard-boiled eggs, cooked yolks separated from whites
- 2 teaspoons Dijon mustard
- 3 tablespoons tarragon vinegar
- Pinch of kosher salt
- Freshly ground black pepper
- ⅓ cup light sesame oil

PREPARATION

Combine the lettuces, English peas, and sugar snap peas in a salad bowl. Chop the egg whites and sprinkle on top of the lettuces.

Put the hard-boiled egg yolks in a blender with the mustard, vinegar, salt, and pepper to taste and whirl it on low speed. Slowly pour in the oil with the blender on low until emulsified. Taste and adjust the seasoning. Thin with a bit more vinegar or water if needed. Toss the salad with the vinaigrette to moisten but not drench. Store any remaining dressing in an airtight container, refrigerated, for 1 to 2 days.

CREAMY CUCUMBER-DILL SALAD

SERVES 4 TO 6

INSPIRATION CAN COME FROM THE MOST UNLIKELY PLACES. LIKE THE PANCAKE Pantry in Gatlinburg, Tennessee, a tiny town on the edge of the Great Smoky Mountains National Park. When the restaurant switches over from breakfast to lunch service (don't worry, you can order a stack of flapjacks at either meal), servers set tiny crocks of quick-pickled creamy cucumbers on every table as a complimentary snack or side to accompany burgers and patty melts. While this isn't the Pancake Pantry's exact recipe, it's close. Similarly sweet, slightly creamier, and with an extra herbal punch from fresh dill, it makes for a fine, refreshing accompaniment to any summer meal.

INGREDIENTS

- 2 English cucumbers, thinly sliced
- ¼ red onion, thinly sliced into quarter moons
- 1 tablespoon kosher salt
- 2 tablespoons sugar
- 2 tablespoons distilled white vinegar
- ¾ cup sour cream or whole-milk plain Greek yogurt
- ¼ cup loosely packed snipped fresh dill

    Kosher salt and freshly ground black pepper

PREPARATION

Combine the cucumber, onion, salt, and 1 tablespoon of sugar in a medium bowl and toss well. Refrigerate for 1 hour or up to 3 hours. Rinse well in a colander, then drain well. Line the bowl with a clean kitchen towel and return the cucumbers and onion to it. Fold the towel over and lightly press excess moisture from the cucumbers and onion. Remove the towel, leaving the vegetables in the bowl.

In a small bowl, combine remaining 1 tablespoon sugar and the vinegar; whisk until the sugar is dissolved. Whisk in the sour cream and dill. Pour over the cucumbers and onion and toss well to combine. Chill for at least 1 hour or until ready to serve; drain off any liquid in the bottom of the bowl before serving cold.

FRIED OKRA, FRIED GREEN TOMATOES, & FRIED PICKLE CHIPS

Walk around any state fair and it becomes pretty clear folks will figure out how to fry just about anything. Snickers bars? Coke? Why not? But frying vegetables is more than just a stunt. It's an act of culinary genius. (Exhibit A: the French fry.) Take something like a crisp, briny pickle or lemony green tomato, encase it in seasoned batter, then bathe it in oil until golden brown, and an already-fine food becomes even better. The trick works for less universally beloved veggies too—like okra.

MASTER FRY BATTER MIX

MAKES 2 CUPS

BEFORE THE FRYING COMES THE COATING. MAKE A BATCH OF THIS DRY MIX and all you'll need is fresh buttermilk for an anytime batter. Think of it as a canvas that you can customize to your liking. For more rustic crunch, up the ratio of cornmeal. For more kick, use a heavy hand with the cayenne or whisk a few dashes of hot sauce into the buttermilk dip when you're ready to fry.

INGREDIENTS

- 1 cup all-purpose flour
- 1 cup cornmeal
- ⅓ cup cornstarch
- 2 teaspoons kosher salt
- 1 teaspoon freshly ground black pepper
- ¼ to ½ teaspoon cayenne pepper
- ¼ teaspoon granulated garlic

PREPARATION

Combine all the ingredients in a lidded container and keep in a cool dark place for up to 1 month.

FRIED OKRA

THE UNIVERSAL LAMENT ABOUT OKRA IS THAT IT'S SLIMY. THE MOMENT YOU slice the pods, they start to ooze a substance that's called mucilage. As soon as the stuff is heated, it begins to thicken, and you can wind up with clumps of okra instead of individual pieces. The easiest way to avoid both the slime and the clumps is to not slice the okra at all. Fry younger, tender pods of okra whole; set any that measure more than 3 inches aside and keep them in the freezer for gumbo, where their thickening powers will play a more purposeful role. Treat the pods like chips or fries and dip them into a side of Comeback Sauce (page 237).

INGREDIENTS

Peanut oil for deep-frying
½ cup cornstarch
1 cup buttermilk
2 cups Master Fry Batter Mix (page 175)
1 pound small fresh whole okra pods
Kosher salt

PREPARATION

In a large, deep-sided cast-iron skillet fitted with a deep-frying thermometer, heat 2 inches of oil to 350°F over medium heat.

Set up a dredging station with a plate containing the cornstarch, a shallow bowl containing the buttermilk, and a shallow bowl containing the batter mix.

Toss the okra in the bowl with the cornstarch and transfer to a fine-mesh sieve. Tap the sieve several times to shake off excess cornstarch.

Working in batches, dip the okra in the buttermilk, shake to remove excess, then place in the batter mix, tossing to coat. Shake off the excess batter mix and carefully slip the okra into the hot oil. Be careful not to overcrowd the pan. Fry for 5 to 7 minutes, turning occasionally, until golden brown. Remove from the oil with a spider or slotted spoon and drain on paper towels or a rack set over a paper towel–lined baking sheet. Sprinkle with salt to taste. Let cool for 2 to 3 minutes before serving.

FRIED GREEN TOMATOES

SERVES 4 TO 6

FANNIE FLAGG'S 1987 NOVEL *FRIED GREEN TOMATOES AT THE WHISTLESTOP CAFE*, loosely based on her aunt's Irondale Cafe in Alabama, put fried unripe tomatoes in the collective consciousness of food lovers coast to coast. Truth is, fried green tomatoes aren't uniquely Southern, having appeared in kitchens in the Midwest and Northeast before Flagg cemented their Southern pedigree. But no matter your locale, this is a dish that's hard not to love.

INGREDIENTS

Peanut oil for frying

3 large green tomatoes, cleaned and thickly sliced (about ½ inch)

½ cup cornstarch

1 cup buttermilk

1 cup Master Fry Batter Mix (page 175)

Kosher salt

White Creole Rémoulade (page 238)

PREPARATION

In a large, deep-sided cast-iron skillet fitted with a deep-frying thermometer, heat 1 inch of oil to 350°F over medium heat.

Set up a dredging station with a plate containing the cornstarch, a shallow bowl containing the buttermilk, and a shallow bowl containing the batter mix.

Working in batches, lightly press the tomato slices, one at a time, in the cornstarch, then dip them in the buttermilk, then lightly press them into the batter mix. Carefully slip the slices into the hot oil, three at a time, and cook for 1 to 2 minutes per side, until golden brown. Remove from the oil with a spatula and drain on paper towels or a rack set over a paper towel–lined baking sheet. Sprinkle with salt to taste. Let cool for 2 to 3 minutes before serving.

Stack two or three to a plate and serve with White Creole Rémoulade.

FRIED PICKLE CHIPS

SERVES 4

FRY SKINNY LITTLE HAMBURGER PICKLE CHIPS, AND YOU'LL WIND UP WITH more breading than pickle. Take a cue instead from Bernell "Fatman" Austin, of Atkins, Arkansas, who claims to have introduced fried dill pickles to the South. He sliced whole dills into thick rounds to get the ratio of crunchy breading to crisp pickle just right. A simpler option: start with a jar of your favorite dill chips, which are usually about a half inch thick.

INGREDIENTS

Peanut oil for frying
1 (16-ounce) jar thick-cut spicy dill pickle chips, drained
½ cup cornstarch
1 cup buttermilk
1 cup Master Fry Batter Mix (page 175)
Kosher salt

PREPARATION

In a large, deep-sided cast-iron skillet fitted with a deep-frying thermometer, heat 2 inches of oil to 350°F over medium heat.

Set up a dredging station with a plate containing the cornstarch, a shallow bowl containing the buttermilk, and a shallow bowl containing the batter mix.

Working in batches, toss the pickles in the cornstarch and transfer to a fine-mesh sieve. Tap the sieve several times to shake off excess cornstarch.

Dip the pickles in the buttermilk, shake to remove excess, then place in the batter mix, tossing to coat. Shake off the excess batter mix and carefully slip the pickles into the hot oil. Be careful not to overcrowd the pan. Fry for 4 to 6 minutes, turning occasionally, until golden brown. Remove from the oil with a spider or slotted spoon and drain on paper towels or a rack set over a paper towel–lined baking sheet. Sprinkle with salt to taste. Let cool for 2 to 3 minutes before serving.

POOL ROOM SLAW

MAKES 3 QUARTS;

serves 24

POOL ROOM SLAW STRADDLES A LOT OF LINES: IT'S A BIT FRESH COLESLAW,
a bit pickled chowchow, a bit north Alabama, a bit middle Tennessee. One line pool room slaw *doesn't*
cross: it's not a cool, creamy, mayo-swaddled salad designed to cut the spice from other foods. Though
it's served cold, this slaw gets heat—and plenty of it—from two sources: yellow mustard's sharpness
and as much red pepper as you dare. The slaw's ambiguity plays out well in the kitchen too. Finely grate
the vegetables, and you have an almost relishlike dish that can do double duty as a side or a topper for
burgers, barbecue, or hot dogs, the traditional accompaniment in pool halls across the rural central
South. Shred instead, and you're in more traditional and familiar coleslaw-as-salad territory.

INGREDIENTS

- 1 head green cabbage
- 1 red bell pepper, stemmed and seeded
- 1 yellow bell pepper, stemmed and seeded
- 4 carrots, peeled
- 1 Vidalia onion, quartered
- 2 cups distilled white vinegar
- ½ cup granulated sugar
- 1 cup yellow mustard
- 1 tablespoon kosher salt
- 1 tablespoon yellow mustard seeds
- 2 teaspoons celery seeds
- 1 to 2 tablespoons red pepper flakes

PREPARATION

Fit a food processor with the shredding (or grating) blade. Cut the
cabbage into wedges that will fit through the feed tube of the processor
and shred or grate. Transfer to a large bowl. Repeat with the bell
peppers, carrots, and onion. Transfer each batch to the bowl with the
cabbage; set aside.

In a 4-quart saucepan, combine the vinegar, sugar, yellow mustard,
salt, mustard seeds, celery seeds, and red pepper flakes over high heat
and bring to a boil, stirring to dissolve the sugar. Reduce the heat to
medium. Add the shredded vegetables to the hot liquid, stirring gently
to combine. Cook for 5 minutes, stirring occasionally. Transfer the slaw
and liquid to a large crock or container, let cool to room temperature,
then refrigerate for at least 4 hours or up to 2 days before serving to
allow the flavors to meld.

MACARONI & CHEESE
WITH VIRGINIA COUNTRY HAM

SERVES 6

IN 1789, THOMAS JEFFERSON RETURNED FROM FRANCE WITH A HANDWRITTEN recipe for *Nouilly a maccaroni* (macaroni noodles). Later, as president, Jefferson would serve White House diners a butter-laden macaroni casserole. *The Virginia Housewife*, published in 1824, included the first recipe for macaroni and cheese to appear in print in the United States. The book's author was Mary Randolph, a relative of Jefferson's. Her sentence-long recipe called only for noodles, cheese, butter, and a sprinkling of salt. While those are still the basic ingredients, Southern chefs have had plenty of time to refine the formula. One of our favorites is the gussied-up version on the menu at the Inn at Little Washington, a resort neatly situated between Washington, D.C., and Jefferson's home in Charlottesville, Virginia. Aged Gouda cheese, which has the consistency of Parmesan, and savory Virginia country ham give this variation a luxurious depth of flavor. It might not be what Jefferson or Randolph would recognize, but don't be surprised if it becomes your new favorite.

INGREDIENTS

Kosher salt

¾ pound dried elbow macaroni or your favorite tubular pasta

1 tablespoon olive oil

2 tablespoons unsalted butter

1 teaspoon minced garlic

1 tablespoon minced shallot

2 cups heavy cream

½ cup freshly grated aged Gouda cheese

¼ cup freshly grated Parmesan cheese

Pinch of freshly grated nutmeg

Freshly ground black pepper

2 slices Virginia country ham, finely julienned

2 teaspoons snipped fresh chives

PREPARATION

In a large pot, bring 4 quarts salted water to a boil over high heat. Add the macaroni and cook for about 6 minutes, until half-done (the interior will be slightly raw). Drain, put the pasta in a bowl, and toss with the oil to keep the macaroni from sticking together. Allow the pasta to cool.

In a 4-quart saucepan over medium-low heat, melt the butter. Add the garlic and shallot and cook for 5 minutes, stirring occasionally, being careful not to let them brown. Add the cream, bring to a rapid boil, then reduce the heat to low and simmer, stirring occasionally, until the cream has reduced by one quarter and coats the back of a spoon.

Whisk in the cheeses and cook for 1 to 2 minutes, until cheese is melted and the mixture is smooth. Season with nutmeg, salt, and pepper. Stir in the cooked macaroni and simmer for 2 to 3 minutes to warm through.

When ready to serve, garnish each portion with ham and chives.

CREAMED COLLARDS

SERVES 8

TRADITION SAYS EATING GREENS ON NEW YEAR'S DAY BRINGS WEALTH.
But there's another reason Southerners cook collards in the winter; they're ripest for picking after a few hard frosts, which turn starches inside the tobacco-size leaves into sugars. Frost-kissed collards don't need to stew for hours and hours to soften their assertive, sulfurous flavor. In this twist on tradition, they're simply sliced into a chiffonade, then given a steakhouse-style creamed spinach treatment, accented with aromatic nutmeg and roasted garlic. If the blanching step seems fussy, know that it's for a good reason. A quick bath in boiling water helps soften the sturdy leaves for quicker cooking. Dunking them in ice water helps preserve their green color.

INGREDIENTS

- 1 whole head of garlic, unpeeled, cloves intact
- 1 teaspoon olive oil
  Kosher salt and freshly ground black pepper
- 4 pounds collard greens, rinsed, tough stems removed, cut into ribbons
- 4 tablespoons (½ stick) unsalted butter
- 1 red onion, finely diced
- 3 cups heavy cream
- ¼ teaspoon freshly grated nutmeg

PREPARATION

Preheat the oven to 325°F. Slice the top quarter off the whole garlic bulb and discard the top. Put the bulb, cut-side up, in the center of a square of foil. Pour the oil on top of the garlic and sprinkle with a bit of salt and pepper. Bundle the foil to make a pouch and roast for 45 minutes. Remove from the oven and, when cool enough to handle, squeeze out the roasted garlic pulp into a small bowl and mash it well.

Bring a large pot of generously salted water to a boil over high heat. In a large bowl, prepare an ice-water bath. Blanch the collards in the boiling water in two batches. Drain, then shock the collards in the ice-water bath, then remove and squeeze with clean hands to extract all the excess liquid from the greens.

Put the butter in a Dutch oven over medium heat and, when it foams, after 2 to 3 minutes, add the onion. Sauté for 3 minutes to just soften. Add the cream and whisk in the roasted garlic, the nutmeg, 1 tablespoon salt, and 2 teaspoons pepper and reduce the heat to medium-low. Add the blanched greens and cook for 5 minutes, stirring frequently, until the cream is slightly reduced and the greens are tender. Taste and adjust the seasoning, if desired. Serve hot.

CORNBREAD OYSTER DRESSING

"THE ONLY PART OF THANKSGIVING DINNERS I LIKED WERE THE CHESTNUTS," says Korean-American chef Edward Lee, who grew up in Brooklyn. "We ate them roasted, boiled, mashed in sticky rice, or right out of the shell." Now the chef and owner of 610 Magnolia and MilkWood in Louisville, Kentucky, Lee is known as one of the most inventive chefs in the South. And as the master of ceremonies at his own holiday gatherings, he harks back to that childhood love with a chestnut-topped twist on traditional oyster stuffing that gives the briny bivalves an extra boost of salty goodness from country ham. It's a complex balance of salt and sweet that will stand up to, or maybe even eclipse, all the other flavors at the Thanksgiving table.

INGREDIENTS

½   cup (1 stick) unsalted butter, melted, plus 5 tablespoons, plus 1 tablespoon for buttering the baking dish

12   cups ½-inch-diced unsweetened cornbread (about 2 prepared rounds; page 215)

2   cups chopped onions (about 2 medium onions)

1½   cups chopped celery (about 3 stalks)

2   garlic cloves, finely minced

6   ounces country ham, finely diced

2   tablespoons chopped fresh sage leaves

2   teaspoons fresh thyme leaves

1½   teaspoons sea salt

1   teaspoon freshly ground black pepper

½   teaspoon freshly grated nutmeg

18   to 20 freshly shucked oysters, roughly chopped, liquor reserved

1   cup chicken stock

¾   cup milk

3   large eggs, lightly beaten

15   roasted chestnuts, peeled and roughly chopped

PREPARATION

Preheat the oven to 400°F. Toss the melted butter with the cornbread and spread on baking sheets, crumbs and all. Bake, stirring occasionally, for 30 minutes, or until well toasted. Keep the oven on.

Meanwhile, in a large skillet over medium-low heat, melt the remaining 5 tablespoons butter. Add the onions, celery, and garlic and cook, stirring occasionally, until translucent, 8 to 10 minutes. Transfer the vegetables to a large bowl and add the toasted cornbread, tossing gently to combine. Add the ham, sage, thyme, salt, pepper, nutmeg, and oysters with their liquor and combine with a rubber spatula.

Warm the stock and milk together in a small saucepan over medium-low heat just until simmering, about 5 minutes. Drizzle the mixture over the cornbread mixture and fold it in. Fold in the eggs.

Lightly butter a 9-by-13-inch baking dish. Spoon the dressing into the baking dish and sprinkle with the chestnuts. Lower the oven temperature to 350°F. Cover the dish with foil and bake for 15 to 20 minutes, then remove the foil and bake uncovered for 15 to 20 minutes more, until the edges and top are browned. Serve immediately.

7

BAKED GOODS

&

DESSERTS

ALWAYS SAVE ROOM FOR DESSERT

*Every meal, no matter how humble, merits a happy ending—
particularly if there's pie*

ROY BLOUNT, JR.

ROY ACUFF, THE KING OF COUNTRY MUSIC, PREFERRED to eat his pie first, to make sure he had room for it. And Acuff, said Charley Pride, *was* (apple) pie. Old Roy was still appearing belovedly on the Grand Ole Opry just before he died at eighty-nine.

Ralph Waldo Emerson, the author of *Self-Reliance*, believed in starting off the day with pie—ate it regularly for breakfast. One morning, according to his friend James B. Thayer, Emerson offered a piece of pie to several guests, one by one. Each gentleman declined. "'But,' Mr. Emerson remonstrated, . . . thrusting the knife under a piece of the pie, and putting the entire weight of his character into his manner, 'But . . . *what is pie for?*'"

There. There you are.

Was breakfast pie bad for Emerson? In only slightly premature old age he began losing his memory, but he retained, by all accounts, a nice smile. "He suffered very little," according to his son Edward Waldo, "took his nourishment well, went to his study and tried to work, accomplished less and less, but did not notice it." More and more, as I get on in years, I think of this as my fallback ambition.

However.

Where do I get off saying "However" to Roy Acuff and Ralph Waldo Emerson when it comes to pie? Well, I wrote a song to pie, which Andie MacDowell sang (music by Steve Dorff, whose other credits include "Every Which Way But Loose") in the movie *Michael*. It goes something like this:

> *Pie.*
> *Oh my,*
> *Nothing tastes sweet, wet, salty and dry*
> *All at once so well as pie.*
> *Peach or pecan, key lime or black-bottom,*
> *I'll come to your place every day if you've*
> *got 'em.*
> *Pie.*

So I have *some* room to talk, when it comes to pie, and here is what I wonder: Might Emerson's golden years have been even mellower if he had *saved room* for pie?

Pie being the highest form of food, it does seem best looked forward to. When we say "sweet as an angel eating pie," we do not mean icky, we mean ultimate. Eudora Welty, in her story "Kin," celebrates the perfect ending to a pleasant day: " . . . wonderful black, bitter, moist chocolate pie under mountains of meringue."

Let us pause to reflect that *bitter* is a key word there. Sweetness is enhanced by a discordant note—the seeds in blackberry preserves or pomegranate pips, the vinegar in chess pie, the cheese on apple pie, those gentlemen's disapproval of Emerson's breakfast pie. I don't know what your mother's pie-top meringue was like, but mine's (that's a double possessive) was ever-so-slightly-burnt-toasty at its high points. When we finally get to our pie, it may be sweetened by the sacrifice we have made in saving room for it.

Unquestionably, pie squeezed into too little room is, in effect, too much pie, and will make you sluggish. It's not what I would call a *bad* sluggish, but it's not you at your keenest, should a reason arise—fire, most obviously—for feeling like you really ought to get up from the table. And here is something to consider: you cannot truly know, except by some rough principle such as "more than one piece" (but what *size* pieces?), how much pie is too much until you have had it. You can, however, know, or believe you know, how much *room* you have for pie. One's room for pie is like one's capacity for love, in this sense: few life-affirming people underestimate their own. So don't worry about that. But you don't want to fritter away, so to speak, your room for pie.

There may be something to be said, even, for pie indefinitely deferred. Imagine a couple, each married to someone else, who work in the same office. The chemistry between them is strong. But they are prudent enough, responsible enough, family-loving enough, job-loving enough, to realize that under the circumstances, romance would be a bad idea.

Then it happens that each of them has an assignment, involving different matters, that will take them at the same time to . . . Paris. As if Cupid were giving them a poke. They make no explicit plans, they just let drop to each other where they will be staying in the City of Love, and when they will be arriving, and in each other's eyes they get the drift.

But on the day her flight is to depart, something comes up—his business in Paris has to be put off for a month. Hers can't be.

So here's what she says to him (and what each of them, we may assume, will think whenever anyone mentions *Casablanca*): "We'll always not have Paris." If something is sufficiently delicious as a prospect, then even doing without it can be sweet.

Right.

SORGHUM-BOURBON PECAN PIE

SERVES 8

WHAT'S BETTER THAN FRESH PECAN PIE? FRESH PECAN PIE WITH BOURBON.
What's better than that? Fresh pecan pie with bourbon and sorghum, which adds a distinctive touch—
the warmth of brown sugar crossed with honey's floral sweetness. Still, the real stars of this show are
the pecans, one of fall's most anticipated treats (and the South's only cultivated indigenous nut). In this
recipe they perform double duty: crushed pecan cookies for the crust, chopped nuts for the filling.

INGREDIENTS

FOR THE CRUST

- 15 shortbread pecan sandies
- 6 tablespoons all-purpose flour
- 3 tablespoons unsalted butter, plus 1 tablespoon for buttering the pie plate

FOR THE FILLING

- 6 tablespoons unsalted butter
- ⅓ cup dark brown sugar
- ½ teaspoon kosher salt
- ¾ cup sorghum syrup
- 3 tablespoons bourbon
- 1½ teaspoons vanilla extract
- 3 large eggs
- 1½ cups (6 ounces) toasted and chopped pecans

PREPARATION

FOR THE CRUST Preheat the oven to 350°F. Butter a 9-inch pie plate.

In a food processor, pulse the cookies and flour together until pulverized. Add the butter and process until the mixture resembles wet sand. Press the mixture into the bottom and up the sides of the prepared pie plate. Bake until lightly browned, 12 to 14 minutes. Let cool completely on a wire rack.

FOR THE FILLING Put the butter, brown sugar, and salt in a saucepan and cook over medium heat, stirring occasionally, until the sugar is melted, about 2 minutes. Whisk in the syrup, bourbon, and vanilla. In a bowl, whisk the eggs together. Temper the egg mixture: slowly whisk ½ cup of the warm butter-sugar mixture into the eggs. Pour the tempered egg mixture back into the saucepan with the butter-sugar mixture and reduce the heat to medium-low. Cook, stirring constantly, until the mixture is glossy, about 3 minutes. Remove from the heat and stir in the pecans.

Pour the mixture into the crust and bake until the center feels set yet soft, 30 to 40 minutes. Let cool completely on a wire rack; this will take about 4 hours. Serve at room temperature.

TIP: **In the unlikely event of leftovers, wrap the pie plate tightly in plastic wrap and refrigerate for up to 2 days.**

MARDI GRAS MOON PIES

MAKES A BAKER'S DOZEN

(12 cookies and 1 small one for the cook)

DAVID GUAS, WHO BRINGS THE FOOD OF LOUISIANA TO THE PEOPLE OF VIRGINIA at his Bayou Bakery in Arlington, developed a Moon Pie obsession early. While growing up in New Orleans, he'd sit atop the family Mardi Gras viewing ladder as the floats passed by, waiting for the krewes that threw mini versions of the Chattanooga-born convenience-store staple. Now that he's an adult, Guas still craves Moon Pies. But instead of the packaged version, he whips up his own. He starts with dough made from finely ground graham crackers to give the cookies their characteristic sandy texture. Then he sandwiches a dollop of honey-kissed marshmallow filling in between and dips the whole thing into bittersweet chocolate. These sweet nostalgia bombs are best the day you make them or perhaps a day later. After that, the cookies lose their snap. Not that they're likely to last long. A homemade Moon Pie is a rare treat.

INGREDIENTS

FOR THE COOKIE DOUGH

- ¾ cup (1½ sticks) unsalted butter
- ¼ cup firmly packed light brown sugar
- ¼ cup cane syrup
- ¼ teaspoon vanilla extract
- 1½ cups all-purpose flour
- 1¼ cups fine graham cracker crumbs (about 9 or 10 rectangular crackers pulverized in a food processor)
- ¾ teaspoon kosher salt
- ½ teaspoon baking powder
- ½ teaspoon baking soda
- ¼ teaspoon ground cinnamon
- 2 tablespoons whole milk

PREPARATION

FOR THE COOKIE DOUGH In the bowl of a stand mixer fitted with the paddle attachment, beat the butter, brown sugar, syrup, and vanilla for 1 minute. In a separate bowl, combine the flour, cracker crumbs, salt, baking powder, baking soda, and cinnamon and mix with a fork. Add the dry ingredients to the butter mixture and mix on low speed; gradually add the milk. Continue mixing until the dough comes together. Press the dough flat, wrap it in plastic, and refrigerate for at least 1 hour.

Preheat the oven to 325°F. Line a baking sheet with parchment paper.

Put the chilled dough on a flour-dusted work surface, then roll to ¼ inch thick. Stamp out cookies using a 3-inch round cookie cutter. Place the cookies on the prepared baking sheet and bake for 10 to 12 minutes. Let cool completely while you make the filling.

RECIPE CONTINUES ▶

FOR THE MARSHMALLOW FILLING

- 4 teaspoons unflavored powdered gelatin
- ½ cup ice-cold water, plus ¼ cup at room temperature
- ¼ cup light corn syrup
- 3 tablespoons honey (clover or wildflower)
- ¾ cup sugar
- 3 large egg whites

FOR THE CHOCOLATE COATING

- 1 pound bittersweet chocolate (61 to 70% cacao)
- 2 tablespoons vegetable oil or canola oil

FOR THE MARSHMALLOW FILLING In a small bowl, sprinkle the gelatin over ½ cup ice-cold water and set aside to bloom.

Combine ¼ cup room-temperature water, the corn syrup, honey, and sugar in a small saucepan, clip a candy thermometer to the side, and simmer until the mixture reaches 240°F. When the thermometer reaches 200°F—but not before—place the egg whites in the cleaned bowl of the stand mixer fitted with the whisk attachment and whip on high speed. (You want to get them to the soft peak stage before adding the gelatin and sugar mixture.)

Once the sugar mixture reaches 240°F, remove from the heat and stir in the bloomed gelatin. Then, while the egg whites are whipping, slowly and carefully drizzle the hot sugar mixture into the bowl. Continue whipping for an additional 8 minutes, until the mixture stiffens.

Flip half of the cooled cookies over. Lightly coat a spoon with nonstick cooking spray, and spoon about ¼ cup of the marshmallow onto each flipped cookie. Use the remaining cookies as tops; gently push down until you can see marshmallow come just to the edge. Place the cookies in the refrigerator to chill for at least 15 minutes while you make the chocolate coating.

FOR THE CHOCOLATE COATING Melt the chocolate in a heatproof bowl set over a small saucepan of simmering water (double boiler). Stir until the chocolate has melted, then remove the bowl from the pan and let the chocolate cool slightly. When the chocolate is no longer hot, but is still warm, slowly whisk in the oil in a steady stream. Let the chocolate cool at room temperature for about 5 minutes before proceeding.

Submerge the chilled cookies in the chocolate, using two forks, slotted spoons, or spatulas to gently lift the sandwiches out of the bowl. Let the coated cookies stand on a cooling rack until the coating hardens, 1 to 2 hours. Store in an airtight container at room temperature for up to 1 day.

BRÛLÉED BUTTERMILK PIE

SERVES 10

IN THE HILLS OF EAST TENNESSEE OUTSIDE OF KNOXVILLE, THE CRUZE FAMILY still does things the old-fashioned way. Patriarch Earl milks pasture-raised Jersey cows and makes the buttermilk himself, starting with the liquid left over from butter making—an acidic, largely defatted milk. In the days before refrigeration, farmers left that liquid in uncovered pitchers, where natural cultures fermented, thickened, and soured it. Cruze adds cultures to his buttermilk more deliberately, but the end result is the same—a dessertlike richness reminiscent of panna cotta or lemon cream. Understand real buttermilk and its presence in a pie seems perfectly natural. Made with farm-fresh or, in a pinch, the dairy-case kind, buttermilk pie does what so many Southern recipes do: turns a simple ingredient into something sublime.

INGREDIENTS

FOR THE CRUST

- ⅓ cup toasted and chopped pecans
- 1¼ cups all-purpose flour
- 1 tablespoon sugar
- ¼ teaspoon kosher salt
- ¼ teaspoon ground cinnamon
- 6 tablespoons cold unsalted butter, cut into pieces
- 2 tablespoons cold lard, cut into pieces
- 6 to 8 tablespoons ice water

FOR THE FILLING

- ¾ cup granulated sugar
- 1 tablespoon cornstarch
- ½ teaspoon kosher salt
- 2 whole large eggs
- 5 large egg yolks
- 1½ cups buttermilk
- ¼ cup heavy cream
- 4 tablespoons (½ stick) unsalted butter, melted
- 1 teaspoon vanilla extract
- 2 tablespoons dark brown sugar

PREPARATION

FOR THE CRUST In a food processor, finely grind pecans. Add the flour, sugar, salt, and cinnamon and pulse to combine. Add the cold butter and lard and pulse until the dough resembles wet sand, about 10 pulses. Add the ice water, 1 tablespoon at a time, and pulse until the dough holds together, about 10 pulses. Shape into a disk; wrap in plastic and refrigerate for at least 1 hour. (The dough may be made up to 2 days ahead.)

Position an oven rack in the center and preheat the oven to 425°F.

On a floured surface, roll the dough to a 12-inch round. Transfer to a 9-inch broiler-safe pie plate, pressing the dough against the bottom and sides. Trim the dough so that the edge is in line with the outer rim of the pie plate. Refrigerate for 20 minutes. Remove from the refrigerator and flute the edge. Prick the bottom and sides of the dough with a fork.

Line the pie shell with foil and fill with pie weights. Bake until lightly browned, about 15 minutes. Remove the weights and foil and bake until the crust is golden brown, 5 to 8 minutes. Let cool completely on a wire rack.

FOR THE FILLING Lower the oven temperature to 300°F.

Whisk the granulated sugar, cornstarch, and salt together in large bowl. Whisk in the whole eggs and yolks until well combined. Whisk in the buttermilk, cream, melted butter, and vanilla. Pour the mixture into the crust and bake on a baking sheet until only the pie center jiggles when moved, 50 to 60 minutes.

Remove the pie from the oven and turn the oven to broil. Shield the rim of crust with a pie shield or strips of foil. Sprinkle the surface with brown sugar and broil until the sugar melts, about 1 minute. Keep close watch so the sugar doesn't burn. Let cool for 45 minutes on a wire rack. Transfer to refrigerator until chilled, about 2 hours. Serve cold.

STRAWBERRY-MOONSHINE FRIED HAND PIES

MAKES 10

CONJURED FROM AN INEXPENSIVE ALCHEMY OF FAT, FLOUR, AND FRUIT, fried hand pies have long been proof that pleasure can be coaxed from hard times. "If I have any money," Georgia bluesman Curley Weaver sang in his 1934 recording "Fried Pie Blues," "I will buy me some." Joe Trull began frying pies as the pastry chef at NOLA, Emeril Lagasse's French Quarter restaurant. Over ten years there, he mastered the art. Now, fried pies are a dessert-menu staple at Grits and Groceries, the restaurant he and his wife, Heidi, run in Belton, South Carolina. Fried hand pies differ from baked pies in a couple of key ways. First, the dough should be a bit softer than a standard piecrust, and meticulously crimped so no filling escapes. That filling needs to be slightly dry, too. "A lot of people don't cook the insides first because that's how their grandmother did it," Trull says, "but using raw fruit makes it too wet." Lately, he's also been stirring in a little legal white lightning, too. "But the real trick," he says, "is that hot oil."

INGREDIENTS

FOR THE FILLING

- 4 cups strawberries, trimmed and cut into quarters
- 1 cup sugar
- 3 tablespoons commercial moonshine or grappa
- 1 teaspoon chopped orange zest
- 1 tablespoon freshly squeezed orange juice
- 2 teaspoons vanilla extract
- 3 tablespoons cornstarch
- 1 tablespoon unsalted butter
- ½ teaspoon kosher salt

FOR THE DOUGH

- 4 cups all-purpose flour
- 2½ teaspoons kosher salt
- 1 cup vegetable shortening or good-quality lard
- ¾ to 1 cup ice water

PREPARATION

FOR THE FILLING Put the strawberries, sugar, 2 tablespoons of the moonshine, the orange zest, juice, and vanilla in a large bowl. Mix gently to combine and refrigerate for at least 6 hours or overnight.

Transfer the strawberry mixture to a large saucepan and bring to a simmer over medium-low heat. In a small bowl, whisk together 2 tablespoons of water, the cornstarch, and the remaining 1 tablespoon moonshine. When the strawberries are tender, after about 5 minutes, stir in the cornstarch mixture, the butter, and salt and cook for 7 to 10 minutes, until the texture resembles jam. Transfer to a bowl and put in the refrigerator to chill.

FOR THE DOUGH In a large bowl, combine the flour and salt. Using a pastry blender or your fingers, rub the shortening into the flour until the mixture resembles coarse meal. Add the ice water ¼ cup at a time, mixing until the dough comes together but is not too sticky. Shape into a disk, wrap in plastic, and refrigerate for at least 1 hour. (The dough can be made up to 2 days ahead.)

RECIPE CONTINUES ▶

FOR THE SUGAR COATING

2 cups sugar

3 teaspoons grated orange zest

Egg wash: 1 egg, beaten with 1 teaspoon water

Peanut oil for frying

Ice cream for serving (optional)

FOR THE SUGAR COATING In a large bowl, combine the sugar and orange zest. Set aside.

ASSEMBLE THE PIES On a floured surface, roll half of the dough into a circle about ⅛ inch thick and cut into 6-inch rounds. (The lid from a large coffee can or plastic container works well as a guide.) Repeat with the remaining dough. Gently gather the trimmed dough into a ball and reroll and cut rounds until you have 10 rounds.

With your finger or a pastry brush, coat the outer edge of a dough round with egg wash. Place 2 heaping tablespoons of the filling in the center, then carefully fold the dough over the filling, making sure no filling touches the rim of the dough. Crimp the edges together firmly to make a seam.

To fry the pies, fill a Dutch oven with 1 to 2 inches of oil and clip a deep-frying thermometer to the side. Place over medium-high heat and bring the oil to 375°F. (The temperature will drop considerably when the pies are added; you want to regulate the heat to maintain a temperature around 350°F during frying.) Gently fry two or three pies at a time, leaving room for them to float freely in the oil. Cook for 8 to 9 minutes, turning occasionally, until the dough is crisp and lightly browned. Use a spider or slotted spoon to remove the cooked pies to paper towels or a wire rack set over a baking sheet. Let cool slightly.

One at a time, place each pie in the bowl of sugar coating and gently toss to coat. Serve plain or with ice cream. Store fully cooled pies in an airtight container, refrigerated, for up to 1 day.

SWEET POTATO SONKER

SERVES 12 TO 14

A POOL OF LUSCIOUS FILLING SURROUNDED AND TOPPED BY BUTTERY CRUST.
That's a cobbler, right? Not in Surry County, North Carolina, where the name of the dessert game is sonker. Like cobblers and pies, sonkers come in all sorts of varieties—cherry, strawberry, peach, blueberry, sweet potato. But what sets sonker apart is the "dip"—a thick sauce drizzled over the top that varies from family to family. At Lorene's Bakery and Catering, a little operation in Dobson, North Carolina, Lorene Moore makes her dip with butter, evaporated milk, sugar, egg yolks, and a spoonful of vanilla extract. The secret to her sonker's rich, flaky crust? Canned biscuits.

INGREDIENTS

- 4 sweet potatoes
- 1 can biscuits (Moore recommends Grands 8-count Homestyle Buttermilk Biscuits)
- ¾ cup sugar
- ½ teaspoon ground cinnamon
- 1 tablespoon butter for buttering the baking dish

FOR THE DIP

- ½ cup (1 stick) unsalted butter
- 1 (12-ounce) can evaporated milk
- 1 cup sugar
- 1 tablespoon vanilla extract
- 4 large egg yolks

PREPARATION

Preheat the oven to 350°F.

Peel the sweet potatoes and cut them into ½-inch-thick slices. Put the sweet potatoes in a large Dutch oven with enough water to just cover them, bring to a boil over high heat, then reduce the heat to low and simmer, covered, until tender, about 15 minutes; don't drain.

Butter a 9-by-13-inch baking dish or coat it with cooking spray. Roll out the biscuit dough, cut it into strips, and use some of it to line the sides of the dish. Pour the sweet potatoes and their cooking liquid into the dish. Sprinkle evenly with the sugar, then the cinnamon. Cover the top with more dough strips. Bake for 45 minutes, or until nicely browned on top.

FOR THE DIP In a medium saucepan, melt the butter over medium heat, then add the evaporated milk, sugar, and vanilla and bring just to a boil. Remove from the heat. In a medium bowl, whisk the egg yolks together, then temper them: whisk ½ cup of the hot milk mixture into the yolks. Pour the tempered egg yolks back into the saucepan with the warm milk mixture, stirring constantly until incorporated. Place over medium-low heat for 8 to 10 minutes, bringing to just below a boil and stirring constantly. Remove the dip from the heat.

Remove the sonker from the oven, pour half of the dip over the top, making sure that it runs down between strips of biscuit dough. Let the sonker rest for 15 minutes to set, then serve with the remaining dip in a bowl to ladle over individual servings.

BANANA PUDDING
WITH PEANUT BUTTER WHIPPED CREAM

SERVES 8 TO 10

THERE SEEM TO BE TWO FAMILY TREES FOR BANANA PUDDING IN THE SOUTH:
the traditional custard-based kind made at home, which places a premium on creamy pudding topped
with fluffy meringue, and the kind bought from barbecue joints, which is often just banana slices and
vanilla wafers suspended in puffy clouds of sweet whipped cream. This recipe combines the best of
both, then gets a little Elvis-y by whipping peanut butter into the topping, inspired by Presley's favorite
sandwich, the grilled PB&B. The result is banana pudding fit for a king.

INGREDIENTS

FOR THE PUDDING

- 4 tablespoons cold unsalted butter
- 4 large ripe bananas, peeled and sliced into rounds
- 4 large egg yolks
- ¾ cup sugar
- 3 tablespoons cornstarch
- ⅛ teaspoon kosher salt
- 2 cups half-and-half
- 1 cup whole milk
- 1 teaspoon vanilla extract
  Vanilla wafers

FOR THE TOPPING

- 2 cups plus 2 tablespoons cold heavy cream
- ¼ cup creamy peanut butter (page 255)
- 3 tablespoons confectioners' sugar
- 1 cup crushed vanilla wafers

PREPARATION

FOR THE PUDDING Melt 2 tablespoons of the butter in a large skillet over
medium heat. Add the sliced bananas, tossing to coat, and sauté for 3
to 5 minutes, tossing occasionally, until the bananas are soft and lightly
browned. Set aside to cool.

In a large bowl, whisk the egg yolks, ¼ cup of the sugar, the cornstarch,
and salt until smooth and pale in color. In a large saucepan, combine
the half-and-half, milk, and remaining ½ cup sugar and cook over
medium heat, stirring occasionally, until warmed and lightly steaming.
Temper the egg yolk mixture: slowly whisk ½ cup of the hot half-and-
half mixture into the yolk mixture. Return the mixture to the saucepan
with the half-and-half mixture and cook, whisking constantly, until
bubbles begin to form and the mixture is thickened and glossy, about
1 minute. Remove from the heat; add the remaining 2 tablespoons
butter and the vanilla and stir until the butter is melted.

Arrange a single layer of vanilla wafers in the bottom of a 2-quart
dish or trifle bowl. Top with half of the sautéed bananas. Spoon half
of the pudding on top of the bananas; layer again with vanilla wafers,
bananas, and the remaining pudding. Press a piece of plastic wrap
directly on the surface of the pudding to prevent a skin from forming
and refrigerate until well chilled, at least 2 hours or overnight.

FOR THE TOPPING Put the 2 tablespoons cream and the peanut butter in a
microwave-safe bowl and microwave until creamy and thinned, about
30 seconds. Let cool completely, then transfer to a large bowl and add the
remaining 2 cups cream and the confectioners' sugar. With an electric
mixer on medium speed, beat until stiff peaks form, about 2 minutes.

To serve, line the rim of the serving dish with more vanilla wafers,
dollop the topping over the pudding, and sprinkle with crushed
vanilla wafers.

APPLEJACK STACK CAKE

SERVES 12 TO 16

APPALACHIAN APPLE STACK CAKE IS COMMUNAL COOKING AT ITS FINEST.
Originally, each layer was baked at home by individual cooks, likely in cast-iron skillets, then brought together and assembled for church suppers and gatherings. Instead of the spongy cakes we're used to today, these layers are more like cookies—firmer, so they slowly soften beneath liberal applications of apple butter and cooked apples. This recipe stays mostly true to those principles. Instead of individually baking the layers one skillet at a time, though, use a cake pan to trace a pattern on parchment paper and trim circles of rolled dough to fit it. Bake two layers simultaneously (more if you have a convection oven). The edges of the cake layers won't be as perfectly neat as if you'd baked them in skillets or cake pans, but that's all right. This is a rustic cake. RECIPE FOLLOWS ▸

INGREDIENTS

FOR THE FILLING

- 3 pounds assorted apples, peeled and cut into ½-inch wedges
- ½ cup brown sugar
- 1 cup apple cider
- ¼ cup applejack, apple brandy, or bourbon
- 1½ cups apple butter (store-bought or see page 253)

FOR THE CAKE

- 5 cups all-purpose flour
- 1 teaspoon baking powder
- 1 teaspoon baking soda
- ¼ teaspoon kosher salt
- ⅓ cup buttermilk
- 1 teaspoon vanilla extract
- ¾ cup (1½ sticks) unsalted butter
- 2 cups granulated sugar
- ¼ cup molasses
- 2 large eggs

FOR THE GLAZE

- 1 cup dark brown sugar
- ¼ cup reserved apple cider mixture (from the filling)
- 1 tablespoon molasses
- 2 tablespoons unsalted butter

TIP: **You only need ¼ cup of the reserved apple cider mixture to make the glaze. That'll leave about another cup or so of liquid left over, depending on how much water the apples released, and it's an elegantly simple cocktail just waiting to happen. Pour some of the cooled cooked cider mixture into a highball glass with a dash of bitters, a squeeze of lemon, and a jigger of bourbon and serve over ice.**

PREPARATION

FOR THE FILLING Put the apples, brown sugar, cider, and applejack in a large saucepan; bring to a boil over medium-high heat. Reduce the heat to medium-low and simmer, covered, stirring occasionally, until the apples are tender, about 20 minutes. Drain the apples and reserve ¼ cup of the liquid. Set aside.

FOR THE CAKE Position the racks in the upper-middle and lower-middle of the oven and preheat the oven to 350°F. Coat two baking sheets with cooking spray.

In a medium bowl, whisk the flour, baking powder, baking soda, and salt together. In a large liquid measuring cup, whisk together the buttermilk and vanilla.

In large bowl, with an electric mixer at medium-high speed, beat the butter and granulated sugar until light and fluffy, about 2 minutes. Reduce the speed to medium-low and add the molasses, beating until incorporated. Add the eggs one at a time and mix until incorporated. Gradually add the buttermilk (the mixture will look curdled); add the flour mixture and mix until a soft dough forms—it should look like cookie dough. Remove the dough from the bowl, pat into a round, cover in plastic wrap, and refrigerate for 20 minutes.

Divide the dough into 6 equal portions, about 8½ ounces each. On parchment paper, roll portions of dough into circles about ¼ inch thick. Use an 8-inch cake pan as a guide to trim into uniform 8-inch circles. Bake one circle on each prepared sheet until golden brown, 10 to 12 minutes, rotating and switching the baking sheets halfway through baking. Transfer the circles to cooling racks and let cool completely. The cakes will harden and set as they cool. Repeat with remaining dough. Reroll scraps to form a seventh layer.

Place the first layer on a serving plate and spread with ¼ cup of the apple butter. Arrange one-sixth of the cooled cooked apples on top of apple butter and top with another layer of cake. Repeat with the remaining filling and cake layers, ending with a cake layer on top. Wrap the cake tightly in plastic wrap and refrigerate until the layers soften, at least 12 hours and up to 2 days.

FOR THE GLAZE In a small saucepan, combine the brown sugar, reserved apple cider mixture, and the molasses. Bring to a low boil over medium-high heat and cook until the sugar is dissolved, about 2 minutes. Remove from the heat and stir in the butter until smooth. Let cool for 5 minutes, then pour the glaze over the top of the cake. Slice and serve, or store the cake, covered, at room temperature for up to 3 days.

SWEET TEA GRANITA

SERVES 6

LIKE SO MANY SOUTHERNERS, ANDREA KIRSHTEIN GREW UP DRINKING sweet tea by the gallon. "I was usually the one who made it," she says, "solely because I had it down to a science." In the summer, Kirshtein, who is now the pastry chef at the Spence in Atlanta, uses the recipe her family came to call "glucose tea" as a base for frozen granita. It's an easy dish to make. The only challenge is tending to it while it's in the freezer. Once the mix just starts to harden, run a fork through the ice crystals every fifteen or twenty minutes. After an hour or two, you've got a fluffy dessert that Kirshtein likes to pair with shortbread made from cornmeal. But, like a glass of good sweet tea, her granita is also perfectly refreshing all by itself.

INGREDIENTS

- ⅔ cup sugar
- 2 black tea bags, preferably English breakfast or other good-quality tea

PREPARATION

In a medium saucepan, bring the sugar and 3 cups water to a boil over high heat. Remove from the heat, add the tea bags, and steep for 5 minutes. Remove the tea bags and let the tea cool to room temperature. Pour into an 8-inch square baking dish (or any shallow freezer-proof dish); cover with plastic wrap and freeze.

After 1 hour, scrape a fork through the mixture to break up any large pieces of ice; return the dish to the freezer. Repeat every 15 to 20 minutes until the consistency is fluffy and no large ice crystals remain, two or three more times. Scoop into glasses and serve.

The granita may be made ahead and stored in the freezer for up to 3 days. Fluff with a fork before serving.

TIP: **For an Arnold Palmer variation, reduce the water to 2½ cups. Zest 2 lemons; then halve and juice them. After steeping the tea, add the lemon juice and zest and begin the freezing process as directed.**

PEACH ICE CREAM

MAKES 1 QUART

SUMMER BRINGS MANY A BLESSED THING—FIREFLY NIGHTS, FRESHLY CAUGHT shrimp, and, especially, perfectly ripe peaches. And while a chin-soaking bite of a just-picked peach is hard to top, nothing cools down a sultry day better than homemade peach ice cream. This version nods slightly to modern-day cooking; instead of being poured straight into the ice-cream mixing canister, the custard base is cooked to safely heat the eggs, then cooled. Simmering the peach pits in milk extracts an extra layer of sweetness, underpinned with almond tones. Creamy goat cheese might seem like a curious addition, but it supplies a slightly savory, grassy element, reminiscent of the fresh milk our grandparents would have used. If you prefer whole chunks of fruit in your ice cream, puree only half of the macerated peaches. Then pour it all into an ice-cream maker and let the anticipation begin.

INGREDIENTS

- 2 ripe peaches, peeled and finely chopped (about 2 cups), pits reserved
- 1½ cups whole milk
- 1 cup heavy cream
- 2 tablespoons freshly squeezed lemon juice
- 1 tablespoon light brown sugar
- ⅔ cup granulated sugar
- 4 large egg yolks
- ½ teaspoon vanilla extract
- ¼ teaspoon kosher salt
  About ½ (3-ounce) log goat cheese, such as Alabama-made Belle Chevre, crumbled

PREPARATION

In a medium saucepan, heat the peach pits, milk, and cream over medium heat until steaming. Remove from the heat, cover, and steep for about 1 hour.

In a medium bowl, combine the peaches, lemon juice, and brown sugar. Let sit for 1 hour. In a blender or using an immersion blender, puree the peaches and any juices that have collected in the bowl. Set aside.

Remove the peach pits from the milk mixture and discard them. Add the sugar to the saucepan with the milk mixture and heat over medium-high heat, stirring occasionally, until the mixture is steaming, about 5 minutes. Remove from the heat.

While the milk mixture heats, whisk the egg yolks, vanilla, and salt in a bowl until smooth. Temper the egg yolks: Slowly whisk ½ cup of the hot milk mixture into the yolk mixture, whisking constantly. Pour the tempered yolk mixture back into the saucepan with the milk mixture and cook over low heat, stirring constantly, until the custard thickens and coats the back of a wooden spoon, about 5 minutes.

Put the cheese in a large bowl. Pour the custard over the cheese and gently whisk until the cheese melts and the mixture is smooth. Whisk in the peach puree. Let the custard cool for 15 minutes over an ice-water bath, stirring frequently. Cover with plastic wrap (pressing it directly onto the surface of the custard so it doesn't form a skin) and place in the refrigerator to chill completely, about 4 hours.

Transfer the chilled custard to an ice cream machine and churn according to the manufacturer's instructions. Transfer the ice cream to an airtight container and freeze until firm, at least 2 hours. Serve.

Store in an airtight container in the freezer for up to 2 weeks.

BROWN BUTTER SMITH ISLAND CAKE

SERVES 12 TO 16

BURY SOMETHING IN FUDGE, AND IT'S NOT LIKELY TO MOVE. THAT'S BASICALLY
the principle behind the very sturdy—and very tasty—Smith Island Cake, made for generations of
Chesapeake watermen to serve as a long-lasting reminder of home when the seas were rough and
the days were long. "A lot of work goes into the cake, so the watermen would know their wives were
thinking of them," says Sarah Malphrus, who mulls over many regional desserts as the executive pastry
chef at Woodberry Kitchen in Baltimore. Her version of the classic cake deviates a little bit from the
standard. Malphrus adds depth to each layer with toasty brown butter. Next, she coats the entire cake
with intensely chocolatey buttercream—a velvety-smooth stand-in for fudge that's still thick enough
so the cake won't budge. The result may take time, but it's a special treat for the hardworking people in
your life.

INGREDIENTS

FOR THE BROWN BUTTER

¾ cup (1½ sticks) unsalted
    butter

FOR THE CAKE

1 cup (2 sticks) unsalted butter,
   at room temperature

4 cups granulated sugar

2¼ cups light brown sugar

12 large eggs

2 cups buttermilk

1⅓ cups sunflower or canola oil

6½ cups cake flour

2½ teaspoons baking powder

3½ teaspoons kosher salt

PREPARATION

FOR THE BROWN BUTTER Slice the butter evenly into tablespoon-size
pieces, then melt in a stainless-steel or light-colored skillet (so you
can observe the color of the butter as it browns) over medium heat,
stirring frequently. The butter will begin to foam after 2 to 3 minutes.
Continue stirring for about 10 minutes, or until the foam begins
to subside and the butter has become golden brown and fragrant.
Remove from the heat and set aside to cool to room temperature.

FOR THE CAKE Preheat the oven to 350°F.

Combine the cooled brown butter, room-temperature butter,
granulated sugar, and brown sugar in the bowl of a stand mixer fitted
with the paddle attachment and beat on medium speed for 5 minutes.
Scrape down the sides of the bowl with a spatula and add the eggs, one
at a time, making sure each is thoroughly incorporated before adding
the next (beating for 1 to 2 minutes each time). Scrape down the bowl
again, and gradually pour in the buttermilk and oil. Beat on medium-
high speed for 6 minutes, or until the mixture is light and fluffy.

In a separate bowl, whisk together the flour, baking powder, and salt.
Add the flour mixture slowly to the butter and sugar mixture, mixing
on low speed until all the ingredients have been incorporated.

FOR THE CHOCOLATE BUTTERCREAM FROSTING

1 pound 2 ounces dark chocolate (70% cacao), chopped

3 cups (6 sticks) unsalted butter, at room temperature

¼ cup milk

6 cups confectioners' sugar, sifted

Trim eight sheets of parchment paper to fit 8- or 9-inch cake pans. Butter each pan, place a parchment round in the bottom, and butter the parchment. Working in batches, scoop 1 heaping cupful of cake batter into each pan and spread with an offset spatula so the batter is even and ¼ to ½ inch deep. Bake for 25 to 30 minutes, until a toothpick inserted in the center comes out clean. (You can bake layers two or four at a time, depending on how many cake pans you have; the more layers you bake, the more cooking time you may need.) As soon as you pull each cake layer from the oven, run a knife along the inside edge of the pan to loosen the cake layer. Let the layers cool in the pans before carefully inverting them to remove from the pans.

FOR THE FROSTING Put the chocolate in a heatproof bowl set over a small saucepan of simmering water (a double boiler). Stir until the chocolate has melted, then remove the bowl from the pan and let the chocolate cool to room temperature.

In the bowl of a stand mixer fitted with the paddle attachment, beat the butter until smooth, 2 to 3 minutes, then slowly pour in the melted chocolate while the mixer is on low speed and mix until combined, about 5 minutes. Add the milk and mix on low speed for about 1 minute. Add the confectioners' sugar 1 cup at a time and mix on low speed until fully incorporated and the frosting is smooth, about 8 minutes total.

ASSEMBLE THE CAKE Place one cake layer on a cake stand. Using an offset spatula, spread ¼ cup of the buttercream evenly over the cake. Repeat with the remaining layers. Refrigerate the cake for 30 minutes. Use the remaining buttercream to cover the top and sides of the cake. Slice and serve, or store, covered, at room temperature for up to 3 days.

SWEET POTATO CANDY

MAKES 36 CANDIES

MANY FAMILY STORIES SUGGEST THAT THIS HUMBLE SWEET, MADE FROM JUST four ingredients, is a Depression-era creation born of frugal ingenuity. But it's more likely that potato candy made its way to the South with Irish settlers and eventually to tables as a confection reserved for special occasions like Thanksgiving or Christmas. Oddly, the candy doesn't taste much like sweet potato; in fact, it's more akin to peanut butter fudge. Cooked sweet potato is simply a binder for nearly *two pounds* of powdered sugar, making this one very sweet treat.

INGREDIENTS

- 1 small sweet potato
- 1 teaspoon vanilla extract
- 1½ to 2 pounds confectioners' sugar
- ½ cup creamy peanut butter (page 255)

PREPARATION

Pierce the sweet potato with a fork and cook in a microwave oven on high until very tender, 5 to 7 minutes. Let cool completely. Remove the skin. With a potato masher or in bowl of a stand mixer fitted with the paddle attachment, mash the potato until completely smooth. Stir in the vanilla. Gradually add the confectioners' sugar, 1 cup at a time, mixing until a soft, slightly sticky dough forms. (It will be the consistency of cookie dough.)

Place the dough in between two layers of waxed paper dusted with additional confectioners' sugar. Roll the dough into a 9-by-12-inch rectangle about ¼ inch thick; spread the dough with the peanut butter. Starting at a long side of the rectangle, roll the dough into a log using the waxed paper to shape it. If the dough begins to stick to the paper, place in the refrigerator for 5 minutes. Wrap the dough in waxed paper and refrigerate for at least 2 hours. Slice into ¼-inch-thick pieces. Serve.

Store in an airtight container at room temperature for up to 3 days.

TIP: Microwave the peanut butter for 30 seconds to help make it more spreadable.

SOUTHERN SKILLET CORNBREAD

SERVES 8 TO 12

CORNBREAD IS A CORNERSTONE OF SOUTHERN—AND AMERICAN—FOOD
tradition: the country's first bread made without yeast. It evolved from nourishing Cherokee corn-and-bean cakes into simple unleavened ash cakes and pones baked on the hearthstones of frontier cabins, then into portable Johnny cakes and hoecakes that fortified soldiers and farmers alike, and finally into the iconic skillet-baked round we treasure today. Unlike the cakey cornbread of the North, traditional Southern cornbread relies on coarser cornmeal and little or no flour or sugar. If there's any secret, it's not so much an ingredient as a technique. Put the fat—melted lard or bacon grease—in a cast-iron skillet, put the skillet into a hot oven while you assemble the ingredients, then pour in the bread batter. The sizzle you'll hear—and the golden crust that results from it—is what truly sets Southern cornbread apart.

INGREDIENTS

- 4 tablespoons melted lard or bacon grease
- 2 cups good-quality coarse-ground yellow cornmeal, such as McEwen & Sons or Anson Mills
- 1 teaspoon baking powder
- 1 teaspoon baking soda
- 1 teaspoon kosher salt
- 2 large eggs
- 1½ cups buttermilk

PREPARATION

Preheat the oven to 400°F. Put 2 tablespoons of the lard or grease in a 10-inch cast-iron skillet. Put the skillet in the oven to preheat.

In a large bowl, combine the cornmeal, baking powder, baking soda, and salt. In a separate bowl or liquid measuring cup, whisk the eggs, buttermilk, and the remaining 2 tablespoons lard together, mixing well to combine. Pour the liquid ingredients into the dry ingredients, stirring just until incorporated. Do not overmix.

Carefully remove the hot skillet from the oven and swirl the melted fat to coat the bottom and sides. Pour the batter into the pan and return it to the oven to bake for 20 to 25 minutes, until the bread is golden on top and has pulled away from sides of the pan slightly. (A toothpick inserted in the center should come out clean.) Slice and serve.

CHEROKEE BEAN BREAD

SERVES 6

THE HOMESTEADERS WHO MOVED INTO THE SOUTHERN APPALACHIANS TWO
and three centuries ago may have introduced cornmeal to buttermilk and cast iron, but their native
neighbors had been eating cornmeal for generations. Cornbread is still a staple in some Cherokee
households in western North Carolina, where cooks mix dense patties of cornmeal with protein-
packed beans. Fifteen years ago, Cherokee elder Nancy Plemmons and her husband wrote a book
that still stands almost alone as a document of native mountain cuisine. *Cherokee Cooking: From the
Mountains and Gardens to the Table*, is a spiral-bound collection of recipes infused with native history
and ingredients: hickory nut soup, ramps and potatoes, pork ribs with corn, and this recipe for bean
bread. The cakes are traditionally garnished with salty fatback and its grease. Don't skimp—it's just as
important as butter to hot biscuits.

INGREDIENTS

- 1 cup dried pinto beans
- 1½ cups white cornmeal, plus more as needed
- ¼ cup all-purpose flour
- 4 to 6 ounces fatback, cut into 1-ounce pieces

PREPARATION

Soak the beans overnight in 5 cups cold water. Drain. Put the beans in
a saucepan with 3 cups water. Simmer until cooked through but still
firm, 2 to 3 hours. Drain, reserving the cooking liquid.

Fill a large Dutch oven with water and place it over high heat.

Combine the cornmeal and flour in a large mixing bowl. Slowly add
½ cup of the beans and 1 cup of the bean cooking liquid to the mixture,
working it with your hands until it begins to form a soft dough—still
wet, but not sticky. Add more bean liquid or cornmeal as needed.

Divide the dough into six equal portions. Then, using your hands,
shape the dumplings into palm-size patties, about ½ inch thick. When
the water in the pot reaches a boil, drop them in. Agitate the dumplings
slightly to keep them from sticking to the bottom of the pot, then let
them cook for 10 to 15 minutes, until they float to the top.

While the dumplings cook, put the fatback in a cast-iron skillet
over medium-high heat. Cook until the pieces are golden, turning
occasionally, about 8 minutes. Remove the fatback to paper towels to
drain, and pour the rendered fat into a bowl. When the dumplings are
ready, remove from pan with a spider or slotted spoon, and allow them
to drain slightly. Serve each one topped with a piece of crispy fatback
and a hearty drizzle of rendered fat. Season the leftover pinto beans
with salt and serve them alongside the dumplings.

CLASSIC BUTTERMILK BISCUITS

MAKES 6 TO 8 BISCUITS,

depending on the size of your cutter

IF YOU ONLY BAKE BISCUITS ONCE OR TWICE A YEAR FOR SPECIAL OCCASIONS, the results may turn out fine, but chances are they won't quite reach the pinnacle of the form: light, fluffy biscuits like so many Southern mothers and grandmothers made 365 days a year for a lifetime. Making great biscuits isn't rocket science, but it requires a certain finesse.

This recipe, distilled from dozens of handwritten recipes and stove-side sessions, doesn't call for any fussy techniques like rolling and folding multiple times, or weird secret ingredients like sour cream. It does rely on a few tried-and-true Southern staples: a mix of butter (for flavor) and lard (for puff); tangy buttermilk; and extra-fine soft winter wheat flour. Beyond that is where the experience and skill of the baker comes in. Two things to keep in mind:

1. Be flexible when adding the buttermilk. If it's a humid or rainy day, there's already moisture in the air (and therefore in your flour), so your dough may need a little less liquid to come together. On a cool, dry winter day, it may need more. Make a well in the center of the dry ingredients (which you've sifted, so the baking powder is thoroughly distributed), slowly pour in the buttermilk, stirring all the while, until the dough just comes together.

2. Don't overwork the dough or touch it too much with your warm hands, which can cause the butter and lard to start to melt. You want those little chunks of fat to melt in the oven, releasing steam and reacting with the baking soda to form bubbles of carbon dioxide, which help the biscuits rise to light and airy perfection. (Okay, so there is *some* science involved.) RECIPE FOLLOWS ▶

INGREDIENTS

- 2 cups all-purpose flour
- 4 teaspoons baking powder
- ¼ teaspoon baking soda
- 1 teaspoon kosher salt
- 1 teaspoon sugar
- 2 tablespoons cold unsalted butter, cut into small pieces, plus melted butter for brushing
- 2 tablespoons cold lard, cut into small pieces
- ¾ to 1 cup cold whole buttermilk (¾ cup on a rainy day; 1 cup on a clear, dry day)

PREPARATION

Preheat the oven to 450°F.

Sift the flour, baking powder, baking soda, salt, and sugar together into a large bowl. Blend the butter and lard into the flour using a pastry blender, two knives, or two forks until the mixture resembles coarse meal with fine flakes of butter and lard dispersed throughout. Make a well in the center of the flour mixture, then slowly pour in the buttermilk, stirring until a dough forms (if this happens with ¾ cup, stop; if not, keep slowly adding buttermilk until the dough forms).

Turn the dough out onto a floured pastry cloth or work surface. Roll or pat the dough out to ½ inch thick and, using a biscuit cutter, cut out as many rounds as possible. Gather leftover dough and roll it out again to get several more biscuits. Transfer to a baking sheet, arranging biscuits on the pan so that each one just touches its neighbor; they'll "climb" each other as they bake. Bake for 10 to 12 minutes, until the biscuits have risen and the tops have begun to brown. Remove from the oven and brush the tops with melted butter. Serve warm.

THE ABCs OF SOUTHERN BISCUITS

ANGEL BISCUITS:
Made extra moist and light by adding yeast to the mix. Some recipes also substitute heavy cream for buttermilk, which may render butter or lard unnecessary. Either addition (or both) makes for a soft, tender biscuit that's more like a dinner roll—a heavenly dinner roll.

BEATEN BISCUITS:
In the days before leavening ingredients like baking powder became common, biscuits were beaten—first by hand, then by contraptions specially built for the purpose—for 30 to 45 minutes to incorporate air into the batter so the biscuits would rise. Even so, a beaten biscuit is not a fluffy biscuit. They're thin and crisp.

CATHEAD BISCUITS:
Extra-large, often domed biscuits that are roughly the size of a cat's noggin. Catheads may be baked in a cast-iron skillet or round baking pan, with scoops of dough (rather than neatly rolled and cut) nestled together; when done, each biscuit will break apart from its neighbor. Sometimes they're also made more savory than traditional biscuits, topped with a pat of butter and pinch of salt before baking.

SAUSAGE-STUFFED KOLACHE

MAKES 24 KOLACHES

SINCE CZECH IMMIGRANTS FIRST BROUGHT KOLACHES TO TEXAS IN THE nineteenth century, everything from fried potatoes to venison has been tucked into the breakfast pastry's pillowy embrace. The sausage kolache, in particular, is a uniquely Texan creation. It comes from Wendel and Georgia Montgomery's Village Bakery, founded in 1952 in the Texas town of West. Wendel saw the traditional Czech pastry as a vehicle for capitalizing on Americans' love of hot dogs. He even trademarked his creation as a *klobasniki*, which means "little sausage." So while anyone can sell a sausage kolache, only Village Bakery can sell the original klobasniki. We've taken Wendel's stroke of inspiration a step further by stuffing the pastry with a spicy mix of crumbled breakfast sausage, jalapeño, and pepper Jack cheese so there's a bit of savory filling in every bite.

INGREDIENTS

FOR THE FILLING

- 2 tablespoons unsalted butter
- 1 onion, diced (about 1 cup)
- 2 jalapeños, seeded and minced
- 1 pound pork breakfast sausage, cooked and crumbled
- 1 teaspoon freshly ground black pepper
- 2 cups shredded pepper Jack cheese

FOR THE DOUGH

- 1 tablespoon plus 1 cup warm milk (103 to 110°F)
- 1 teaspoon plus 6 tablespoons sugar
- 2 envelopes (4½ teaspoons) active dry yeast
- 14 tablespoons unsalted butter, melted, plus 1 tablespoon for the bowl
- 3 large egg yolks
- 4 cups all-purpose flour, sifted
- ½ teaspoon kosher salt

PREPARATION

FOR THE FILLING Melt the butter in a large cast-iron skillet over medium heat. Add the onion and jalapeños and cook until softened, about 3 minutes. Add the sausage and cook until browned, about 5 minutes. Add the black pepper. Transfer the mixture to a paper towel–lined plate to drain and cool for 5 minutes. In a medium bowl, combine the cooled sausage mixture with the cheese; set aside.

FOR THE DOUGH In a 4-cup liquid measuring cup, whisk the warm milk and 1 teaspoon sugar together. (The milk needs to be warm—103 to 110°F—but not so hot that it kills the yeast. Check the temperature with a kitchen thermometer.) Add the yeast and stir until dissolved. Let the yeast sit until foamy, about 10 minutes. Whisk 12 tablespoons of the melted butter and the egg yolks into the yeast mixture.

In the bowl of a stand mixer, whisk the flour, the remaining 6 tablespoons sugar, and the salt together. Fit the stand mixer with the dough hook; gradually add the yeast mixture to the flour mixture and mix on low speed until no dry flour remains, about 1 minute. Increase the speed to medium and knead until a dough forms in the bowl but still sticks to the bottom, 2 to 3 minutes (the dough should be smooth and glossy).

Transfer the dough to a lightly buttered mixing bowl, turning it to butter all sides. Cover the bowl and let the dough rise in a warm spot until it has doubled in size, about 1 hour.

RECIPE CONTINUES ▶

FOR THE MUSTARD DRIZZLE

¼ cup Dijon mustard

1 tablespoon honey

ASSEMBLE THE KOLACHES Preheat the oven to 350°F. Line two rimmed baking sheets with parchment paper.

Punch down the dough and divide it into four equal portions. Place each piece of dough on a lightly floured counter and knead for 1 minute, until uniform and not sticking. Shape 6 dough balls of equal size from each quarter. Flatten the dough balls with your hand, shaping them into disks 2 to 3 inches wide. Place 2 to 3 tablespoons of the sausage mixture in the center of each and wrap the edges around, sealing the dough with your fingers and forming a small ball. Place the stuffed rolls seam-side down on the prepared baking sheets. Continue until all the dough and filling have been used. Cover the rolls with a clean towel and let rise in a warm spot for about 20 minutes.

Brush the rolls with the remaining 2 tablespoons melted butter and bake until golden brown, 20 to 25 minutes. Transfer to a wire rack.

FOR THE MUSTARD DRIZZLE Combine the mustard and honey in a microwave-safe bowl. Microwave for about 15 seconds, then drizzle on the baked kolache or serve on the side.

ORANGE ROLLS

MAKES 24 ROLLS

IN CULLMAN, ALABAMA, THE ALL STEAK RESTAURANT HAS BEEN LURING travelers with the promise of world-famous orange rolls—a citrusy-sweet take on cinnamon breakfast rolls—since before Interstate 65 cut a swath west of town. All Steak's current owner, Matt Heim, keeps the recipe close to the vest, although he'll be happy to package a dozen to go. Since Alabama's other iconic purveyor, Sister Schubert, recently discontinued her frozen, ready-to-bake version, we applied some ingenuity to re-interpret these puffy little pinwheels for home cooks. Nothing succeeds like excess, so we went for orange in every step: tender yeasty dough sweetened with juice, buttery filling flecked with zest, and tangy marmalade stirred into the glaze.

INGREDIENTS

FOR THE DOUGH

- 1⅓ cups warm water (103 to 110°F)
- ¼ cup sugar
- 1½ teaspoons active dry yeast
- 2 tablespoons unsalted butter, melted
- 2 tablespoons vegetable shortening, melted
- 1 tablespoon freshly squeezed orange juice
- 1 teaspoon freshly squeezed lemon juice
- 1 large egg
- 1 teaspoon kosher salt
- 4 cups all-purpose flour

FOR THE FILLING

- ½ cup sugar
- 2 tablespoons orange zest
- 4 tablespoons (½ stick) unsalted butter, melted

FOR THE GLAZE

- 1 cup confectioners' sugar
- ¼ cup orange marmalade
- 2 tablespoons freshly squeezed orange juice

PREPARATION

Preheat the oven to 400°F. Place paper muffin liners on two baking sheets. Spray the liners with cooking spray.

FOR THE DOUGH In the bowl of a stand mixer fitted with the whisk attachment, combine the warm water, sugar, and yeast. (The water needs to be warm—103 to 110°F—but not so hot it kills the yeast. Check the temperature with a kitchen thermometer.) Let the mixture sit until foamy, about 10 minutes. Whisk the melted butter and shortening, the orange juice, lemon juice, egg, and salt into the yeast mixture until combined. Gradually add the flour and mix until just combined. Change the whisk attachment to the dough hook and knead on medium speed until a smooth dough forms, about 7 minutes (the dough will be sticky).

FOR THE FILLING Combine the sugar and zest in a small bowl; set aside.

Turn the dough out onto a heavily floured surface. Divide the dough in half. Roll one piece of dough into a 20-by-12-inch rectangle about ¼ inch thick. Brush the dough with 2 tablespoons of the melted butter and sprinkle evenly with half of the sugar mixture. Using a pizza wheel or knife, cut the dough into 1½-inch strips. Tightly roll the strips and place them in the prepared muffin liners. Repeat with the remaining dough, butter, and sugar mixture. (If the spiral forms a cone, press the middle of the roll to flatten it.) Cover the rolls with a clean towel and let rise in warm spot for about 30 minutes.

FOR THE GLAZE Whisk together the confectioners' sugar, marmalade, and orange juice in a medium bowl; set aside.

Position a rack in the center of the oven and preheat the oven to 400°F. Bake the rolls until golden brown, 12 to 16 minutes. Brush the hot rolls with the glaze. Serve.

8

CONDIMENTS,
SAUCES,
&
SPREADS

WELL DRESSED

Thanks to an abundance of condiments, Southern dishes
are always in good company

JOHN T. EDGE

WHEN I READ A MENU, I LOOK FOR CONDIMENTS. Promise me smoked chicken swabbed with Cheerwine barbecue sauce and you earn my fidelity. Tell me that the coins of fried okra come with a bullet of buttermilk ranch for dunking, and I order two baskets. My perfect pork chop has a pink core and arrives in a puddle of sage pan sauce. Serve me a flute of fries and I'll stir a dipping sauce from mayo, mustard, and three hits of Tabasco.

Gravy is just sauce by another name. From sawmill to red-eye, Southerners sop up the stuff. When I sit for breakfast, I cap over-easy eggs with tomato gravy. Buttermilk biscuits taste better drenched in sawmill gravy. Swamped in chocolate gravy, which is to say chocolate sauce, biscuits are a countrified dessert worthy of my mother's damask.

My mother believed that black-eyed peas were naked without chowchow. She thought collards weren't worth their weight in cornbread without the vinegary bite that condiment delivered. As is the case with many things, including the virtues of a well-shined pair of shoes, I've realized, many years later, she was right.

I came to condiments in my Georgia youth, when I learned to cook steaks from my father, who marinated rib eyes in Dale's, that vaguely Asian soy-based sauce from Alabama, and served them charcoal-singed from the embers and dolloped with butter. Since moving to Mississippi, I've learned to rely on Hoover Sauce, a thicker and sweeter take on the same formula, made in the Delta town of Louise and favored by hunters who swear by its effects on venison haunches.

The South does hot sauce well. Tabasco, which harvests its salt from a Louisiana dome and ferments a sauce that tastes like distilled Cajun sunshine, is our most storied artisanal good. Up in North Carolina, a tray of Piedmont-style pork, hacked into smoky nubs, tastes best when drizzled with Texas Pete, a sauce conceived and produced in North Carolina, sold with an incongruent lasso-wielding cowboy on the label.

Barbecue sauce is contentious. "It's all about the sauce, all about the sweet cover," a Memphis pitmaster once told me. "Sauce is a plaything," a pitmaster in Texas once said when I dared suggest his brisket might benefit from a douse. In South Carolina, the styles of sauce, from sweet and mustardy to thin and vinegary, are so divergent that a geographer once color-coded a map of the state to illustrate the balkanizations.

My favorite Arkansas sauce, from Craig's in De Valls Bluff, contains lemon and apple leavings from making pies, and pork drippings collected from the pit. I can still recall the first time I ordered a chicken plate in Alabama and the bird arrived stippled with mayonnaise-based white sauce, thinned with vinegar and pocked with black pepper. At home now in Mississippi, I make my own Georgia-style sauce by adding a pinch of sugar and a drift of red pepper flakes to a pint of apple cider vinegar.

Not long after I moved to Oxford, I went rummaging through the cupboard at Rowan Oak, William Faulkner's columned home just a few blocks south of my own. In addition to a few tins of sage, two bottles of filé, enough cloves to perfume the Caribbean, and enough dry mustard to devil the detritus from three hams, I spied a bottle of Escoffier-brand Sauce Diable, thick with tomatoes, tamarinds, dates, mangoes, and raisins. I've never come across a bottle of the stuff since. Alecia's Tomato Chutney, made in Alabama, is the closest modern analog. Made from tomatoes, sugar, vinegar, ginger, and raisins, it's as elemental and honest a condiment as you can source. Following the lead of Frank Stitt of Highlands Bar and Grill in Birmingham,

I now use that ferrous and funky stuff for a salad dressing base.

I develop many of my condiment crushes on the road. Traveling Kentucky, I learned that, if cathead biscuits taste better with a swirl of sorghum and butter, then so do hamburgers. Down in Florida, especially in St. Augustine, datil peppers, born of Minorcan migration, are the heat of choice. Locals dip fried shrimp in a pink sauce made from mixing tartar with datil. After a week of eating in those parts, I did too.

Mississippi has been my home now for twenty years. My assimilation takes many forms. When the University of Georgia plays the University of Mississippi in football, I no longer root for the Bulldogs. And when talk turns to most-favored condiments, I now reach for comeback, a kind of country-boy rémoulade.

Comeback was popularized by Greek-Southern restaurants in the 1930s, like the Mayflower in Jackson. Here in Oxford it's customary to drizzle comeback on salads or dip fries in bowls of the stuff. More recently, I've learned you can trowel comeback on a cracker and eat the combo as a canapé. In the recipe on page 237, Adam Evans, chef of the Optimist in Atlanta, adds diced celery to the usual mix before his comeback hits the blender. One try of his recipe later, I can tell you that the extra body gained has no adverse effect on cracker cling.

BARBECUE SAUCES

Southerners can agree about lots of things: a cast-iron skillet is the most versatile kitchen tool ever invented, SEC football (period), and thank-you notes, always handwritten. Barbecue sauce, however, isn't one of those things. Loyalties largely break down by region, and countless words have been written and fights waged over what kind of sauce reigns supreme. Is it the thin, vinegary sauce that slices like a cleaver through luscious pork pulled from a whole hog across eastern North Carolina? The brown sugar–sweet, thick tomato-y gravy draped across spice-rubbed shoulder meat in Memphis? The mustard-based tradition in South Carolina? Alabama's peculiar though awfully tasty white sauce? The debate rages on. And that's the beauty, really. Barbecue sauce is personal, and everyone has a favorite style. The only way to pick a winner is to try them all yourself.

MEMPHIS-STYLE TOMATO BARBECUE SAUCE

MAKES ABOUT 2 CUPS

MEMPHIS-STYLE IS CLOSEST TO WHAT MOST FOLKS OUTSIDE OF THE SOUTH think of as barbecue sauce. This simple stir-together version gets a little extra kick—but not too much—by cutting the ketchup with chili sauce.

INGREDIENTS

- 1 cup ketchup
- 1 cup Heinz chili sauce (about half of a 12-ounce bottle)
- ⅓ cup apple cider vinegar
- 1 to 2 tablespoons hot sauce, such as Frank's Red Hot or Tabasco
- 1 tablespoon tomato paste
- 1 tablespoon chili powder
- 1 teaspoon Colman's dry mustard
- 3 garlic cloves, minced to a paste
- 2 tablespoons finely grated white onion with juice
- 2 tablespoons packed dark brown sugar
- ½ teaspoon liquid smoke, or 1 tablespoon smoked paprika

PREPARATION

Combine all the ingredients in a saucepan over medium-high heat. Bring to a boil, stirring often, then reduce the heat to low. Simmer for 20 minutes. Serve immediately. Let any remaining sauce cool to room temperature and store in an airtight container, refrigerated, for up to 1 week. To serve again, reheat by microwaving for 30 seconds to 1 minute.

TEXAS-STYLE BEEF BARBECUE SAUCE

MAKES 2 CUPS

MORE THAN ANYWHERE ELSE, LONE STAR STATE BARBECUE IS ABOUT THE meat itself. So it comes as little surprise that barbecue sauce, if it's used at all, starts with the rich, intensely smoky meat drippings that slowly ooze out of briskets set to smoke over many a soot-crusted Central Texas pit. This recipe fudges just a bit; bacon grease from the smokiest bacon you can find and a pinch of cumin supply the smolder. Although if you have a vat of meat drippings standing by, sauté the onion in a bit of bacon grease or neutral oil, such as canola, and then use the drippings in place of the beef stock for an even thicker, richer sauce.

INGREDIENTS

- 2 tablespoons bacon grease, or 2 thick-cut smoked bacon slices, such as Tennessee-made Benton's, minced
- ½ cup minced onion
- ½ teaspoon ground cumin
- ¼ teaspoon cayenne pepper
- ½ cup cider vinegar
- 1 cup beef stock
- 1 cup ketchup
- 1 tablespoon hot sauce
- ½ teaspoon kosher salt
- ½ teaspoon freshly ground black pepper

PREPARATION

Melt the bacon grease in a cast-iron skillet over medium heat. If starting with whole bacon slices, put the minced bacon in the skillet and cook over medium heat, stirring occasionally, for 5 to 6 minutes, until the fat is rendered and the bacon is browned; remove the crisped bacon from the pan and reserve for another use.

Add the onion, cumin, and cayenne to the bacon grease and continue to cook until the onion is softened, about 3 minutes. Add the vinegar and stock and increase the heat to high to bring to a boil. Stir in the ketchup and hot sauce, then reduce the heat to medium-low, add the salt and black pepper, and simmer uncovered for 30 minutes, stirring occasionally. Serve immediately.

Let any remaining sauce cool to room temperature, then store in an airtight container, refrigerated, for up to 1 week. To serve again, reheat by microwaving for 30 seconds to 1 minute.

EASTERN NORTH CAROLINA–STYLE VINEGAR-PEPPER SAUCE

MAKES 2 CUPS

JUST FOUR SIMPLE INGREDIENTS—VINEGAR, SALT, BLACK PEPPER, AND CRUSHED red—produce a tart, spicy liquid contrast to smoky, fat-basted pork. Blending in a small amount of cider vinegar adds a hint of sweetness. For the light-tomato version of this sauce that dominates once you cross into western North Carolina, replace the apple cider vinegar with ketchup and whisk in 1 tablespoon tomato paste.

INGREDIENTS

- 1½ cups distilled white vinegar
- ½ cup cider vinegar
- ½ teaspoon kosher salt
- ½ teaspoon freshly ground black pepper
- 1 to 2 tablespoons red pepper flakes, depending on desired heat level

PREPARATION

Put the vinegars in a microwave-safe bowl and warm for 30 seconds. Add the remaining ingredients, stir to dissolve the salt, and pour the mixture into a jar. Set aside for at least 1 day to let the flavors fully meld, then serve.

Store any remaining sauce in an airtight container at room temperature for up to 2 weeks. Shake well before using.

SOUTH CAROLINA–STYLE MUSTARD BARBECUE SAUCE

MAKES ABOUT 2 CUPS

BORN OF FLAVORS BROUGHT TO THE STATE BY GERMAN IMMIGRANTS, traditional South Carolina mustard-based sauces start with plain yellow mustard. No need to get high falutin' with Dijon.

INGREDIENTS

- 1 teaspoon vegetable oil
- 1 tablespoon grated white onion
- 2 garlic cloves, minced
- 1 cup yellow mustard
- ½ cup apple cider vinegar
- ¼ cup honey
- 2 tablespoons dark brown sugar
- 1 teaspoon Worcestershire sauce
- 1 teaspoon freshly squeezed lemon juice
- 1 teaspoon freshly ground black pepper
- 1 teaspoon red pepper flakes
- ½ teaspoon celery seeds
- 1 teaspoon hot sauce

PREPARATION

Place a saucepan over medium heat and add the oil. Add the onion and garlic and sauté for 2 minutes, stirring frequently. Whisk in the remaining ingredients, stirring well to combine. Cook over medium heat until bubbles break the surface. Reduce the heat to low and simmer for 10 minutes. Serve immediately.

Let any remaining sauce cool to room temperature, then store in an airtight container, refrigerated, for up to 2 weeks. To serve again, reheat by microwaving for 30 seconds to 1 minute.

ALABAMA-STYLE WHITE BARBECUE SAUCE

MAKES ABOUT 2 CUPS

MAYONNAISE ADDS SILKINESS TO THIS SURPRISINGLY LIGHT SAUCE THAT is a Decatur, Alabama, original, created in 1925 by barbecue master Big Bob Gibson as a condiment for his hickory-smoked chicken. If you like it peppery, add more black pepper. If you like heat, boost the cayenne.

INGREDIENTS

- 1 (15-ounce) jar mayonnaise (about 1½ cups)
- ¼ cup distilled white vinegar
- 1 tablespoon apple juice
  Juice of ½ lemon
- 2 teaspoons freshly ground black pepper
- 2 teaspoons prepared horseradish
- ¼ teaspoon kosher salt
- ¼ teaspoon cayenne pepper

PREPARATION

Combine all the ingredients in a bowl and whisk well to combine, then serve.

Store any remaining sauce in an airtight container, refrigerated, for up to 1 week. Stir before serving.

CREAMY MAYONNAISE SAUCES

COMEBACK SAUCE

MAKES ABOUT 3 CUPS

FIRST STIRRED UP IN A GREEK RESTAURANT IN JACKSON IN THE 1930s, THIS sauce kept folks "coming back" from all over Mississippi and beyond. It falls somewhere between a classic white Creole rémoulade and McDonald's secret sauce. This version, created by Alabama-born chef Adam Evans to pair with his Salt-Baked Shrimp (page 19), gets base and body from celery, which gives it a cool crispness that also pairs perfectly with fried foods.

INGREDIENTS

- 1 cup mayonnaise
- 2 tablespoons grated fresh or jarred horseradish
- 2 tablespoons grainy mustard
- 5 celery stalks, diced
- 1 tablespoon diced shallot
- Juice and grated zest of ½ lemon
- 1 garlic clove, minced
- 2 tablespoons chopped fresh parsley
- 2 tablespoons chopped cornichons
- 1 tablespoon capers, drained
- ¾ teaspoon kosher salt
- ¾ teaspoon freshly ground black pepper
- ¾ teaspoon cayenne pepper

PREPARATION

Combine all the ingredients in a blender or food processor and pulse until the mixture is incorporated. Set aside for 15 minutes to allow the flavors to meld, then serve.

Store any remaining sauce in an airtight container, refrigerated, for up to 1 week. Stir before serving.

WHITE CREOLE RÉMOULADE

EVEN THOUGH IT'S TECHNICALLY A LITTLE MORE BLUSH-COLORED THAN white, this version of Creole rémoulade gets its name from its primary ingredient: mayonnaise. Like Creole culture, this sauce's flavor profile is a mix—creamy, spicy, sweet, tart, and briny—which is why you can douse anything from steamed shrimp to fried green tomatoes with it.

INGREDIENTS

- 1 cup mayonnaise
- ¼ cup finely diced gherkins
- 3 tablespoons freshly squeezed lemon juice
- 3 tablespoons chili sauce
- 2 tablespoons Creole mustard
- 1 tablespoon capers, drained, rinsed, and chopped
- 1 small garlic clove, minced
- 1 teaspoon Tabasco sauce
- ½ teaspoon Worcestershire sauce
- ¼ teaspoon paprika
- ¼ teaspoon cayenne pepper
- 3 tablespoons finely chopped fresh parsley
- Kosher salt and freshly ground black pepper to taste

PREPARATION

Combine all the ingredients in a large bowl and set aside for 15 minutes to allow the flavors to meld, then serve.

Store any remaining sauce in an airtight container, refrigerated, for up to 1 week. Stir before serving.

TARTAR SAUCE

TARTAR SAUCE ORIGINATED WITH THE FRENCH TO PAIR WITH SLIMY RAW beef (i.e., tartare), but it wasn't long before Southerners discovered that the creamy, briny condiment made a great pairing with crisp fried seafood and began tweaking it accordingly, adding sweet (pickle relish) and heat (hot sauce) to the Gallic base of mayo and Dijon.

INGREDIENTS

- ¾ cup mayonnaise
- 1½ teaspoons Dijon mustard
- Juice of ½ small lemon
- 1 medium shallot, minced
- 1 teaspoon Tabasco sauce
- 1 tablespoon capers, drained, rinsed, and roughly chopped
- 1 tablespoon sweet pickle relish
- Kosher salt and freshly ground black pepper to taste

PREPARATION

Combine all the ingredients in a large bowl, then serve.

Store any remaining sauce in an airtight container, refrigerated, for up to 1 week. Stir before serving.

BLACK PEPPER RANCH DRESSING

MEET YOUR NEW FAVORITE RANCH. THIS IS THE VERSION THAT CHEF JESSE Houston, of Saltine restaurant in Jackson, Mississippi, uses to tame his rendition of Nashville-hot fried birds—usually Cornish hens or quail. The refreshingly herbal concoction also makes a perfect dip for vegetables or chicken wings.

INGREDIENTS

- ½ cup buttermilk
- ½ cup sour cream
- ½ cup mayonnaise
- ½ tablespoon minced fresh parsley
- 1¼ teaspoons minced fresh chives
- 1 teaspoon minced fresh dill
- 2 teaspoons freshly squeezed lemon juice
- ½ teaspoon onion powder
- ¼ teaspoon granulated garlic
- ½ teaspoon kosher salt
- ¾ teaspoon freshly ground black pepper

PREPARATION

Whisk all the ingredients together in a mixing bowl until smooth, then serve.

Store any remaining sauce in an airtight container, refrigerated, for up to 3 days. Stir before serving.

SAVORY SAUCES & SPREADS

CHEERWINE ONION MARMALADE

MAKES ABOUT 2 CUPS

IT'S AMAZING HOW A LITTLE TIME AND HEAT CAN TURN AN ORDINARY ONION into an irresistible delicacy. Use a Vidalia, and you're already a step ahead. The onion's natural sweetness intensifies as its sharpness evaporates away. Cheerwine—a soda with North Carolina roots a hundred years deep—adds a signature cherry flavor. You only need half a 12-ounce bottle for this recipe; sip the rest while the onions do their thing. Once caramelized, they're amazingly adaptable—use this marmalade to top vegetable dishes (like the Not-Quite-So-Cooked-to-Death Green Beans on page 154), spread on a pizza, or tuck into sandwiches.

INGREDIENTS

3 tablespoons unsalted butter

4 large Vidalia onions, thinly sliced

6 ounces Cheerwine or cherry-flavored Dr. Pepper

1 tablespoon sherry vinegar

2 teaspoons kosher salt

PREPARATION

Melt the butter in a large cast-iron skillet over medium heat. When foamy, after about 2 minutes, add the onions and toss to coat; reduce the heat to low and cook for 30 minutes, stirring frequently, until the onions are soft and golden vanilla in color (they should not become crispy or browned). Add the Cheerwine and increase the heat to medium. Cook, stirring frequently, until most of the liquid has reduced to syrup and the onions are meltingly soft, about 15 minutes. Stir in the vinegar and salt. Serve immediately.

Let any remaining marmalade cool, then store in an airtight container, refrigerated, for up to 1 week.

SAVORY CREOLE TOMATO JAM

MAKES 2 CUPS

THIS CHUNKY JAM FROM CHEF TORY McPHAIL OF COMMANDER'S PALACE, in New Orleans, is especially good slathered over grilled chicken, though you can also use it with other meats. Or pour it over a block of cream cheese for a super-simple party spread. The recipe calls for a whole *head* of garlic, not just one clove. (Creole varieties, if you can find them, have a high sugar content.) Go lighter if you like, but the long simmer will blunt its bite.

INGREDIENTS

- ½ teaspoon vegetable oil
- 1 head of garlic, cloves peeled and sliced
- 1 Vidalia onion, thinly sliced
- 3 large tomatoes, peeled, cored, and coarsely chopped
- 2½ teaspoons kosher salt
- ½ teaspoon freshly ground black pepper
- ½ teaspoon cayenne pepper
- 1 cup dark brown sugar
- 2 teaspoons Crystal hot sauce
- 2 teaspoons Worcestershire sauce
- Juice of 1 lemon

PREPARATION

Place a Dutch oven over medium heat and add the oil. Add the onion and cook, stirring occasionally, until softened, 4 to 6 minutes. Add the garlic and cook, stirring, until fragrant, about 1 minute. Add the remaining ingredients and stir to combine. Reduce the heat to low and simmer uncovered, stirring occasionally, for 2 to 3 hours, until the jam is dark and thick. Serve immediately or let cool to room temperature. (It's excellent either way.)

Let any remaining jam cool, then store in an airtight container, refrigerated, for up to 1 week. To serve again, reheat by microwaving for 30 seconds to 1 minute.

MUSCADINE MOSTARDA

MAKES 1 CUP

MOSTARDA IS AN ITALIAN CONDIMENT MADE FROM FRUIT, VINEGAR, SUGAR, mustard, and spices, typically served with cheeses and meats. Old World meets new South when muscadine grapes are prepared this way. The jammy texture of the sweet-and-sour concoction comes from the muscadine skins and pulp, both of which are loaded with pectin that thickens the mixture. Spread it on hot ham biscuits, serve with a log of fresh goat cheese and crackers, or use as a garnish on grilled meats.

INGREDIENTS

- 1 quart (1½ pounds) muscadines, halved
- ¼ cup apple cider vinegar
- ¼ cup sugar
- 1 tablespoon yellow mustard seeds
- ½ teaspoon kosher salt
- ¼ teaspoon cayenne pepper
- 2 teaspoons Dijon mustard
  Juice of ½ lemon

PREPARATION

Squeeze the muscadine pulp from each grape half into a small saucepan. Put the skins in a second small saucepan. Set each pan over medium heat and when the pulp begins to simmer, reduce the heat beneath both pans to low. Cover and cook the skins and pulp, stirring occasionally, for about 15 minutes, until the skins are soft and have given up some moisture and pulp is syrupy and seeds have separated from the flesh.

Push the pulp through a fine-mesh sieve, pressing the solids with the back of a spoon, into the saucepan with the skins. Stir in the vinegar, sugar, mustard seeds, salt, and cayenne and continue to cook, covered, over low heat for 8 to 10 minutes more. Transfer the mixture to a blender with the mustard and lemon juice. Blend until smooth. Pour into a bowl and let cool to room temperature. Serve at room temperature.

Store any remaining mostarda in an airtight container, refrigerated, for up to 1 week.

PEACH-TOMATO SALSA

MAKES 2 CUPS

SOME MIGHT ARGUE THAT THE ONLY FRUIT MORE PERFECT THAN A RIPE peach is a ripe tomato (which, yes, is a fruit). With this Southern-infused salsa everybody wins. Adjust the heat level with yet another fruit, the jalapeño—seed it completely for mild, or halfway for more kick. Same with the lime. Squeeze half into the salsa mix, then taste for acidity, adding more juice if desired. Then bring on the tortilla chips or spoon the salsa onto anything from grilled fish to chicken, tacos to quesadillas.

INGREDIENTS

2   ripe peaches, peeled and diced

2   ripe tomatoes, seeded and diced

½   small Vidalia onion, diced

¼   cup chopped fresh cilantro

1   small jalapeño, seeded (if desired) and minced

  Juice of ½ lime

  Grated zest of ½ lime

1   teaspoon kosher salt

1   teaspoon freshly ground black pepper

PREPARATION

Toss all the ingredients together in a large bowl, mixing well to thoroughly combine. Serve immediately.

Store any remaining salsa in an airtight container, refrigerated, for up to 3 days.

CHUNKY SWEET ONION JEZEBEL SAUCE

MAKES 1 CUP

THIS COMMUNITY COOKBOOK STAPLE DELIVERS A MUCH HAPPIER ENDING than its biblical namesake to whatever grilled or roasted meats you choose to pair with it. The charred Vidalia onion lends a sweet and smoky flavor to this versatile sauce, and is balanced with a little spice from the horseradish and mustard, plus bright notes of citrus that keep it well out of cloying territory.

INGREDIENTS

- 1   small Vidalia onion
- 1   teaspoon vegetable oil
- 3   tablespoons grainy mustard
- 3   tablespoons prepared horseradish, drained
- ¼   cup apple jelly
- ¼   cup pineapple preserves
- ½   teaspoon grated lemon zest
- 1   teaspoon freshly squeezed lemon juice

PREPARATION

Trim the ends from the onion and cut into 4 rounds about ½ inch thick. Remove the skins. Place a large cast-iron skillet over high heat and add the oil. Add the onion slices and cook for 3 to 5 minutes per side, until well charred and soft.

Transfer the onion slices to a cutting board and finely chop. Put in a mixing bowl with the mustard, horseradish, apple jelly, pineapple preserves, lemon zest, and lemon juice, stirring well to combine. Let cool to room temperature. Cover and refrigerate overnight to allow the flavors to meld. Serve at room temperature.

Store any remaining sauce in an airtight container, refrigerated, for up to 1 week.

COLLARD PESTO

MAKES 1½ CUPS

WINTER GREENS LIKE COLLARDS, MUSTARD, KALE, OR CHARD MAKE HEARTY substitutes for summer basil in this easy no-cook pesto, replacing the herb's anise flavors with stronger mustardy tones. It's a natural, of course, for pasta, but its earthy accent also lends itself well to roasted meats, as a base for pizzas, or as a sandwich spread.

INGREDIENTS

- ⅓ cup toasted pecan halves
- 1 to 2 garlic cloves, peeled
- About 1 cup good-quality extra-virgin olive oil, such as Georgia Olive Farms
- ½ cup freshly grated Parmesan cheese
- ½ teaspoon grated lemon zest
- 1 tablespoon freshly squeezed lemon juice
- 3 cups stemmed and chopped collard greens
- ½ teaspoon kosher salt, or more to taste
- ¼ teaspoon freshly ground black pepper, or more to taste

PREPARATION

In a blender or food processor, combine the pecans, garlic, ¼ cup of the oil, the cheese, lemon zest, and lemon juice and blend or pulse several times to combine. Add the greens a handful at a time and blend or pulse to combine. Slowly pour in the remaining ¾ cup oil, with the motor running, until the pesto reaches the desired consistency. Add the salt and pepper, adjusting the seasoning if desired, pulsing one final time to combine. Serve immediately.

Store any remaining pesto in an airtight container, refrigerated, for up to 1 week or freeze for up to 6 months. Before sealing the container, pour a thin layer of olive oil on top of the pesto to prevent discoloration.

SWEET SAUCES & SPREADS

BOURBON CARAMEL SAUCE

MAKES ABOUT 1 CUP

SUGAR IS INTEGRAL TO DISTILLING: IT'S WHAT CREATES THE ALCOHOL.
So it's only natural that the end result of the process shows up at dessert. Here, a touch of bourbon lights up the richest, smoothest caramel sauce you've ever tasted, courtesy of pastry chef Eric Wolitzky, of Cakes & Ale in Decatur, Georgia. He uses it to top apple dumplings—a perfect pairing. You won't have to think hard to come up with more—drizzle it over ice cream, shortbread, pecan pie, waffles, bacon . . .

INGREDIENTS

½ cup heavy cream
¼ cup sour cream
1 cup sugar
2 tablespoons light corn syrup
2 tablespoons bourbon

PREPARATION

In a small saucepan, whisk together the heavy cream and sour cream. Warm over medium-low heat. In another saucepan, combine the sugar, ¼ cup water, and the corn syrup. Boil, without stirring, until the mixture turns a light amber, about 6 minutes. Remove from the heat and carefully whisk in the bourbon. (The mixture will spatter.) Whisk in cream mixture. Transfer to a serving dish, gravy boat, or pitcher. Let the caramel cool slightly and thicken, then serve.

Store any remaining sauce in an airtight container, refrigerated, for up to 1 week.

BLACKBERRY SAUCE

MAKES 2 CUPS

MAKE THIS SIMPLE SAUCE WITH ANY FRESH BERRIES IN SEASON; THE SAME formula works for dewberries, raspberries, blueberries, even strawberries. A touch of salt and a hint of lemon juice boost both the sweetness and tartness of the fruit. Spoon it over ice cream, sliced pound cake, or even oatmeal at breakfast.

INGREDIENTS

- 2 (12-ounce) packages fresh blackberries
- ⅓ cup sugar
- 1 tablespoon unsalted butter
  Pinch of kosher salt
- 1 teaspoon freshly squeezed lemon juice

PREPARATION

Rinse the blackberries well in a colander. Transfer to a small saucepan with the sugar, butter, and salt and cook over medium heat for 5 minutes, or until the berries release some of their juices, the sugar is dissolved, and the fruit has warmed through. (For a thicker sauce, reduce the heat to low and simmer for 20 minutes, stirring occasionally.) Stir in the lemon juice. Serve warm or pour into a bowl, cover, refrigerate, and serve cool.

Let any remaining sauce cool, then store in an airtight container, refrigerated, for up to 1 week. To serve again, reheat, if desired, by microwaving for 30 seconds to 1 minute.

SORGHUM BUTTER

MAKES 1 CUP

SORGHUM ADDS AN ELEMENT OF COMPLEX SWEETNESS TO THIS HEAVENLY
compound butter, inspired by the kind sometimes found on breakfast tables at Blackberry Farm, a luxury resort in Tennessee's Smoky Mountain foothills. Eat with lots of warm biscuits. Lather it on thick.

INGREDIENTS

- ½ cup sorghum syrup
- 1 cup (2 sticks) unsalted butter, at room temperature

PREPARATION

Stir together. That's it. Serve at room temperature.

Wrap any remaining butter tightly in plastic wrap and store in an air-tight container, refrigerated, for up to 1 week.

SLIGHTLY BOOZY APPLE BUTTER

MAKES 4 CUPS

AT HARVEST TIME THROUGHOUT THE SOUTHERN MOUNTAINS, FAMILIES would gather to make apple butter in large copper kettles over open fires—all-day affairs that helped feed entire communities. For the modern cook making apple butter, the labor is just as rewarding. After nine hours of largely passive stovetop simmering, as more and more liquid evaporates, the butter takes on a rich caramel color, aromatic with cinnamon and nutmeg. It's perfect with biscuits and just as good spread on slices of roast pork, too.

INGREDIENTS

- 4 tablespoons (½ stick) unsalted butter
- 4 pounds assorted apples, peeled, cored, and chopped (8 to 9 medium apples)
- 2 cups unfiltered apple cider
- ¼ cup bourbon, Tennessee whiskey, or spiced rum
- ½ cup molasses
- ½ teaspoon ground cinnamon
- ¼ teaspoon freshly grated nutmeg
- ⅛ teaspoon kosher salt

PREPARATION

In a Dutch oven, melt the butter over medium heat. Add the apples and cook until slightly softened, about 5 minutes. Increase the heat to high and add the cider and liquor; bring to a boil. Reduce the heat to low and simmer, covered, stirring occasionally, until the apples are completely soft and light brown, about 45 minutes. Remove from the heat.

In batches, puree the apples and liquid in a food processor for 1 to 2 minutes, until smooth. Return the puree to the Dutch oven and add the molasses, cinnamon, nutmeg, and salt. Bring to a boil over medium-high heat. Reduce the heat to low and cook, stirring occasionally, until the mixture is thickened and caramel in color, 8 to 9 hours. Let cool to room temperature and store in an airtight container, refrigerated, for up to 2 weeks.

PEANUT BUTTER

MAKES 1½ CUPS

THE FAMOUS SOUTHERN BOTANIST GEORGE WASHINGTON CARVER DIDN'T
invent peanut butter (the Aztecs get credit for that). But from his perch in the agriculture department
of Alabama's Tuskegee University, he certainly put it in the pantheon of favorite Southern foods thanks
to his work promoting peanuts as a crop in the rural South. It's plenty easy (and a lot more rewarding)
to make it yourself.

INGREDIENTS

- 2 cups roasted, lightly salted peanuts (skins removed)
- 1 tablespoon peanut oil
- 2 teaspoons honey, cane syrup, or sorghum syrup
- Kosher salt

PREPARATION

Put the peanuts in a food processor or high-powered blender and process or blend for 1 minute. Scrape down the sides of the bowl with a spatula, then process for 2 minutes more, slowly pouring in the oil and honey. Scrape down the sides of the bowl, then process for 3 minutes more, or until the mixture is smooth. Taste, adding salt (start with ¼ teaspoon) if desired, then process for 1 to 2 minutes more to reach the desired consistency.

Store in an airtight container, refrigerated, for up to 2 weeks.

9

COCKTAILS

WE'LL DRINK TO THAT

A toast to the South's long tradition of imbibing

KATHLEEN PURVIS

WE ARE A DRINKING PEOPLE HERE IN THE SOUTH. We are Bloody Mary brunchers, tailgate tipplers, and business-deal toasters. We are julep sippers and eggnog beaters, punch dippers and flask-packers. We are aficionados of bourbon and tellers of moonshine tales. With full respect for those who don't imbibe for reasons of health, recovery, age, or taste, social occasions here tend to be powered by your higher-octane fuels. As Southern Episcopalians often joke, wherever four of us shall gather, there will always be a fifth.

You can place part of the blame on the historical tradition of Southern hospitality. When the South was a much more sparsely populated place, feeding and welcoming guests and even wayfaring strangers was expected. Bending an elbow hurried conviviality even faster than lifting a fork.

And yes, some of our tendency to give strong spirits a role in daily life may descend from drinking styles that date to the seventeenth and eighteenth centuries. It's startling to realize that many of our forefathers used to drink alcoholic beverages from morning until night, a habit sometimes blamed on lack of access to water they could trust. The book *Travels of Four and a Half Years in the United States of America*, by John Davis, printed in London in 1803, describes a julep as "a dram of spiritous liquor that has mint steeped in it, taken by Virginians of a morning." Good morning to you, too, sir.

There are other reasons, though, for the alcohol that sometimes seems to flow through the South. Geology, history, and commerce all played roles in making this region the headwaters of American spirits.

To put it in perspective, think back to the early years of European settlement. With ports that were easily reached from the Caribbean and the West Indies, rums and Madeiras began arriving early in the colonies, particularly in New Orleans and Savannah, to be dispersed and sold farther north.

Away from the ports, there were vast stretches of wilderness waiting to be tamed and farmed. Despite a skirmish called the Whiskey Rebellion—in which the new American government enforced its first domestic tax on distilled spirits—turning corn and wheat into whiskey was a popular way to earn money in the Southern frontier, especially among settlers who came from Scotland and Ireland, where distilling was common.

Corn grew well all over the South, and it was particularly suited for making into whiskey. Handy, too: dried and ground, corn could be sold as food. But dried, ground, mashed, fermented, and cooked into alcohol, it could be sold for a lot more. That started a pattern in the backwoods of the South that continued into the twentieth century: if you live way back up in the mountains, revenue agents have a hard time keeping you from running a still or taxing what you make with it.

Moving into the mountain regions of North Carolina, Tennessee, and Kentucky, those early distillers discovered something else: very good water. Great slabs of limestone, the foundations on which the mountain ranges of the South stand, act as natural filters for underground water sources. Limestone not only filters out iron and sulphur that would ruin whiskey, it also adds calcium, which has the handy effect of making yeast work better when you're fermenting ground-up corn.

Pretty soon, the mountains of the South were awash in very strong alcohol. The moonshine made in those backwoods stills would certainly take the chill off a predawn morning or hurry you toward sleep on a frosty night. But it was rough stuff. It was drinkable, but tasty could be a debatable point.

Turning that fiery, clear liquid into something that was smooth, rich, and brown took two things: time, and an oak barrel that was charred on the inside. Hang around bourbon distilleries long enough and you'll hear all kinds of tales about how that charred barrel came into the picture, everything from a cheap Scots minister who reused a barrel that had held fish to a cheap Scots minister who had a fire in his barn and used the barrels anyway.

More likely? Much of the whiskey sold in those days was placed in barrels and floated downriver on rafts, to New Orleans. French merchants there were already familiar with cognac, which is aged in oak barrels that are sometimes toasted to control tannins.

It's not a big jump to figure out that if it's good for brandy, it's good for corn whiskey.

Kentucky and Tennessee became known all over the world for beautifully made whiskeys and bourbons, and eventually for cocktails and high-balls made from them.

Skip forward a couple of hundred years—over that buzzkill called Prohibition, over the still-dry counties where it lingers (although most have thriving liquor stores right across their borders)—and what do you find in the South today? A renaissance in Southern distilling, with new whiskeys, rums, brandies, and even gin being made in small batches. Old names in bourbon are being rediscovered and embraced so enthusiastically that shortages are common. The craft beer industries in several states, including Georgia and North Carolina, rival those of Colorado and California for energy and creativity. Wine production has broken out from Texas to Virginia. There's even new interest in old traditions like hard cider.

All of these artisan producers might sound like they're on the cutting edge, but really, they're just new bricks in an old foundation that's been around for a long time. The South has always attracted individuals with stubborn streaks and a belief that they can make whatever they desire, and make it so much better.

One thing we know for sure: gather here long enough and a glass will be raised. What's in it is up to you.

CHARLESTON BROWN WATER SOCIETY PUNCH

SERVES 28

IN CHARLESTON, SOUTH CAROLINA, NEARLY EVERY SOCIAL CLUB OF NOTE has its signature drink—a tradition that dates back at least as far as the late eighteenth century, when the dashing young socialites who called themselves the Light Dragoons paraded through the streets, raising glasses of rum-and-brandy punch. So it's only natural that the Charleston Brown Water Society, a dedicated group of bourbon drinkers and proselytizers, has one too. Roderick Weaver, who mixes drinks at the Bar at Husk, created this punch to serve at society events, where you'll typically find a pitcher tucked among many bottles of bourbon. The punch isn't strictly whiskey-driven. There's a hit of dark rum and a sweet citrusy mix to tame the burn, and it makes for a great sipper at any gathering. Serve it in a punch bowl, and, per Brown Water tradition, be sure to raise a toast to the society after you ladle out the first round.

INGREDIENTS

- 3 cups bourbon, preferably Johnny Drum Private Stock
- 2 cups dark rum, preferably Mount Gay
- 1½ cups freshly squeezed orange juice
- ½ cup freshly squeezed lemon juice
- 2 cups honey simple syrup (1 cup honey dissolved in 1 cup water)
- 2 cups demerara sugar syrup (1 cup demerara sugar dissolved in 1 cup water)
- 3 cups soda water

GARNISH
- Orange slices

PREPARATION

Combine all the ingredients except the soda water. Chill. Pour into a punch bowl with a large block of ice, and add soda water just before serving, with orange slices for garnish.

THE TALLULAH (COKE, PEANUTS, & WHISKEY)

MAKES 1 DRINK

EVER DROP A HANDFUL OF ROASTED PEANUTS INTO AN ICE-COLD COCA-COLA?
No, seriously. The sweet and salty pairing, rare above the Mason-Dixon line and vanishing below, conjures vivid memories for Southerners of a certain age. The folks at Mountain Brook, Alabama, gastropub Ollie Irene have reinvented this treat as a cocktail with the Tallulah, a drink made with Coca-Cola, peanut syrup, and a healthy pour of Jack Daniel's. Named for co-owner Chris Newsome's great-aunt Tallulah, who was a lifelong whiskey drinker, it is a smooth, nutty, and respectably boozy tribute to rural Southern tradition.

INGREDIENTS

1¾ ounces Jack Daniel's
1 ounce Peanut Orgeat (recipe follows)
Coca-Cola

GARNISH
Roasted peanuts

PREPARATION

Pour the whiskey and peanut orgeat into a rocks glass over ice. Stir, and top with Coca-Cola. Garnish with roasted peanuts.

PEANUT ORGEAT

While the three-ingredient cocktail couldn't be much easier to assemble, the peanut syrup—known to the savvy cocktailian as an orgeat—takes a little time to prepare. Make a batch up to 2 weeks ahead. Store in an airtight container, refrigerated, until your get-together.

INGREDIENTS

2 cups roasted, unsalted peanuts
1½ cups sugar
1 teaspoon orange flower water
1 ounce brandy or vodka

PREPARATION

Pulverize the peanuts in a food processor.

Combine the sugar and 1¼ cups water in a saucepan over medium heat, stirring constantly until the sugar dissolves. Allow the mixture to boil for 3 minutes, then add the peanuts. Reduce the heat to low and simmer for 3 to 5 more minutes, then gradually increase the temperature to medium-high. When the mixture is just about to boil, remove from the heat and cover the pan. Let sit for at least 6 hours.

Strain the cooled mixture through a fine-mesh sieve or cheesecloth and discard the peanuts. Add the orange flower water and brandy. Store in an airtight container, refrigerated, for up to 2 weeks.

THE 610 MAGNOLIA OLD FASHIONED

MAKES 1 DRINK

COCKTAIL LORE TRACES THE OLD FASHIONED TO LATE-NINETEENTH-CENTURY Louisville, specifically the Pendennis Club, where it was purportedly invented by (or perhaps in honor of) Col. James E. Pepper, a patriarch of Kentucky bourbon whiskey. To this day, the Pendennis remains a private club, but you can do just as well at 610 Magnolia, a New American bistro located in the heart of historic Old Louisville. The elements of the drink aren't exotic by modern cocktail standards: its eponymous glass; a strip of lemon peel, cut large and uneven to help release essential oil from the rind and a little tang from the pith during the muddle; and cubed brown sugar, which acts as an abrasive to further expedite the process and adds a touch of molasses flavor. No syrups. No fancy garnishes. No cocktail hijinks. Just proof—about 90, in fact—that some things never go out of fashion.

INGREDIENTS

1 large uneven slice of lemon peel

1 brown sugar cube

2 dashes Angostura bitters

1 dash Regan's Orange Bitters No. 6

1 ounce water

2 large ice cubes

2 ounces Jefferson's Reserve Very Old bourbon or Elijah Craig 12-Year bourbon

GARNISH

Thin slice of orange

PREPARATION

Put the lemon peel, sugar cube, and both bitters in the bottom of an Old Fashioned glass. Using a wooden muddler, muddle the ingredients firmly, working the muddler in a circle. (The tapered shape of the glass allows you to perform this task with ease.) Add the water and continue to muddle for a bit longer. Add the ice cubes and then the bourbon. Stir with a spoon. To garnish, float an orange slice on top.

DARK & STORMY

BERMUDA'S NATIONAL DRINK, THE DARK AND STORMY IS "OFFICIALLY" MADE with the British territory's largest export, Gosling's Black Seal rum—the two-century-old family business actually holds the drink's trademark—and Gosling's Stormy ginger beer. But don't fear, the British Royal Navy won't throw you in the brig if you deviate from the standard. Michael Schwartz, chef/owner of Michael's Genuine Food & Drink in Miami, came up with his own version using homemade syrup in place of the ginger beer. "I wanted to stay true to the Dark and Stormy's classic flavors while giving it a handcrafted element that makes the drink unique," he says. The syrup gives his take a fresher taste: nice and gingery, with some kick thanks to added jalapeño. "We use Myers's Dark Rum because it is a tad lighter than the traditional Gosling's, allowing the spice and flavor to really shine through," Schwartz says. While it isn't exactly authentic, we can assure you this Dark and Stormy is smooth sailing.

INGREDIENTS

2½ ounces Myers's dark rum
2 ounces homemade Ginger Lemongrass Syrup (recipe follows)
Club soda or sparkling water

GARNISH

Candied ginger

PREPARATION

Fill a Collins glass with ice. Add the rum and syrup, then top with club soda, stirring to mix. Garnish with candied ginger.

GINGER LEMONGRASS SYRUP

Makes about 8 ounces, enough for 4 drinks

INGREDIENTS

1 large piece of fresh ginger (4 to 5 ounces), peeled
1 large stalk lemongrass, lower bulb end and tough outer leaves removed (this will give you a 4- to 5-inch piece)
½ cup sugar
½ jalapeño (split but with seeds)

PREPARATION

Finely chop the ginger and lemongrass. In a saucepan over medium heat, dissolve the sugar in 1 cup water. Add the ginger, lemongrass, and jalapeño and increase the heat to high to bring to a boil. Reduce the heat to low and simmer until the syrup is infused with flavors, about 20 minutes. Remove from the heat and strain in a fine-mesh sieve. Discard the solids. Let cool completely before using.

ANTEBELLUM JULEP

MAKES 1 DRINK

AS A VETERAN OF THE HOUSTON COCKTAIL SCENE, ALBA HUERTA HAS PLENTY of classic drinks in her repertoire. Most days, however, she is particularly focused on just one—the julep, for which her charming Washington Avenue bar is named. Though the julep we're all familiar with is usually made with bourbon, Huerta's antebellum version hews closely to the early-nineteenth-century Southern recipe, historically made with cognac and rum. In another nod to tradition, Huerta includes a touch of sorghum syrup in place of simple syrup for extra depth. As for the mint, Huerta's go-to variety is spearmint, which has a mild, slightly sweet and fruity profile. Just don't overmuddle the leaves or you risk releasing bitter chlorophyll into the drink. Three or four good twists of the muddler is plenty.

INGREDIENTS

- 8 to 10 fresh mint leaves
- 2 bar spoons sorghum syrup
- 2 ounces cognac
- ½ ounce Jamaican rum

GARNISHES

Fresh mint sprig and confectioners' sugar

PREPARATION

In a julep cup, lightly muddle the mint leaves and syrup. Pour in the cognac to rinse off the muddler; remove the muddler. Fill the cup three-quarters full with crushed ice and stir with a bar spoon. Add a small dome of crushed ice and pour rum over the top. Garnish with a mint sprig and a dusting of confectioners' sugar.

SLURRICANE

MAKES 1 DRINK

BORN AT BOURBON STREET BAR PAT O'BRIEN'S IN THE 1940S, THE HURRICANE has since sent many a New Orleans tourist on a drunken, and probably embarrassing, waltz through the French Quarter. Though the drink was originally a potent blend of lemon juice, passion fruit syrup, and rum, today's Hurricane is easy to dismiss as little more than a Kool-Aid sugar bomb made from powdered mix and served up all over town in gimmicky souvenir cups. In the hands of New Orleans cocktail scholar Jeff "Beachbum" Berry, however, the Hurricane returns to its roots—and its deserved place right alongside other, more revered Crescent City classics like the Sazerac, Pimm's Cup, and Ramos Gin Fizz.

INGREDIENTS

- ½ ounce freshly squeezed lime juice
- ½ ounce freshly squeezed lemon juice
- ¾ ounce passion fruit syrup
- ¼ ounce grenadine
- ¼ ounce guava juice or nectar
- 2 ounces dark Jamaican rum

GARNISHES

Lime wedge and brandied cocktail cherry

PREPARATION

Fill a cocktail shaker with ice and add all the ingredients. Shake well and strain into a tumbler filled with fresh crushed ice. Garnish with a lime wedge speared to a brandied cocktail cherry.

SIR ISAAC NEWTON

MAKES 1 DRINK

"APPLE BRANDY IS ONE OF MY FAVORITE SPIRITS TO WORK WITH," SAYS Jeremy Wingle of Poole's Downtown Diner in Raleigh, North Carolina. Though the spirit doesn't exactly scream Southern, the region has a long tradition of cultivating the fruit and distilling its essence into spirits too. As late as the 1870s, there were nearly two thousand active brandy distilleries in the South, many in states that are still top apple producers, like North Carolina and Virginia. Wingle's Sir Isaac Newton cocktail is a variation on a classic sour, but with a symphonic level of apple flavors. Lemon juice provides the tart, but the sweet comes from an intense, simple-to-make syrup that a simmered-down reduction of fresh apple cider yields. Add a base of apple brandy, and the effect is almost deliriously autumnal.

INGREDIENTS

- 1 ounce Apple Cider–Cinnamon Syrup (recipe follows)
- ½ ounce freshly squeezed lemon juice
- 1½ ounces apple brandy
- 2 dashes Angostura bitters

GARNISH

Thin slice of apple

PREPARATION

In a cocktail shaker full of ice, combine the syrup, lemon juice, brandy, and bitters. Shake vigorously, then strain into a chilled cocktail glass. To garnish, float an apple slice on top of the drink.

APPLE CIDER– CINNAMON SYRUP

Makes 4 ounces, enough for 4 drinks

INGREDIENTS

- 4 cups apple cider
- 1 cinnamon stick

PREPARATION

In a saucepan, bring the cider to a boil over medium-high heat. Reduce the heat to medium-low, add the cinnamon stick, and continue to cook, stirring occasionally, for about 25 minutes, or until the cider has reduced to the consistency of syrup. Let cool to room temperature, then refrigerate in an airtight container for up to 2 weeks.

THE SEELBACH

MAKES 1 DRINK

A CENTURY AGO, THE SEELBACH HOTEL, IN LOUISVILLE, WAS A GLITZY destination where big spenders from all over the country would gather to clink glasses of Kentucky whiskey. That was the age that produced the Seelbach cocktail, a glamorous concoction of bourbon, orange liqueur, bitters, and champagne that guests like F. Scott Fitzgerald and Al Capone might have enjoyed. The drink disappeared somewhere in the chaos of Prohibition but was rediscovered by a hotel manager in 1995. Today, Eron Plevan, bartender at the hotel's stately Oakroom, doesn't veer too far from the original recipe. You don't need to, either.

INGREDIENTS

- 1 ounce Old Forester bourbon
- ½ ounce Cointreau
- 4 dashes Peychaud's bitters
- 3 dashes Angostura bitters
- Cold champagne or sparkling wine

GARNISH

- Long twist of orange peel

PREPARATION

In a chilled champagne glass, stir together the bourbon, Cointreau, and both bitters. Top with champagne and garnish with an orange twist.

MICHELADA

MAKES 1 DRINK

THERE ARE AS MANY THEORIES ABOUT THE ORIGINS OF THIS LONE STAR STATE cocktail—a spicy beer-over-ice concoction—as there are variations on it. Travel north and the mix includes tomato juice, for example. But there's one constant: south-of-the-border beer. This version, from the Hotel San José in Austin, is light with a tart edge. First-timers might want to start with a pale lager, such as Modelo Especial. For a step up in flavor, try one of these two San José–bar mainstays: Pilsener of El Salvador or Xingu, a Brazilian black lager with a rich, roasty flavor, medium body, and a clean, malty finish. Serve the beer on the side, giving each drinker the freedom to pour it into the mix to taste—a very Texas touch.

INGREDIENTS

- 2 dashes Tabasco sauce
- 2 dashes Worcestershire sauce
- ¼ ounce soy sauce
- 2 to 3 ounces freshly squeezed lime juice
- 4 to 6 twists coarsely ground black pepper
- 1 bottle south-of-the-border beer, such as Modelo Especial or Xingu

GARNISHES

Coarse sea salt or kosher salt and thin slice of lime

PREPARATION

Rim a straight-sided 20-ounce glass with salt. Fill the glass halfway with ice cubes. Pour all the ingredients except the beer into the glass and garnish with a lime wheel. Serve with a stirring straw and the beer on the side (add the beer to the glass to taste).

COCHON BLOODY MARY

SERVES 10 TO 12

THE BLOODY MARY IS MORE THAN A DAY-DRINKING TRADITION IN THE SOUTH, it's practically a religion. Sure, plenty of folks swear by bottled mixes like Mr. & Mrs. T and Zing Zang. And while those get the job done, true connoisseurs make their own mixes, some with recipes as closely guarded as the family silver. Fortunately, Donald Link is happy to share. The executive chef and co-owner of Cochon in New Orleans makes the queen of Bloody Marys. His secret lies in some unmistakably Southern ingredients, including a heavy splash of pickled okra brine and authentic pork *jus*, which adds to the drink's savory depths. If you don't happen to be the chef of one of the most famous pork restaurants in America, substitute canned beef stock for the *jus*. (The pickled okra, and its brine, are a requirement, though.) Then stir up a pitcher and let brunch begin.

INGREDIENTS

- 1 (46-ounce) bottle V8 juice
- 2 tablespoons freshly ground black pepper
- 2 tablespoons grainy mustard
- 1 tablespoon granulated garlic
- 3 tablespoons pork *jus* or beef stock
- 3 tablespoons freshly squeezed lime juice
- 5 tablespoons freshly squeezed lemon juice
- 7 tablespoons hot sauce, preferably Crystal brand
- 4 tablespoons green hot sauce
- 3 tablespoons red wine vinegar
- 2 tablespoons olive juice (the brine from a jar of olives)
- 3 tablespoons okra juice (the brine from a jar of pickled okra)

  Vodka of choice

GARNISH

  Pickled okra and celery stalks

PREPARATION

Combine all the ingredients except the vodka in a pitcher and stir to combine. (The mixture can be made ahead of time and kept in a sealed pitcher for up to 1 week.) To serve: Fill a glass with ice. Add about 2 ounces vodka. Fill with Bloody Mary mix. Stir, garnish with pickled okra and a stalk of celery, and serve.

GLOSSARY

COOK LIKE A SOUTHERNER, SPEAK LIKE ONE TOO

Southerners have a flair for language. See:
William Faulkner, Margaret Mitchell, Tennessee Williams,
Harper Lee, Truman Capote . . . So it's no surprise
that our linguistic skills combine with our culinary ones in
curious ways. And we don't mean "heapin'
helpin's of vittles and fixin's."

This glossary is not intended to be a complete list of
Southern culinary terminology. Nor is it intended
to catalog our region's countless dishes—from Creole gumbo
to Lowcountry Frogmore Stew, with all their
hyper-regional subvarieties. You'll find recipes for many of
those elsewhere in this book. It's simply a collection
of terms that have special meaning in the Southern kitchen.

BARBECUE: A noun or adjective only, never a verb: meat slowly smoked over hardwood or charcoal. Usually pork or beef; smoked chicken or turkey might be described as "barbecue chicken" or "chicken barbecue." In Kentucky, it may also include lamb or mutton.

BARK: The charred, extra-smoky exterior of barbecue. Rarely on the menu, but nearly always available at barbecue joints, where you can place an order of pulled pork with "extra bark." Also called "outside brown" or just "brown."

BOIL: A generic term, both noun and verb, for Southern outdoor gatherings at which shellfish (enough to feed a good-size crowd) is boiled, along with potatoes, corn, and seasonings in a large pot. The dish is inseparable from the event. In coastal South Carolina and Georgia Lowcountry boils, shrimp and crab go into the pot. In Louisiana, crawfish.

BUGGY: The wheeled shopping basket you use to hold groceries at Piggly Wiggly (aka "the Pig"), Publix, Harris Teeter, or any other Southern grocery store.

CHICKEN-FRY: The verb describing the process by which chicken is prepared—dredged in seasoned flour, then fried in oil or melted lard until golden-crisp. Also applies to other foods cooked in this manner. (See Chicken-Fried Short Ribs, page 88.)

CRACKLINS OR CRACKLINGS: Crisp, savory leavings—may be skin, meat, or membrane— from the rendering of pork fat. Not to be confused with chitlins or chitterlings, which are hog intestines that have been turned inside-out for a thorough, laborious and . . . shall we say *fragrant* cleaning, then simmered to soften. For more detail on the many other pork parts commonly used by Southerners, from jowl to streak-o'-lean, see page 72.

DEBRIS (*DAY-BREE*): In New Orleans, a rich beef gravy full of pan drippings and bits of meat. Elsewhere in Cajun cuisine, the term refers to a more rustic gravy made with organ meats and other parts left over from hog butchering.

DEVILED: Made spicy, usually with the addition of cayenne pepper or hot sauce. As with eggs, crab, or ham.

DINNER: The midday meal, historically quite large, as it was the primary fortifying meal of the day. The evening meal, usually smaller, may be called "supper."

FRYING PAN: A common term for the cast-iron skillet, which is used for frying as well as searing, sautéing, simmering, and even baking. About ten inches in diameter, on average, although many sizes are available, and frequently notched on one side for easily pouring off grease. Does not refer to stainless-steel, copper, or nonstick pans—Teflon, ceramic, or otherwise.

GREASE: Flavorful, semi-solid bacon-fat renderings or drippings, which can be used in place of butter or oil to start a sauté. Often kept at room temperature in dedicated canisters, some with filters that remove any particles or browned bits, although coffee cans work fine for this purpose too.

GREENS: Most frequently applies to hearty winter greens, like collard, mustard, and turnip. (See also "mess.") In Appalachia, may also refer to more tender spring lettuces, which may be eaten raw in salads or cooked. (See also "kil't.")

HOLY TRINITY: The Father, Son, and Holy Ghost, yes. Also the combination of celery, onion, and bell pepper at the heart of nearly every Cajun or Creole dish you can imagine, from grillades to gumbo.

ICE, ICING: Applied to a cake, the same as "frost" or "frosting." Refers to both a thin sugary glaze or a thick buttercream.

ICEBOX DESSERTS: Frozen concoctions, similar to ice cream, but without all the churning. Similar to Italian semifreddo, often with fanciful names that might include such words as "delight" or "delectable." Usually molded in loaf pans, though the term may also apply to pies made with frozen fillings. The "icebox" refers back to a time when refrigeration was accomplished with large blocks of ice stored in insulated cabinets or chests.

KIL'T: An adjective commonly used for greens that have been wilted, or "killed." (See page 168.)

LIGHT BREAD: A synonym for store-bought loaf bread made from white flour. As opposed to "bread," which for much of Southern history automatically meant cornbread in its many variations. (See page 215.)

MEAT AND THREE: Exactly what it seems: a plate containing one meat with three vegetable sides (which includes mac and cheese), served, often cafeteria-style from steam tables, by restaurants also known as "meat-and-threes." The dishes are deliciously homey—think hamburger steaks with brown onion gravy (page 90) or fried catfish (page 110).

MESS: Frequently applied to greens, but can also apply to any food cooked in large quantity. Implies an amount that would require using a stockpot.

MILK: As a verb, the process by which the milky liquid inside individual kernels of corn is removed, usually accomplished by firmly running the back of a knife down the length of an ear of trimmed corn. (Only when the ear is shucked, de-kerneled, and dried does it become a "cob.")

OLD HAM: A synonym for salt-cured country ham, which can be aged for years before eating. (See page 76.) Ordinary ham, the moist, tender kind, is often called "city ham," to distinguish it from its country cousin. For more on old ham's preferred partner, the biscuit, and its many forms, see page 217.

PEA: Less likely to refer to round green English peas than starchy field peas (black-eyed, pink-eyed, etc.), which can be cooked from fresh or frozen, or rehydrated from dried. (See page 161.) Similar to—but not the same thing as—butter beans, which are a small, pale yellow-green variety of lima beans.

PICKING: A noun used to describe the party that commences as soon as a whole-smoked and roasted hog comes off the pit. Also the process by which its meat is hand-pulled.

POKE OR POLK: In conjunction with "salad" or "sallet," refers to pokeweed, a common wild green that's both edible and poisonous. Young leaves—never stems, berries, or roots—must be boiled, like other greens, changing the water at least two or three times to remove the toxins naturally present in the plant. "Poke" may also refer to a bag or sack used to carry food.

POTLIKKER: The meaty, nutrient-rich liquid left behind after a "mess of greens" is cooked, usually with a smoked ham hock or a piece of salt pork. "Beanlikker" is similar, but thicker-bodied than potlikker due to starches leached from the beans.

PUT UP: As a verb, to preserve by canning or pickling; jars of canned fruits or vegetables, pickles, jams, or preserves are sealed in sterilized lidded jars and then stored (i.e., "put up") for later use. As an adjective, the description of said preserved items (e.g., "put-up green beans").

ROAST: As a noun, an oyster roast. Like a "boil" or a "picking," a gathering at which the dish and event are one.

SEASON: A cast-iron skillet must be periodically "seasoned" with oil or lard to maintain its nonstick properties. When slowly heated, the oil polymerizes and bonds to the pan's surface. Despite popular myth, soap won't remove that polymer; feel free to gently wash your frying pan after every use.

SMIDGE: A small amount, roughly analogous to a pinch, but likely even less, as determined by intuitive cooks. Similar to—but not the same as—"skosh," also a small amount, but more often applied to libations.

SWEET MILK: Whole cow's milk, called "sweet" to distinguish it from tart buttermilk. Not to be confused with sweetened condensed or evaporated milk, which may often be described by their brand names (e.g., "PET milk").

CONTRIBUTORS

Except where indicated, all recipes developed by Katherine Cobbs

Photography by Peter Frank Edwards

Food styling by Cynthia Groseclose

Prop styling by Kenneth Hyatt and Justin Schram

Illustrations by John Burgoyne

ADDITIONAL RECIPES FROM THE FOLLOWING CHEFS AND CULINARY PROFESSIONALS: Hugh Acheson, Greg Baker, Jeff "Beachbum" Berry, John Besh, Bill Briand, Griffin Bufkin, Walter Bundy, Kevin Callaghan, Ashley Christensen, John Currence, BJ Dennis, Justin Devillier, Adam Evans, Spike Gjerde, Linda "the Ya-Ka-Mein Lady" Green, David Guas, Trevor Higgins, Jesse Houston, Alba Huerta, John Lasater, Mike Lata, Edward Lee, Donald Link, Andrea Kirshtein, Sarah Malphrus, Tory McPhail, Ouita Michel, Lorene Moore, Carrie Morey, Chris Newsome, Robert Newton, Whitney Otawka, Nancy Plemmons, Eron Plevan, Andrea Reusing, Leon Rosato, Harrison Sapp, Steven Satterfield, Michael Schwartz, Chris Shepherd, Stephen Stryjewski, Alzina Toups, Joe Trull, Roderick Weaver, Tandy Wilson, Callie White, Jeremy Wingle, Eric Wolitzky. Duck & Oyster Gumbo recipe (page 132) reprinted with permission from *My New Orleans* by John Besh, courtesy of Andrew McNeel Publishing.

ESSAYS BY: Roy Blount, Jr., Rick Bragg, John T. Edge, Allison Glock, Randall Kenan, Matt Lee and Ted Lee, Jonathan Miles, Kathleen Purvis, Julia Reed

ADDITIONAL CONTRIBUTIONS FROM: Cathy Barrow, Meredith L. Butcher, Kate Connor, Jenny Everett, Bettina Fisher, Vanessa Gregory, Jack Hitt, Margaret Houston, Maggie Brett Kennedy, CJ Lotz, Francine Maroukian, Dave Mezz, Jessica Mischner, Jed Portman, Hanna Raskin, Phillip Rhodes, Kim Severson

SPECIAL THANKS TO: The Commons, Nickie Cutrona, Nathalie Dupree, Edward's Hams, Rachel Feinberg, Wayne and Katherine Guckenberger, Hunter Kennedy, Manchester Farms, Elizabeth Marks, Sunburst Trout Farms, Dan Xeller

ACKNOWLEDGMENTS

DEVELOPING A COOKBOOK THAT COVERS THE MODERN South means relying heavily on the past while remaining cognizant of what's next for our foodways. Wrangling that past, present, and future was the job of Phillip Rhodes, *Garden & Gun*'s executive managing editor. He sifted through eight years of food coverage in *G&G*, orchestrated the development of the new recipes, and then took on the mammoth job of putting it in cookbook form. His expertise, dedication, and hard work cannot be overstated, and his deft touch is evident in every page of this book.

Maggie Brett Kennedy, *G&G*'s photography director, brought the same attention and talent to these pages that she brings to every issue of the magazine. From overseeing the two-week photo shoot to digging in her attic for the perfect plate or fork to accompany an image, she made sure the photos stayed true to the magazine and the South. Associate photo editor Margaret Houston tackled any unforeseen task that arose—and there were many. The photos themselves are the hard work of Peter Frank Edwards, a regular in the pages of *G&G*. His photography is as good-looking as the dishes are tasty, and he's a delight to work with. The actual food styling was done by another *G&G* favorite, Cynthia Groseclose. And thanks to Wayne and Katherine Guckenberger for the use of their wonderful house as a backdrop for the photo shoot.

The development of new recipes was handled by the talented Katherine Cobbs. She did a lot of work in short order and she did it well, while always thinking about the reader. Her recipes were then put through their paces by our testers, Kate Connor and Bettina Foster.

As a staff, the entire *G&G* edit team made this a better book, including art director Marshall McKinney and associate art director Braxton Crim. They consulted on the book's design and worked with illustrator John Burgoyne. Speaking of design, Laura Palese brought her own sensibilities to the project while keeping the DNA of *Garden & Gun* at the core. When it came to the actual words, deputy editor David Mezz helped fine-tune the manuscript, and senior editor Jessica Mischner, assistant editor Jed Portman, and research editor C. J. Lotz all happily pitched in when their skills and knowledge were needed.

The magazine's literary agent, Amy Hughes of Dunow, Carlson & Lerner, has been a champion of this project, and all *G&G* books, from the start. A huge helping of thanks goes to the team at HarperWave. Publisher Karen Rinaldi and executive editor Julie Will take good content, make it better, and package it beautifully. And for that we're grateful. Also at HarperWave, Sydney Pierce kept us in line and on time—no easy task. Additionally, design director Leah Carlson-Stanisic, jacket designer Gregg Kulick, senior publicity manager Martin Wilson, and marketing director Brian Perrin made sure this book was everything it could be on all fronts.

None of this happens without the owners of *Garden & Gun*, Rebecca Wesson Darwin, Pierre Manigault, and J. Edward Bell III. They believe in editorial independence, integrity, and quality. I couldn't ask for more.

Truly, it takes a village. Thank you all.

INDEX

Page numbers of photographs appear in italics.

B

ABOUT GARDEN & GUN MAGAZINE

Garden & Gun is a national magazine that covers the
best of the South, including its sporting culture,
food, music, art, and literature, and its people and their ideas.
The magazine has won numerous awards for journalism,
design, and overall excellence. Garden & Gun was
launched in the spring of 2007 and is headquartered
in Charleston, South Carolina.

OK

AR

TX

Dallas

HILL
COUNTRY

Austin

Houston

LA

GULF